CRITICAL INCIDENTS
IN GROUP COUNSELING

Edited by

LAWRENCE E. TYSON
RACHELLE PÉRUSSE
JIM WHITLEDGE

AMERICAN COUNSELING ASSOCIATION
5999 Stevenson Avenue
Alexandria, VA 22304
www.counseling.org

Critical Incidents in Group Counseling

Copyright ® 2004 by the American Counseling Association. All rights reserved. Printed in the United States of America. Except as permitted under the United States Copyright Act of 1976, no part of this publication may be reproduced or distributed in any form or by any means, or stored in a database ore retrieval system without the prior written permission of the publisher.

10 9 8 7 6 5 4 3 2 1

American Counseling Association
5999 Stevenson Avenue
Alexandria, VA 22304

Director of Publications
Carolyn C. Baker

Production Manager
Bonny E. Gaston

Copyeditor
Lucy Blanton

Cover design by Martha Woolsey

Library of Congress Cataloging-in-Publication Data

Critical incidents in group counseling / [edited] by Lawrence E. Tyson, Rachelle Pérusse, Jim Whitledge.
    p. cm.
    ISBN 1-55620-190-7 (alk. paper)
    1. Group counseling. 2. Critical incident technique.
 I. Tyson, Lawrence E. II. Pérusse, Rachelle. III. Whitledge, Jim.
BF637.C6C72 2004
158'.35—dc22

2003023830

ACKNOWLEDGMENTS

The editors of this book thank the contributors who made this effort possible. The incident and response writers of *Critical Incidents in Group Counseling* work in a variety of settings and share a common interest in group counseling.

Group counseling is a specialty area in counseling, a specialty that requires unique skills and knowledge. The professionals whose names are listed in the Table of Contents have agreed to share their knowledge, experience, and expertise. The editors are very grateful for their contributions to the profession.

It is within this spirit that this book is dedicated to the counseling professionals who identify themselves as *group counselors*, and especially to the *counselors in training* who are about to enter into a truly rewarding and stimulating profession.

TABLE OF CONTENTS

PART I
GROUP LEADER CONCERNS

PART II
GROUP MEMBER CONCERNS

PREFACE

Critical Incidents in Group Counseling is a practical text for counselor educators, group counseling practitioners, and counseling education students as well as those who have a general interest in the counseling profession. Each chapter contains a description of a critical incident, followed by two responses. The incidents are based on common experiences, specific to the group counseling setting, and challenge the reader to think about the factors present in the described incident and how those factors may be addressed.

The responses allow the reader to view two approaches in deciding on appropriate professional behaviors the group counseling practitioner may follow to meet the challenges presented in the described incident. Opportunities for further learning exist for group discussion or individual analysis of the incident and responses to provide insight into what might be considered as best practice in group work.

The topics for the group counseling incidents, generated by the editors based upon their experience and knowledge of group work and group work techniques, are placed in one of three categories representing a broad range of group work issues: Group Leader Concerns, Group Member Concerns, and Leadership Techniques. The basic plan is to provide group counseling incidents that might occur across a variety of work settings (i.e., school, private practice, community agencies, hospital, and university counseling centers). Further, with the number of contributing writers and the differences among them, a variety of presenting problems in group work are presented.

The editors each had responsibility for one of the three sections. Once an incident was received, it was edited and sent out to the two respondents who independently wrote their responses and sent them back to the appropriate editor. The editors communicated with each other via email and telephone to maintain a consistent editing approach and format for the book. The second and third editors are listed alphabetically and contributed equally.

A broad approach was used in soliciting writers to contribute to this book. The editors developed a list of professionals in the group counseling field perceived to be well-known authors, skilled practitioners, or knowledgeable educators. An invitation was developed and sent to those professionals, asking them to contribute to *Critical Incidents in Group Counseling* by writing an incident or a response in connection with the topics that had been generated. The invitation included an example of a chapter (i.e., an incident and two responses) to explain the expected format. Each contributor could write one or two incidents, and/or one or two responses, with a limit of two contributions in total. A contributor could not write both an incident and a response on the same topic. In addition, a general call for contributions was placed on the Counselor Education and Supervision NETwork – Listserv (CESNET) and the International Counselors Network (ICN) to provide for a wider range of contributions.

Contributors were asked to consider the ethical and legal implications as well as the training standards that might apply to their incident or response. The law, ethics, and training standards guide the work of professional counselors in striving to serve the best interest of their clients, whether it is in a group or individual counseling setting. The citations made by the contributors include the American Counseling Association *Code of Ethics and Standards of Practice* (ACA, 1995), the American School Counselor Association *Ethical Standards for School Counselors* (ASCA, 1998), and the Association for Specialists in Group Work *Best Practice Guidelines* (ASGW, 1998).

The editors consider this book to be a valuable resource for group counselors and group counselors in training. The novice as well as the experienced group worker will benefit from *Critical Incidents in Group Counseling*. As a text or supplementary text, or as a reference for advanced or beginning courses in, for example, group work, ethical and legal issues, and practicum, this book will enable counselors in training to benefit from working on some of the real issues they will face in group counseling situations. After reading the incident, the student as well as the experienced practitioner may analyze the factors presented and reflect upon what they might have done the same or differently if and when faced with a similar situation in their own group experience. In addition, the reader may focus on the two responses and reflect upon points of agreement and disagreement in deciding on an appropriate course of action. Consideration of the ethical codes, the law, and standards of practice and care should be applied as well. It is recognized that there can be more than one appropriate course of action applied to a specific incident. The responses to incidents are provided not as ideal responses but as viewpoints that can be discussed and debated.

The editors hope that readers will embrace *Critical Incidents in Group Counseling* as a practical text that provides the means to examine critical incidents that occur in the group counseling setting. Readers are encouraged to be actively involved in determining appropriate courses of action, based upon their reflections in reading the two responses to each incident as well as upon their own training, education, and level of group counseling skill development.

Lawrence E. Tyson
Rachelle Pérusse
Jim Whitledge

REFERENCES

American Counseling Association. (1995). *Code of ethics and standards of practice*. Alexandria, VA: Author.

American School Counselor Association. (1998). *Ethical standards for school counselors*. Alexandria, VA: Author.

Association for Specialists in Group Work. (1998). Best practice guidelines. *Journal for Specialists in Group Work, 23*(3), 237–244.

ABOUT THE EDITORS

Lawrence E. Tyson, PhD, NCC, NCSC, is an associate professor in the Department of Human Studies in the Counselor Education Program at the University of Alabama at Birmingham. Dr. Tyson can be reached at ltyson@uab.edu

Rachelle Pérusse, PhD, NCC, NCSC, is an associate professor in counselor education at Plattsburgh State University. Dr. Pérusse can be reached at perussr@plattsburgh.edu

Jim Whitledge, PhD, LPC, NCC, NCSC, is the counseling and guidance program consultant for Oakland Schools, an intermediate school district that provides educational support services for 28 school districts in Oakland County, Michigan. Dr. Whitledge can be reached at Jim.Whitledge@oakland.k12.mi.us

ABOUT THE CONTRIBUTORS

Patrick Akos, PhD, LPC, NCC, NCSC, University of North Carolina at Chapel Hill
Charleen Alderfer, EdD, College of New Jersey
Jackie M. Allen, EdD, MFT, NCC, NCSC, California Department of Education
Mary L. Anderson, MA, LPC, NCC, Oakland University
Randall L. Astramovich, PhD, NCC, NCSC, University of Nevada at Las Vegas
Sheri Bauman, PhD, NCC, MAC, University of Arizona
John A. Bayerl, PhD, LPC, Northern Michigan University
James J. Bergin, EdD, LPC, NCC, NCSC, Georgia Southern University
Nancy Bodenhorn, PhD, Virginia Tech University
Ford Brooks, EdD, NCC, CAC, Shippensburg University
Beverly A. Burnell, PhD, NCC Plattsburgh State University
Craig S. Cashwell, PhD, NCC, ACS, University of North Carolina at Greensboro
Angela D. Coker, PhD, LPC, NCC, University of Alabama at Birmingham
J. Kelly Coker, PhD, NCC, LADC, University of Nevada at Las Vegas
Robert K. Conyne, PhD, LCC, LP, NCC, ACS, CGP, University of Cincinnati
Doris Rhea Coy, PhD, University of North Texas
Stephen E. Craig, PhD, LPC, Western Michigan University
John R. Culbreth, PhD, LPC, NCC, MAC, University of Virginia
Carol A. Dahir, PhD, New York Institute of Technology
Charlotte Daughhetee, PhD, LPC, LMFT, University of Montevallo
Thomas E. Davis, PhD, PCC, CPC, Ohio University
Janice L. DeLucia-Waack, PhD, State University of New York at Buffalo
Joyce A. DeVoss, PhD, NCC, Northern Arizona University in Tucson
Ginger L. Dickson, PhD, NCC, Lincoln University
Jill D. Duba, MA, PC, NCC, Kent State University
Marcheta Evans, PhD, LPC, NCC, University of Texas at San Antonio
John V. Farrar, EdD, LPC, Central Michigan University
Jody J. Fiorini, PhD, NCC, State University of New York at Oswego
Cheryl W. Forkner, PhD, Clemson University
Louisa L. Foss, MEd PCC, NCC, Kent State University
Linda H. Foster, PhD, NCC, LPC, McAdory High School, Birmingham, Alabama
Perry C. Francis, EdD, NCC, LPC, Texas A&M University at Commerce
S. Lenoir Gillam, PhD, LPC, NCC, Columbus State University

Jane Goodman, PhD, LPC, NCC, NCCC, Oakland University
Jeri L. Goodman, MA, University of Cincinnati
Gary E. Goodnough, PhD, NCC, LCMHC, Plymouth State University
Patricia Goodspeed, EdD, NCC, Alfred University
Valerie L. Guay, MS, NCC, Conifer Park, Plattsburgh, New York
Douglas A. Guiffrida, PhD, NCC, University of Rochester
Judith A. Harrington, PhD, LPC, LMFT, Private Practice
Trish Hatch, PhD, Moreno Valley Unified School District,
    Moreno Valley, California
Suzanne M. Hedstrom, EdD, NCC, LPC, Western Michigan University
Carolyn Henshaw, MA, Midfield High School, Midfield, Alabama
Barbara R. Herlihy, PhD, NCC, LPC, University of New Orleans
Mary A. Hermann, JD, PhD, LPC, NCC, Mississippi State University
Nicole R. Hill, PhD, Idaho State University
Suzanne M. Hobson, EdD, LLP, LPC, NCC, Eastern Michigan University
N. Joan Hornak, EdD, LPC, Central Michigan University
Stephanie Rogers Howard, PhD, Alexander City Schools/
    Alabama State University
Mike Hubert, MEd, ESA, Bremerton High School, Bremerton, Washington
Diana Hulse-Killacky, EdD, LPC, NCC, University of New Orleans
Steven F. Hundley, PhD, NCC, NCSC, ACS, North Dakota State University
Shelley A. Jackson, PhD, Texas Women's University, Denton, Texas
Jennifer C. Lewis Jordan, PhD, NCC, LPC, Clemson University
David M. Kaplan, PhD, LP, NCC, NCCC, CFT, Emporia State University
Virginia A. Kelly, PhD, Fairfield University
Kurt L. Kraus, EdD, LPC, NCC, ACS, Shippensberg University
Gerard Lawson, PhD, LPC, CSAC, Virginia Tech University
Michael LeBlanc, PhD, State University of New York at Oswego
Vivian V. Lee, EdD, NCC, Old Dominion University
Robin Wilbourn Lee, PhD, LPC, NCC, University of Tennessee
    at Chattanooga
Vivian J. Carroll McCollum, PhD, LPC, NCC, University of New Orleans
Kelly A. McDonnell, PhD, Western Michigan University
Gail Mears, PsyD, NCC, LCMHC, Plymouth State University
James L. Moore III, PhD, Ohio State University
Jodi Ann Mullen, PhD, State University of New York at Oswego
Patricia J. Neufeld, PhD, LCPC, NCC, Emporia State University
Edward Neukrug, EdD, LPC, LP, Old Dominion University
Mary Ni, EdD, Salem State College
Carolyn Noël, MS, NCC, Argosy University, Washington, DC Campus
Seth Olson, MA, Kent State University
Linda R. Osborne, MA, CAGS, NCCMHC, LCMHC, Rhode Island
    Department of Corrections
Rachelle Pérusse, PhD, NCC, NCSC, Plattsburgh State University
Jean Sunde Peterson, PhD, LPC, LMHC, NCC, Purdue University
Emily Phillips, PhD, NCC, State University of New York at Oneonta

Stephanie G. Puleo, PhD, LMFT, NCC, University of Montevallo
Tommie R. Radd, PhD, LPC, LMHP, CRC, NCC, University of Nebraska
at Omaha
Deborah E. Renard, PhD, LPC, CRC, University of Wisconsin-Milwaukee
Walter B. Roberts, Jr., EdD, LPC, LSC, NCC, NCSC, Minnesota
State University
P. Clay Rowell, EdS, University of North Carolina at Greensboro
Kathryn Russ, MA, University of Cincinnati
Mark B. Scholl, PhD, NCC, St. John's University
Rebecca A. Schumacher, EdD, NCC, University of North Florida
Muhyiddin A. Shakoor, PhD, State University of New York, College
at Brockport
Howard B. Smith, EdD, LPC, NCC, NCMHC, South Dakota State
University, Brookings
Shannon D. Smith, PhD, PCC, NCC, DAPA, NSC, The University of Akron
Pamela A. Staples, EdD, NCC, George Washington University
Heather Trepal, MEd, PC, Kent State University
Robyn L. Trippany, EdD, LPC, RPT, Troy State University at Montgomery
Linwood G. Vereen, PhD, NCC, St. Cloud State University
Ann Vernon, PhD, LMHC, NCC, University of Northern Iowa
Debbie Vernon, MEd, LPCC-S, ACS, Kent State University
Kelly L. Wester, PhD, LPC, University of North Carolina at Greensboro
Jim Whitledge, PhD, LPC, NCC, NCSC, Counseling and Guidance Program
Consultant, Oakland Schools, Michigan
James V. Wigtil, EdD, LPC, LPCC, NCC, North Dakota State University
Cathy Woodyard, EdD, Texas Woman's University

PART I

GROUP LEADER CONCERNS

CHAPTER 1

PREGROUP PLANNING: "I THINK WE'RE READY"

This incident explores some of the issues that accompany novice group leaders who negate the preplanning details involved with facilitating a successful group experience.

CRITICAL INCIDENT

Debbie Vernon

Background

Allison and Bridget have recently started their first jobs as counselors at a community mental health center. They are under the supervision of one of the Licensed Professional Counselors who work in the center. They went to graduate school together and have been friends for most of that time. They each had experience running groups as part of their practica and internships during their master's programs. Additionally, they were required to lead a personal growth group as part of their group counseling class. Allison worked with adolescents during her internship while Bridget worked with college-age students at the counseling center on campus. They are also roommates.

Incident

The two counselors decided to put together a teen process group. One day during lunch they decided when they would hold the group and what they wanted to cover. After lunch, they spoke to their supervisor and received the green light to facilitate the group. With 3 weeks remaining until the group was supposed to start, the counselors began to develop thoughts about how to prepare for this endeavor. However, because they were such good friends and lived together, they individually decided there was little, if any, pregroup work to do. Both of them delayed holding official meetings due to seeing each other all the time. Actually, they believed all they had to do was wait for the referrals to arrive and begin their group; especially because the local high school counselor stated she would be happy to refer students to them. As expected, the referrals arrived. They briefly discussed the number of participants, and a date was set for the first session. Allison and Bridget were excited about their first group and especially happy they would be co-leading. This idea gave them an extra degree of comfort.

The time for the first session arrived. Bridget and Allison confidently introduced themselves as they eagerly anticipated the group process starting. They decided to engage the group members in an icebreaker activity, just as they learned in their practica. However, the activity finished sooner than expected. After what seemed like an eternity of silence, Allison began asking the members why they had elected to participate in this group. Again, after a short while, the group fell silent. Bridget whispered to Allison, "What do you want to do now?" Allison quickly thought of a solution. She asked each member to take out paper and something to write with. Her instructions to the members were to describe what they wanted to accomplish as a result of participating in this group. As the group members were busy writing their answers, Allison whispered to Bridget, "This will use up some of the time left." After the activity, the members shared their thoughts and were reminded when the next session would be held. Allison and Bridget thanked the members for coming and said they looked forward to seeing them next week.

Discussion

After the session ended and the last teenager left, Allison and Bridget realized that something needed to be done. Allison commented that these teenagers were not as talkative as the others she had worked with. As they continued to discuss their thoughts, they realized the first session had been a bit rocky, but thought the sessions would iron out and they could quickly begin to work on adolescent issues. They hurriedly gathered their belongings and headed toward the door. As they were leaving, their supervisor stopped them and inquired about the session. They happily replied, "The first session went great!" and with that, headed out the door. Watching them leave, the supervisor thought how lucky he was to have Allison and Bridget working at the center.

QUESTIONS

1. What preplanning strategies are these two counselors taking for granted?
2. Are these two counselors suitable for leading such a group?
3. What are the leader issues exhibited in this incident that may or may not interfere with the success of this group?
4. Are there any concerns with the relationship between the counselors and their supervisor?
5. What other ethical issues are important regarding the planning, implementing, and postreview of this session?

RESPONSE

Rachelle Pérusse

These two counselors are not engaging in any meaningful preplanning activities. Group counseling does not just happen; a great deal of work is required in the preplanning stages. This initial preplanning may include a meeting with their supervisor to discuss the basic purpose of the group, the member selection process, group format, and methods of evaluation. In addition to consulting with their supervisor, Bridget and Allison can meet with potential group members on a one-to-one basis in order to screen them for the group experience. This screening process will allow the group leaders to ensure these teens know what to expect from the group experience and allow the teens to ask questions about what will be expected from them and to express concerns they may have about group counseling.

Other preplanning decisions need to be made in addition to deciding upon the number of participants. It is unclear how much, if any, direction Bridget and Allison have given to the school counselor who is referring clients to them. The school counselor could be referring clients to them on a wide variety of issues that may benefit from different types of interventions, or may lead to individual goals that are incompatible with group goals. For example, the school counselor may be referring students who have behavioral issues, anger management issues, grief issues, gay/lesbian coming-out issues, academic concerns, or developmental issues. In other words, Bridget and Allison need to decide if they want a homogeneous or heterogeneous group prior to selecting group members. It is also unclear whether this group is voluntary or involuntary: That is, because they are being referred by the school counselor, are these students required to be in group counseling? Other issues that seem to have been glossed over include the frequency of meetings, whether clients are expected to commit to short-term or long-term goals, and whether the group will be closed or open.

In addition to these preplanning activities, Allison and Bridget need to set up official meetings in which they can plan for the initial group meeting. Even though they know each other as friends, they do not necessarily know each other as group leaders. Before the first session begins, they can decide what needs to be covered during the first session, especially ground rules, informed consent, confidentiality, and potential risks of being involved in this group. During the initial stages of a group, some amount of structuring of the group may be necessary to help group members begin the process of learning to interact with each other and build trust, as opposed to the "make it up as we go along" mentality that both counselors seem to exhibit.

It is difficult to determine whether these two are suitable for leading such a group. It is clear that Allison has worked in some capacity with adolescents during her internship and that Bridget has worked with college-age students. It is less clear how many hours of group work each has logged and whether these group experiences were supervised. Certainly, it is not enough that each has been a part of experiential activities in one group counseling class. An issue that does make them unsuitable for working together as co-leaders is their perception that because they are friends they do not have to meet regularly to prepare for their group. Co-leaders need to be able to give each other feedback and discuss what is going on in group sessions in order to learn from each other and improve their skills. Co-leaders should meet with each other before and after sessions to process the previous session and plan for the next session. In addition to challenging each other, the counselors and their supervisor need to make time for a formal meeting with each other that encompasses more than just passing each other in the hall.

There is no mention of whether Bridget and Allison upheld their ethical responsibilities to the group members. Before joining a group, leaders obtain the informed consent of group members by explaining the purpose of the group, basic ground rules, possible risks involved with participation in group counseling, confidentiality, and the limits to confidentiality. When working with minors, it is advisable to seek written permission from parents or guardians before proceeding with the group.

RESPONSE

Jim Whitledge

Allison and Bridget appear to believe that their familiarity with each other and being roommates will result in things falling in place for their cofacilitation of the teen process group. Yet their group work training and education probably emphasized that they should conduct a meeting to discuss and plan what direction a group might take and that they should discuss parameters, such as the number of participants, screening responsibilities, confidentiality, ground rules, potential topics, and group goals as well as division of facilitator roles before a group meets for the first time. Consulting more thoroughly with their supervisor about the nature of the teen process group and what they hoped to accomplish by running such a group might have helped Allison and Bridget. The supervisor should have been more active in questioning Allison and Bridget about the group and in ensuring that appropriate planning took place.

Allison and Bridget seem unaware of, or are straying from, the basic training and education guidelines for group work they may have experienced in their university programs. They seem to miss the point completely in regard to planning strategies and addressing the best interests of the young people in the group. The American Counseling Association *Code of Ethics and Standards of Practice* (ACA, 1995, section C.2.a) specifies that "Counselors practice only within the boundaries of their competence, based on their education, training, supervised experience, state and national professional credentials, and appropriate professional experience." The implication is that Allison and Bridget should not be running groups at this time if their level of competence does not support their working in the best interests of their clients who are participating in the group experience.

The main leader issue that emerged in connection with this incident is that neither Allison nor Bridget took responsibility for focusing on what was in the best interest of the group members. Instead they agreed with each other that they did not have to do much planning for the group members to have a successful group experience. In addition, there is a leader issue concerning the supervisor. To be consistent with the ACA Code of Ethics, the supervisor should have taken more of a leadership role in assisting Allison and Bridget in overcoming any limitations they had in connection with leading groups.

The relationship between the two counselors and their supervisor appears to be a limited one. The supervisor has an overall responsibility to the clients who participate in the group facilitated by Allison and Bridget. Therefore, the supervisor should have been thorough in discussing the needed planning strategies. After the first session, the supervisor should have provided the environment in which that session could have been discussed in more detail. He or she could have provided input that would have served to address what took place in the session and create awareness as to what might take place in ensuing sessions to enhance the opportunities for a successful group experience.

In addition, Allison and Bridget should have been honest in responding to their supervisor's question after the first session concerning how the group went. This would have provided an opportunity for formal follow-up supervision and the assistance that would benefit the two counselors in the future.

If Allison and Bridget had been thorough in their preplanning strategies, they would have been more specific with the referring high school counselor as to the type of students who might be suitable and possibly benefit from the group experience. The ACA Code of Ethics, in section A.9.a, emphasizes that counselors screen prospective group members and work toward selecting those whose goals and needs are compatible with group goals. Further, it is considered important to include those who will not obstruct the group process and "whose well-being will not be jeopardized by the group experience."

Group counselors, like all counselors, have the responsibility to address informed consent and to disclose to clients information about what takes place in the group counseling experience, including information about limitations, potential risks, and benefits, and any other information that may be considered pertinent. This takes place when the group counseling is initiated and throughout the counseling process as needed. The ACA Code of Ethics, in section A.3, focuses on client rights and the necessity of providing information to enable clients to make an informed choice as to their participation in the counseling experience.

The important role that the supervisor should play in this incident must be emphasized as well. Although the ACA Code of Ethics, in section F, is specific to teaching, training, and supervision involving programs of counselor educators and trainers, the ethical inferences may be perceived as being similar for the supervisor in the community mental health center as well. Therefore, this supervisor had a responsibility to ensure that the planning and levels of competence were appropriate and that ethical guidelines were complied with, so as to best serve the interests of these counselors' clients.

REFERENCE

American Counseling Association. (1995).   *Code of ethics and standards of practice.* Alexandria, VA: Author.

CHAPTER 2

SCREENING OF MEMBERS: "EVERYONE IS WELCOME"

One of the most critical factors in the preparation for group counseling is preselection of group members.

CRITICAL INCIDENT

Doris Rhea Coy

Background
Emily has just obtained emergency certification as a school counselor and has been hired by a local school district. She has not taken the group counseling course nor has she taken practicum or internship. She is, however, eager to begin her first group. She sent a note to teachers indicating that she is requesting the names of students who might benefit from group counseling. The teachers are prompt in returning names of students to Emily. She receives the names of 20 students from grades four to eight. She sends for each student to see if the student is available for group during third period every Wednesday. If students are available, they are accepted into the group. The total number of students accepted is 12. There are two students from each of grades four, five, and six, and three from each of grades seven and eight. The only room that will accommodate a group of 13 people is the cafeteria, so it is determined by the counselor that this will be the location for the group counseling sessions.

Incident
At the first meeting of the group, the school counselor requests that students give their name, grade level, and age; tell something about themselves; and explain what they want to work on while in the group. The following issues are shared with the group: four of the students are siblings, one student is suicidal, a seventh grader is sexually active, two students have been reported to the principal for lying and stealing, one student just completed alcohol treatment, two students have experienced the recent death of a parent, one student states that he has been physically abused, three students are failing at least one subject, and one student is a gang member. The ages of the students range from 9 to 15. One child lives with both parents, eight live with their mother, one lives with the father, one lives with grandparents, and one lives in a group home. Three students have limited speaking skills in

English. The students come from a variety of socioeconomic settings, racial groups, and cultural backgrounds.

Discussion

After the sharing that occurred in the first session, the school counselor is overwhelmed and announces that at this time there will be no further group counseling sessions. She has no idea what she should do next. She becomes very anxious, but tries to review what has occurred. She reviews the American Counseling Association *Code of Ethics and Standards of Practice* (ACA,1995), which her first counseling theories course had addressed. She is convinced that she has violated several of the items listed. She believes that she did not have the skills and knowledge necessary to conduct a group. She wonders about the steps and procedures one should follow in organizing the group experience. She wonders if she did any damage to any of the students. If she did, is there a chance that she could be sued? There were too many students in the group, and she cannot believe the diverse developmental differences of the students. Certainly some of the students should not have been in the group. She questions who should and should not have been selected for the group. She wonders what procedures should be followed in narrowing the issues to be addressed. Another concern she has is how she will explain what has occurred to her principal and to the teachers who made referrals. She is convinced that the students need help, but she questions how these students can receive the services that they desperately need. Out of desperation, she calls her college adviser for advice. She shares her frustrations and requests help.

QUESTIONS:

1. What knowledge and skills should a counselor have to conduct a group?
2. What areas of the ACA Code of Ethics may have been violated?
3. What prescreening procedures did the counselor neglect to take into account?
4. What procedures should be conducted at the first group meeting?
5. What procedure should the counselor follow before conducting her next group counseling session?

RESPONSE

Patrick Akos

Concepts of group stages, group dynamics, leadership styles, therapeutic forces, planning, dealing with problem members, and skills and techniques (e.g., dyads, rounds, deeper focus, drawing out, cutting off) are but a few examples of specific content knowledge and specific competencies that a counselor should have in order to lead a group experience.

Beyond the knowledge and skill competencies, a school counselor should have participated in co-leading with a trained counselor and received supervised practice in running a group. Because Emily has not taken a group course or practicum, or internship, it is likely that she has never participated in group counseling.

Emily has violated a basic ethical principle of the American School Counselor Association—"The professional school counselor functions within the boundaries of individual professional competence" (ASCA, 1998, standard E.1.a)—because she is operating outside her professional competence. Further, specific to group work, Emily apparently did not secure student and parent consent. Emily also did not do a variety of pregroup procedures necessary to ethically proceed. In addition, Emily potentially exposed group members to psychological harm given the wide range of developmental levels and presenting needs in the group.

Prescreening and pregroup procedures in school counseling are extensive and important to utilizing group work in an ethical and helpful way. The use of group counseling should be purposeful. Without knowledge of presenting needs (in asking for general referrals), Emily proposed a group intervention when it might not be appropriate. It would have been useful for Emily to do some prescreening of students who were referred to her. Ritchie and Huss (2000) have suggested using individual interviews, group interviews, interviews in team staffing, or completion of written questionnaires to screen students. In this way, she might have recognized the difficulty of helping all of the students in a group setting. She would have also been able to identify needs, expectations, and appropriateness of group members. Because Emily did not identify a particular group focus, it is difficult to determine what criteria would have been useful for selection of group members based on content or the group format (although developmental levels, availability, siblings, and limited English proficiency seem like obvious problems). In fact, the particular treatment needs of students in this group (harm to self/others, aggression) should be addressed by other counseling interventions.

Parent and student consent are also important to obtain before running a group. Information should be given to students and parents about the leader's qualifications, purpose and goals of the group, expectations of members, risks, confidentiality, and important logistical information (Ritchie & Huss, 2000). In acquiring parental consent, group leaders may also want to discuss privacy limits and confidentiality with parents. Also, prior to group, Emily should have thought through planning for the group intervention, which needs to include, but not be limited to, opening and closing rituals, content and/or exercises for group, sequencing for group content, process or techniques for group, and group evaluation.

Along with pregroup procedures, the components of a first session may be the most important aspect of establishing a school counseling group. A first group meeting sets the tone and purpose of the group and is often instrumental in teaching participants the nature of group process. An appropriate introduction to the school counselor, the purpose of the group, and the logistics associated with the group are important first steps. The leader should start the group by creating an opening ritual that helps students understand the beginning of group process. The school counselor needs to be certain that all students understand and agree to participate in the group. Another component common in school groups is participatory rule making for the group. Often school counselors engage students in deciding on a group name, several group rules, and consequences for rule infractions. Emily certainly should discuss the need for confidentiality and communicate that she is not able to ensure confidentiality by all members. Group members should also discuss expectations of the group leader, other group members, and themselves.

The next step may be an icebreaker activity. It can be in the form of introductions, as Emily did in the incident, but depending on grade level, it may also involve a game, drawing, or interactive procedure to connect students to each other. It may be useful to combine this activity with more information about the purpose of group. Depending on the group topic, it may be appropriate to form individual and group goals important to the leader and members. With most school counseling groups, these components will fill the available time, and Emily will do well to introduce a closing ritual, which may or may not involve homework (e.g., think about the topic, keep a journal, record your grades) for participants.

Under the current circumstances, it is inappropriate for Emily to run another group, especially with the current configuration. Emily needs to report to her principal and teachers her enthusiastic error of jumping in to helping students in group process without having appropriate training. She may also alert the administration to the ethical violations and potential legal ramifications of the incident. She needs to immediately address the suicidal student situation. Immediate contact needs to be made with an appropriate counselor or school psychologist, and ethical, legal, and school policy should be followed with this student. It is also imminent that Emily speaks with the student reporting abuse. Again, ethical, legal, and school policy should be followed in the referral to Child Protective Services (or similar agency) if appropriate. After Emily receives appropriate training to conduct groups, she could determine the best way to serve the students who were referred.

RESPONSE

James L. Moore III

After thoroughly examining this critical incident, it is quite clear that the school counselor is engaging in traditional school counseling practices (e.g., group counseling) that are beyond her scope of training. Several ethical and professional dilemmas surface in this critical incident related to Emily not having proper course work, training, and supervision in group counseling. In many ways, Emily's lack of training and supervision lead to her shortcomings with the group.

In group counseling, screening has an important function. It is essential to implementing effective groups. For this reason, screening is a standard of practice for counselors who desire to use group counseling as a counseling intervention in schools, mental health agencies, and other counseling settings. ACA's Code of Ethics (1995) related to group work (see section A.9.a) illustrates to counselors the importance of identifying and selecting group members who are least likely to impede or even sabotage the group process. The importance of taking necessary safety measures to protect the well-being of all members of the group is also emphasized. In this critical incident, it is obvious that Emily has violated several areas of ACA's Code of Ethics, particularly the one related to group work.

In order to be a viable intervention strategy, group counseling requires that school counselors have a grasp of basic counseling knowledge and skills as well as a clear assessment of the group members' needs. This understanding helps the school counselor put together a cohesive membership, one that can work toward the goals of the group. Before meeting with the group, the school counselor should determine the overall focus of the group, develop the plan of action for implementing the group, determine the number of group members, decide on the appropriate grade level, screen and select appropriate group members, obtain necessary parental permission, allocate adequate time for facilitating the group, and articulate the purpose of the group to group members.

It is worth noting that group counseling in schools serves as one of the many components of a comprehensive developmental school counseling program. Such programs focus on the academic, career, and personal/social needs of students. The extent to which school counselors are successful in organizing, implementing, and facilitating a group counseling experience for students is a function of their training and confidence in leading such an experience from start to finish. Based on Emily's lack of coursework, practicum, and internship experiences with group counseling, it is evident that she was neither equipped nor qualified to plan and lead a group experience. For example, at the first group meeting, she neglected to explain the purpose of the group, articulate to the group members how group counseling works, and emphasize to the group members their responsibility to the group.

Before facilitating her next group counseling session, it is imperative that Emily, first, seeks supervision from her college adviser and/or another counseling faculty member. Second, Emily needs to enroll in the next group counseling course offered at the university where she is working on her school counseling graduate degree. Third, she needs to consult and seek advice from other school counselors about her group. Fourth, she needs to begin to read books, monographs, and journal articles on group counseling. Fifth, she needs to consider dividing the one group into different groups, based on ages and presenting problems. Last, but not least, Emily should consider co-leading this group with another experienced school counselor.

REFERENCES

American Counseling Association. (1995). *Code of ethics and standards of practice.* Alexandria, VA: Author.

American School Counseling Association. (1998). *Ethical standards for school counselors.* Alexandria, VA: Author.

Ritchie, M., & Huss, S. (2000). Recruitment and screening of minors for group counseling. *Journal for Specialists in Group Work, 25,* 146–156.

CHAPTER 3

EQUAL TREATMENT OF MEMBERS: "BRIDGING THE GAP OF RURAL VERSUS INNER-CITY FELONS"

This incident explores issues in which group members have great diversity but one common ground: criminal activity. Skills in bridging the obvious gaps between seven inner-city-environed members and one rural-environed member, and the apparent prejudice of both, involve both unconditional acceptance and an atmosphere of defusing the escalating situation.

CRITICAL INCIDENT

Linda R. Osborne

Background

The group is entitled "Cognitive Self-Change" and is an intensive 6-month program that meets biweekly for 2 hours a session. This group is held inside the prison in the education area of the security department. All candidates are interviewed and screened on multifaceted issues, including their willingness to speak about their criminal activity in front of the group. Group rules and issues of confidentiality are discussed individually during the interview, reviewed at the initial group session, and reviewed again whenever a situation warrants clarification. All members have been convicted of crimes that included either assault charges or the potential for assault (armed robbery). Members include two Caucasians, two Latinos, and four African Americans.

Incident

The group had met for seven or eight sessions before this incident. The inmate from rural America presented his Fearless Criminal Inventory in front of the group. This activity involves a thorough list of rule-breaking behaviors from the individual's earliest recollection. This individual presented his list of rule-breaking activities that included many items such as stealing gas from a neighbor's car and shooting a gun on another's property. The rest of the group belittled the offenses presented by this participant. This member was the youngest member of the group and was quite immature. His anger quickly surfaced, and his frustration tolerance and level of self-control were sorely taxed. Beyond ribbing him for his offenses, the group's discussion continued into the dynamics of urbanization and ruralization. The situation led to heated discussion regarding the "innocence" and magnitude of hardship and severity of the city offenders versus the rural offender. The rule breaking reported by this one member was considered harmless fun by the rest of the group. Indeed, although the crime that sentenced this person to a lengthy prison sentence was very serious, the morality of his rule-breaking activities was such that the majority of group members could not begin to relate. With some modulating behavior by the group leader, the group was left to work this out among themselves. The discussion often led to heated arguments, angry tones, and scorn. It was imperative that the group leader show no bias or leniency toward any group member as they spoke. To the individual presenting, the reported events of his life were as significant as any other individual's report.

Discussion

At the end of the session with the group, anger on the part of the group member who had presented had dissipated for the most part. Although some of the other group members were still snickering and some were befuddled by the code of ethics the presenting individual held, allowing them to have an open, sometimes unfriendly, and often hostile communication resulted in a bonding of all group members. It created the opportunity for all to gain a perspective not available before this interaction. Later group sessions demonstrated a respect for the environmental conditions of others, even though a gentler teasing continued. This was a critical turning point for this particular group that was successful and productive in many ways for all involved in the group.

QUESTIONS

1. Did the group leader demonstrate unconditional regard for all group members and their input and presentations?
2. Did the group leader put any group members, or the continuance of the program itself, at risk by not taking a more assertive role?
3. Was the makeup of group participants screened carefully enough for admission into the group?
4. Would a more homogeneous group been suitable?

RESPONSE

Kathryn Russ

A prison group is, by definition, a coerced or nonvoluntary group; all of the members prefer to be somewhere else. It requires more structure and control from the leader than a voluntary group. This group leader did not demonstrate unconditional regard for all group members, their input, and their presentations when he failed to actively intervene during the rural inmate's presentation. He failed to demonstrate respect for the rural offender, and respect is a necessary ingredient for successful group experiences. By permitting the urban inmates to belittle the rural inmate, the leader was not demonstrating regard for this member. The rural offender's revelations about his life were as significant to him as any other member's report.

It is not necessary to eliminate the majority's responses, but the leader should have intervened assertively to redirect the other members' replies for several reasons. There are usually three underlying goals in offender groups: to replace aggressiveness with assertiveness, to increase personal responsibility, and to increase self-esteem (self-respect). The leader missed the chance to appropriately model assertiveness and respect as the preferred behavior for this group. Giving respect to another and feeling respect in turn has a circular relationship with increased self-esteem, improved sense of achievement, and the propensity for taking personal responsibility. When one achieves something, one takes personal responsibility for it, which, in turn, increases self-respect and respect from others.

The leader also permitted the urban group members to focus on the hardships and severity of their background as a reason or contributing factor to their crimes. This may be true, but such an emphasis does not encourage personal responsibility. The members received support from one another during the discussion that reinforced the belief that their crimes were the result of what they had endured in the way of hardships in their urban environment. By not redirecting the responses to a nonjudgmental discussion of the differences between rural and urban ecologies, the leader was not furthering the goal of personal responsibility.

The critical incident notes that "Later group sessions demonstrated a respect for the environmental conditions of others." The same end could have been achieved without using the rural member as a victim. The information could have been elicited and shared with all group members using more socially acceptable methods that the leader should have been modeling.

The group leader, by not intervening more actively, took a chance that the young rural offender would be able to handle the negative feedback that he received from the group. In this incident, the young man did manage to control his emotions of anger and frustration, but it could very easily have gone the other way, and he could have exploded either verbally or physically. In a closed, controlled environment such as a prison, what happens in the group is frequently not an isolated interaction. The interchange could easily have spread to other areas of the facility. This sort of reaction to the group meeting could have resulted in discontinuation of the program by prison authorities.

Homogeneity and heterogeneity of group members is an ongoing question for group leaders. Too much commonality can lead to stagnation; too little can lead to problems in communication and relationships. The ethnicity of the group was fairly well balanced with two Caucasians, two Latinos, and four African Americans. They all had the same inmate status, but the background and experience of urban and rural dwellers are very different. If I had included the rural offender in the group, I would have screened more thoroughly to include at least two or three people with a rural background. The balance of rural and urban in this group was very lopsided and led to ganging up on the minority member. Section A.9.a of the American Counseling Association *Code of Ethics and Standards of Practice* (1995) addresses the need for screening to ensure that no one is included in the group who might suffer from the experience. The exposure of the urban members to different environmental conditions appears to have been valuable and resulted in their gaining a wider perspective and respect for these differences. By planning in advance, the leader could have achieved this same goal by better balancing of urban and rural members. A more homogeneous group of all-urban offenders could also have been appropriate, and probably with less conflict. Adding heterogeneity, however, contributes to a more valuable and richer experience for all members.

RESPONSE

Shannon D. Smith

This critical incident is a very difficult situation for the group leader to manage. Under the described conditions, if the leader does not respond to the group in an appropriate manner, two unfortunate scenarios could unfold. In the first scenario, the group members could turn their anger and frustration toward the group leader and attack his or her power and leadership authority, thus rendering the group therapy useless. In the second scenario, the group members could seriously verbally attack the inmate from rural America due to his perceived weakness as a criminal. Further, there is potential danger for the group members to take their anger outside of the group setting and attack this inmate in a more serious and harmful way, including physical assault. Therefore, it appears that the group leader demonstrated unconditional regard for all group members and their input and presentations as neither of these scenarios occurred.

However, although the group leader demonstrated unconditional regard for all group members and their input, it appears that there were some unnecessary consequences as a result. First, by not taking a more assertive role in directing the members, the leader put the group at risk for verbal harm and embarrassment through belittling, snickering, and heated arguments and angry tones. This was particularly true for the inmate from a rural environment, who was provoked to anger and whose ability to self-regulate was taxed. Second, the lack of assertiveness on the part of the group leader could inadvertently lead to strengthening the criminal mentality that "a crime is not a crime unless it is a very serious offense," thus minimizing the serious nature of the crime committed by the group member who had presented. Although these could have been consequences from the lack of assertiveness of the group leader, the lack of assertiveness could have also led to the success of the group. For example, participants gained a new perspective not available prior to this interaction, and the members demonstrated a respect for the environmental conditions of others in later sessions.

Member selection for a group is very important because the success of the group process often depends on the established goals and purpose as well as the continuity and homogeneity of the participants. Based on the behavior of the group members, it is difficult to estimate whether or not individuals were screened carefully enough for admission into the group. Indeed members of this group may have been screened appropriately, yet upon entrance into the group they chose to respond to one member in an aggressive manner. This particular incident highlights the importance of proper screening procedures and appropriate member selection as well as the potential for a group to take on a life of its own. Even after a group leader establishes all of the proper selection procedures for group membership, the group members ultimately choose how they interact with each other. This fact does not negate proper selection procedures for group membership; however, it does point out the potential dangers associated with group processes. This case further points out the difficulty for group leaders in finding the balance between intervening too much versus too little in a group situation as well the challenge of selecting the appropriate timing for an intervention.

Finally, a more homogeneous group might or might not have been more suitable for this particular population. Certainly a more homogeneous group would have produced different results. It is important to point out that there are strengths that can be utilized by each of the participants from diverse populations. In this group, for example, one member who might have otherwise been excluded (on the premise that he was not a hard-core criminal) was indeed able to form a bond with the other group participants based on respect for the environmental conditions of others. Obviously this was a difficult and challenging lesson for this group. Participants may learn the most valuable lessons when less homogeneous people are placed together and share their differing opinions, which allows each member to examine his or her own beliefs and prompts reflection. In some instances, however, these participants might have felt more comfortable in a more homogeneous environment. Although it is difficult to speculate on the effectiveness of a more homogeneous group, this diverse group was ultimately successful. In displaying open and honest communication, the members were able to establish personal connections and develop mutual respect.

REFERENCE

American Counseling Association. (1995). *Code of ethics and standards of practice.* Alexandria, VA: Author.

CHAPTER 4

MEMBER LEAVING A GROUP: "NO GOOD-BYES"

This incident explores what happens when a group member leaves.

CRITICAL INCIDENT

Heather Trepal

Background

Luis and Susan both work in a community college counseling center. Together they run an ongoing group for women's issues. The rotating members of the group are comprised of each therapist's individual clients whom they invite to become members of the group. Over the years they have attempted to get women who have similar goals and who are experiencing similar developmental life stage transitions to join the group.

Incident

The women's issues group has been up and running for a number of years. Over the course of this time, several members have come and gone. In the past, when someone left the group and a new member joined, the members seemed to accommodate, and the new member appeared to adjust well. The women in the group quickly transitioned to the working stage. Most of the topics discussed in the group focused on common developmental transitions associated with being in college: relationships, coursework, maintaining balance, and family issues. The group members interacted well with each other and with the co-leaders.

One of the group members graduated over the summer leaving an open spot. Susan reported to Luis that she had been working with Amy in individual counseling over the past few months and felt that it might be beneficial both for Amy and the other members of the group if she were asked to join. Luis agreed, and Amy was invited to attend group sessions.

During the first session Amy was fairly quiet. Other group members introduced themselves, and as was the routine, two members asked for time to be set aside to discuss their particular issues. Susan noticed that Amy was withdrawn and was looking at her throughout the session. Luis processed Amy's first session with Susan after the group, and both decided that she was just getting warmed up. Susan assured Luis that this was not Amy's personality, as she had experienced her to be both outgoing and talkative in individual sessions.

During the second session Amy again said little. She made eye contact with Susan, her individual counselor, a little more than last session but did not seem to interact with the other group members. One member shared an issue that Susan knew that Amy could also relate to. Susan attempted to encourage Amy to share her feelings about the other person's concerns. Susan made prolonged eye contact with her and asked the entire group for feedback. She hoped that Amy would respond, but she still remained silent.

Discussion

After the session, both Susan and Luis wondered about Amy's silence. They wondered what, if anything, she was getting from the group. They also wondered how the other group members were reacting to her behavior. They decided to let it go one more week and then either speak to Amy privately or phone her to consult about the group sessions. Amy never returned to group or individual counseling and did not respond to a follow-up letter.

During the next session the group was very interested in discussing Amy's leaving. They appeared to blame themselves, and the group as a whole, for her leaving. Both Susan and Luis were confused by this and did not know how to process the situation within the group.

QUESTIONS

1. Could the co-leaders have prevented the client's silent departure from the group sessions? If so, how?
2. Are there any techniques that the counselors could have employed in session to get the group members involved?
3. What are the issues that remain in the group when a member unexpectedly and abruptly leaves?
4. What are the ways in which this issue could be processed with the remaining group members?

RESPONSE

Muhyiddin A. Shakoor

I think that the co-leaders might have prevented Amy's silent departure from the group sessions. Upon first reading the incident, it seemed unlikely; but after carefully reviewing the details, several alternative possibilities emerge. The very first consideration is screening. If Amy was, in truth, a poor candidate for the group, her silent departure could have been prevented if the group leaders recognized that she was not a good candidate before she came. This raises questions about Luis and Susan's experience and sense of competence in groups. If they have limited experience with this type of incident, then they must simply be honest with themselves, and learn new more effective methods.

Further, I believe that screening and issues of selection merit serious and thoughtful attention on the part of group leaders (Carroll & Wiggins, 1997;

Corey, 2000; Donigian & Malnati, 1997; Gladding, 2003; Kline, 2003; Shakoor & Rabinowicz, 1978; Yalom, 1995). In this regard, the group work literature appears to support the wisdom of the Benjamin Franklin adage that "An ounce of prevention is worth a pound of cure." The saying is well applied to issues of premature termination in groups. Because this group is open, the issues are more emphatic. Each time someone exits or enters the group, he or she fosters a transition that has impact for both the member and the group.

Part of Luis and Susan's responsibility as effective therapists and group leaders is to insure that individual counseling clients being referred to their group are carefully considered and qualify for their group. In other words, they are encouraged to think about each client and their personal experience of the client in individual counseling. Further, they are encouraged to consider whether the client is or is not a candidate for the group. It is entirely possible that Amy was a poor candidate from the outset. There are many clues that Susan might have noted if she had considered the following questions: Is Amy psychologically-minded? Does she relate well or with difficulty interpersonally? Did relationship issues bring her to therapy in the first place? Is she able to form relationships and be appropriately close or is she challenged by intimacy? Does she relate well to persons of the same gender? What was she like in her family? Is she depressed? Is she secretive? Is she in the grips of a strongly negative self-image? Is she strongly attached to or dependent on the therapist? Does she have highly pressing external problems that are stressful for her at this time in her life?

If after considering these questions, Susan still believes Amy should be selected as a candidate, she should proceed to help orient Amy to the group. This includes telling Amy why she believes that she is a good candidate for the group and what motivates her as the therapist to make such a recommendation. I think Susan's transparency in this regard is essential. Some honest talk can go far. Susan may let Amy and other candidates know what is likely to happen in the group and what will be expected in terms of sharing and what the ground rules are for leaving. Susan may ask Amy to project herself into a group of women who are focusing on the issues that have been identified and ask Amy for a commitment if she sees herself fitting in. This approach may help Amy be more proactive and more involved in selecting or deselecting herself. It will also help Amy be better informed of the benefits and challenges of entering the group. She is then given an opportunity to choose. If she enters the group with some awareness of what needs she is bringing to the group and some sense that her needs may be satisfied, she is more likely to stay. Susan and Luis may also make the kinds of questions that Susan should have asked Amy a part of their discussion and review process whenever transitions occur, whenever there is the possibility for new members to join their group.

The group members could do more to welcome new members. They have already spent considerable time together as a group, and a member like Amy may be challenged to enter the group. Any new member to the group who is overly dependent, who has authority issues, or who tends to compare herself to others in self-depreciating ways may struggle. Group leaders could also model welcoming and taking interest in new members. Group members could express interest in getting to know Amy and share about themselves, thus acknowledging her joining the group before jumping into their issues. As a facilitator, I make every effort to model welcoming, and were group members self-absorbed or distracted, I might comment that the group seemed not ready to welcome Amy. If certain issues are highly prevalent, such as hesitation, anxiety, or fear, it may be helpful to think of more fluid activities such as the use of dyads or quartets for a few minutes at the beginning of a session following a major transition in the group. Inside the dyad or quartet, members may share one or two things personally that they can do to make the group stronger in handling transition. They may also consider things that they can individually do to help the new person more easily make his or her transition in to the group.

Issues that may remain in the group after a transition include loss, disappointment, anger, hurt, relief, surprise, guilt, unresolved feelings/remnants of abandonment or dysfunctional family experiences, and lurking questions about personal responsibility. Members may explore and share feelings they have about the group, here and now in the face of this change. They may share how they feel about other members or how the leaders could be more productive in identifying issues that challenge the equilibrium of the group.

Honest talk and forthright interpersonal sharing can be a helpful way to process this issue with the remaining group members. Members may share as follows: "Here's how I am feeling now that Amy has gone." "Here's how I want to be when new members come into this group or when they leave it. Here's what I want to do." "Here's what I think I expect from you, Susan, or Luis." "Here's what I desire or hope for in this group, and here's what I fear will happen or that I will or will not get." "Here's what I did, and here's my sense of personal effectiveness or ineffectiveness in our group today."

RESPONSE

Valerie L. Guay

Luis and Susan faced an interesting challenge in the presented incident. When a group member like Amy enters a group, says next to nothing for 2 weeks, and then never returns, the group members may blame themselves for the person's departure, and the counselors will usually be left scratching their heads over the person's behavior. These two undesirable outcomes might have been avoided if Luis and Susan had discussed Amy's behavior with her following her first group session. Deciding between them that Amy was just getting warmed up, Luis and Susan denied Amy the opening she might have needed to discuss why she was not feeling comfortable in the group. Amy's discomfort might have been due to many possible factors, including social phobia, performance anxiety, stage fright, or differences in age, racial/ethnic, or socioeconomic background. The description of the incident does not provide us with enough information about Amy to lead us to a conclusive reason for her group behavior. However, Susan's comments about Amy's personality being "outgoing and talkative in individual sessions" are quite interesting. Many clients do not behave the same way in individual sessions and group sessions; for example, clients may be open and talkative in one-on-one sessions where they feel comfortable with the counselor but may verbally shut down in group situations where the expectations of others and the pressure to participate may be too overwhelming. Luis and Susan should have discussed this with Amy immediately following the first group meeting and certainly following the second group meeting. Susan also had the opportunity to discuss the situation alone with Amy during their next individual session (which, presumably, occurred between the two group sessions Amy attended).

The other issue in this incident involves the rest of the group members and their feelings of blame and guilt over Amy's departure. This presented the group leaders with a somewhat tricky situation. Of course, it is not necessarily the fault of the group members if a member decides to leave. However, it is perhaps unavoidable that the group members blame themselves for not being welcoming enough or possibly too aggressive in their welcoming. The group leaders may simply bring up the group member's leaving directly. This will allow the remaining group members to discuss their thoughts and feelings regarding the departure while receiving feedback from the counselors. The counselors may also discuss with the group members the role of the group leaders versus the role of the group members in regard to membership retention. It is not the sole responsibility of the group members to encourage participation and draw out a quiet group member; this is one reason groups have facilitators, and Luis and Susan could have done a better job in this respect.

Seeking guidance and supervision from a more experienced group leader and/or counselor might also have benefited Luis and Susan. Hearing an outside, objective opinion might have helped Susan and/or Luis realize that speaking with Amy immediately might have prevented these issues.

REFERENCES

Carroll, M., & Wiggins, J. (1997). *The elements of group counseling: Back to the basics* (2nd ed.). Denver, CO: Love.

Corey, G. (2000). *Theory and practice of group counseling* (5th ed.). Pacific Grove, CA: Brooks/Cole.

Donigian, J., & Malnati, R. (1997). *Systemic group therapy: A triadic model.* Pacific Grove, CA.: Brooks/Cole.

Gladding, S.T. (2003). *Group work: A counseling specialty* (4th ed.). Upper Saddle River, NJ: Merrill Prentice Hall.

Kline, W. (2003). *Interactive group counseling and therapy.* Upper Saddle River, NJ: Merrill Prentice Hall.

Shakoor, M., & Rabinowicz, S. (1978). The Sought Membership Model: A model for conceptualizing person-group relationships in groups where membership is sought. *Small Group Behavior, 9*(3), 325–329.

Yalom, I. (1995). *Theory and practice of group psychotherapy* (4th ed.). New York: Basic Books.

CHAPTER 5

CO-LEADERSHIP: "WHOSE NEEDS ARE GETTING MET HERE?"

This incident explores some of the issues involving co-leadership of groups.

CRITICAL INCIDENT

Heather Trepal

Background

Jeanette and Claire are master's-level counselors at a rape crisis program. They are both under the supervision of an outside consultant who is a Licensed Professional Clinical Counselor (LPCC) and has years of experience working with rape and sexual assault issues. Jeanette is interested in starting a group for adult survivors of incest. She knows Claire well from staff meetings and has always found her comments to be both insightful and thought provoking. In addition, they often socialize together, and Jeanette considers Claire a friend. They work together for several months in the pre-planning group stages (i.e., developing the group format, recruiting participants, screening potential participants).

Incident

The first group meeting begins, and as planned Jeanette and Claire lead the eight members in introductory activities. The group members are invited to say three things about themselves that will allow other members to get to know them. They are also encouraged to ask each other questions and to get to know one another. In addition, members are asked to share their expectations regarding the group with the other members. The co-leaders feel that this is important as it allows everyone to know where each member stands in terms of what they want from the group. The co-leaders also feel that sharing expectations may encourage ownership of the group by the members. The group members are also asked to read the ground rules and to discuss them with each other and the co-leaders. Ground rules focus on one person talking at a time, being on time and present for group sessions, confidentiality and the limits of confidentiality, and agency policies.

One of the goals of the first session is to allow each participant to tell her story, what she hopes to get from the group, and what her worries are about the group. As they had planned, Jeanette begins the sharing by describing her excitement about the group and the opportunities for healing that it affords members. After each of the members takes a turn, Claire announces that she wants to share something.

Claire informs the group that she, too, is a survivor of incest. She further explains that she is interested in co-leading this group because she feels that it will help her in her healing. After sharing an emotional story about her abuser, Claire begins to cry and is comforted by several members of the group. Although she is surprised by this self-disclosure, Jeanette attempts to refocus the group members on joining and discussing closure of the session.

Discussion

After the session, Jeanette and Claire meet and discuss the first group. Jeanette decides to confront Claire about her self-disclosure and asks, "What was that all about? Telling your abuse story to the group sure seemed like a bad way to get some sympathy." Claire responds, "It is part of my theoretical orientation to share my story with all of my clients. I just thought that everyone who worked with survivors did that." The co-leaders both leave feeling a little confused and overwhelmed by the first group session but decide that they will continue next week.

QUESTIONS

1. Is either of these counselors suitable for leading this type of group?
2. What are the co-leader issues presented in this incident that may interfere with the success of this group?
3. What are the differences in the leaders' theoretical orientations? Is this an important issue to consider in co-leadership of groups?
4. What are the ethical implications of counselor self-disclosure?
5. What are some of the advantages and disadvantages of this type of co-leadership model?

RESPONSE

Beverly A. Burnell

Claire and Jeanette seem to have experienced some benefits from their co-leadership approach, having spent several months "developing the group format, recruiting participants, screening potential participants." Jeanette and Claire also identified goals and related activities for the first group meeting, including using member self-disclosure; sharing expectations, hopes, and worries to encourage ownership by members; and setting ground rules. The overall purpose of the group was not identified, however, so it is unclear whether the leaders defined it. During Jeanette and Claire's pregroup planning, their friendship probably also developed. However, it appears this might have created a barrier to development of a healthy co-leadership team within which differences in theoretical orientations and life experiences could provide complementary perspectives for the good of the group.

In addition to graduate course work, counselor suitability for group leadership requires experience leading or co-leading groups, an understanding of the applicability of a variety of theoretical orientations and how these influence co-leadership, and an array of personal and leadership characteristics beyond those required for individual counseling. We do not know much about these factors in this situation, nor do we know the role the outside consultant/supervisor took in overseeing the development of this co-leadership team. Most critical, however, is the preparation and knowledge each leader had with regard to the topic/purpose of this particular group. It appears that Claire and Jeanette were not open with each other regarding their motivations for developing this group. The incident suggests this type of group was new to both leaders. Claire and Jeanette seem to have not discussed their personal experiences and potential problems and conflicts around the issues for which the group was being formed or the compatibility and applicability of their theoretical orientations to the work of this group and how these would affect their leadership decisions. The co-leaders' knowledge of group dynamics seems inadequate as well, particularly given their intention to foster disclosure of the members' specific experiences in the first session, but also evidenced by Claire's naïve expectations about her use of self-disclosure.

Of additional concern is Claire's suitability for individual counseling if, as she says, she discloses her story to all her clients. Self-disclosure that comes from a theoretical rationale is expected to be intentional and timely and for the purpose of helping the client. Therapy and support for Claire's healing from her experience as a survivor of incest must precede and, if necessary, be concurrent with any professional role she undertakes in providing therapy for other survivors. Claire and Jeanette seem to have discussed the use of counselor self-disclosure as a catalyst to meet their goal of allowing each member to tell her story, though their timing of this goal for the first session is also questionable. The consequences of Claire's disclosure to the co-leadership relationship include betrayal of the trust between the leaders, possibly an inappropriate expectation that Jeanette provide support for Claire's healing process (about which Jeanette has already expressed resentment), and changes in leadership status for both Claire and Jeanette. It is unclear whether or not Jeanette had prior knowledge of Claire's experiences. Jeanette's confrontation of Claire about her disclosure suggests either she did not know or that they began the group with the issue of self-disclosure unresolved between them. Ethical implications of the disclosure for the group members include the potential for harm from participating in a group co-led by an impaired professional and a co-leadership team with critical leadership incompatibilities. The co-leaders had intended for ownership of the group to be held by the members and had undertaken their last activity in the group to assist this. The hopes and worries about the group that each member shared in that activity, and the potential for group ownership by the members, became tainted by Claire's disclosure and need to attend to her own healing. Claire lost her potential as a role model, which a more timely and appropriate disclosure (with the foreknowledge of her co-leader) could have provided.

RESPONSE

Gary E. Goodnough

The incident describes Jeanette and Claire as under the supervision of an LPCC who has significant experience working with issues of sexual assault and rape. It is not clear how much involvement the supervisor has had with the two counselors as they planned the group. Effective supervision of group work includes supervision of the planning process and a facilitation of a discussion about the role of self-disclosure. The supervisor's role is important for many reasons. Formal pregroup supervision would have uncovered the differing perspectives of the group leaders and set the stage for either a resolution of the issue or a delay or cancellation of the group.

The issue of whether Jeanette and Claire are "suitable" for leading this group suggests that counselors have stable personal traits that render them fit or unfit to lead. I assume each counselor has strengths and knowledge that could lead her to be an effective group counselor for this population. In responding to the incident, it is perhaps more helpful to investigate the appropriateness and ethical behavior of each counselor. Currently, both of them seem unready to be a leader of such an important and complex group. Claire's behavior suggests she is using the group for her own continuing personal work. Although it is important that she continue to heal from the trauma she has suffered, doing so within the context of providing counseling services to others is unethical. Jeanette's present approach seems more appropriate for being a group leader, but her willingness to go forward with the group given her sense of being overwhelmed and confused is troubling. The fact that Jeanette did not mention taking the issue to the supervisor is of concern.

It seems clear that the two counselors have vastly different perceptions as to the appropriateness of Claire's revelation in the first group. The counselors are friends. Friendship can create a dual role for group leaders. It is not that friendship is unethical per se, but such a preexisting relationship can create a situation where co-leaders are less than honest with each other and seek to spare each other's feelings. Despite working together for several months to plan the group, they apparently never discussed the role of self-disclosure. Regardless of whether not discussing it was a friendship issue or one of poor communication, such a lack of communication resulted in this issue not being raised. Again, I wonder about the supervisor's role in this situation.

As theory guides practice, counselors are trained to have a theoretical orientation that helps them effectively implement their counseling interventions in a logical and consistent manner. It is not clear to what theory Jeanette ascribes. The only clue seems to be that she is excited and hopeful that the group will help the clients with their growth and healing. As long as such enthusiasm is grounded, genuine, and helpful, it might be an expression of an underlying theoretical construct. It is also not clear to what theory Claire ascribes. She seems to support her self-disclosure and consequent crying and support-seeking behavior as somehow being part of some theory. She also assumes that all rape crisis counselors communicate their abuse histories to their clients in an emotion-laden manner. This justification suggests that she does not have extensive experience nor has she read widely on the topic of group therapy for sexual assault victims.

It seems that Claire believes she has been genuine with her clients and that, because she understands their pain from personal experience, she will be able to be of great help to them. One downside of this type of "I'm like you" self-disclosure is that each person's experiences are unique and personal. Just because she has experienced abuse does not mean that her experience is helpful or meaningful to others. It also subtly suggests to the group that Jeanette, who revealed no such abuse, is somehow not as qualified to lead the group. But Claire's self-disclosure goes beyond just informing the group that she, too, has experienced abuse. Her disclosure results in the focusing of group energy on her. This violates a fundamental rule of counseling: it is for the benefit of clients. Clients must not be placed in the position of comforting the counselor—ever. By behaving in the way she did, the group members took care of her. Claire's self-disclosure and emotional recounting of her abuse suggests that she is not, at present, sufficiently healthy or knowledgeable enough about group counseling to co-lead the group.

CHAPTER 6

IMPOSING COUNSELOR VALUES:
"GRADES ARE MORE IMPORTANT!"

Group counselors often assist clients in sorting through problems that are value laden. Some of the most notable examples of these include issues related to religion, abortion, divorce, or sexuality. It is important that counselors recognize and define their own values on issues such as these to avoid imposing them on their clients. However, it is not only controversial social or political issues in which value conflicts arise. In fact, value-laden problems habitually surface during groups in more subtle forms, as this incident demonstrates.

CRITICAL INCIDENT

Douglas A. Guiffrida

Background

Tom is 22-year-old White male from a middle-class background who is in the second year of his master's degree program in counseling. As part of his internship, he is leading a voluntary group of college students who are seeking to improve their academic performances. During the first group meeting, Tom begins by conducting an ice-breaking activity designed to introduce members of the group to one another. After the icebreaker, he asks the students to write down their perspectives on why they are not doing well academically.

Incident

Tom asks for volunteers to share what they had written regarding reasons for not doing well at college. Michael, an African American male student who is a junior, says, "For me, it is my involvement in activities. I am the president of the college's NAACP, and that has really taken a lot of time. Between running meetings, organizing speakers on campus, and planning the last race dialogue, I have not had any time for school work."

Tom responds by saying, "Wow, it sounds like your plate is really full. Have any other students experienced problems like this?" Connie, a Latino female student who is a sophomore, adds, "I had a similar problem. I was in charge of pledging for my sorority this year. That has taken a lot of my time, plus one of my sorority sisters has been having a lot of problems at home and I have been helping her, and that has also kind of pulled me away from my studies."

Tom responds by saying, "It sounds as if both of you are having problems staying focused on academics because of outside distractions. Does anyone in the group have any suggestions for them on how they can eliminate or reduce these distractions?" Marsha, an African American female student who is a junior, answers by saying, "I am not sure they really can eliminate those things. I mean, when people have problems, you can't just ignore them to do your own thing. Sometimes you just have to sacrifice yourself to help your family. Like last semester, I had to miss a final because my great aunt was sick, and I had to go home to help take care of her."

Connie adds, "Yes, and my sorority sisters really are like my family. It was scary last year when I left home and I hated it here. My sisters really took me in and made me feel like I was home. It is the only place where I feel comfortable on campus and can speak Spanish. They are the only reason I am here, so I can't just turn my back on them. I think professors need to be more understanding of students when they have personal problems."

Michael jumps back in and adds, "I agree. NAACP has been so great for me that there is no way I could just drop it. Plus, I have really done a lot of important things for the Black community on campus through my involvement. Besides, the leadership experience is going to be very valuable when I am looking for a job." Connie adds, "Employers really value those leadership experiences more than grades. It shows that you can think beyond just regurgitating answers on a test."

At this point, Tom asks John, a White student who is a sophomore, if he wants to share his reason for not doing well in school. John says, "It's just managing my time better and not hanging around with my friends as much. I just need to focus and remember why I am here and I think I will do fine." Tom adds, "Yes, I agree. It sounds as if some of you have been very helpful to your friends and families and that you have done a lot for your organizations. But as John points out, you have to remember why you are here. I can't say I disagree with professors who don't seem understanding when you miss a final. Doing well in school requires a great deal of commitment, which includes not getting distracted by outside issues. We can spend the next few weeks helping you to prioritize things a little better."

Discussion

The session continues until everyone shares his or her reasons for not doing well. Tom ends the session by summarizing each student's perspective of the problem. Throughout the session, he continually felt resistance from some of the culturally different students, and he is discouraged that they were not able to see how their outside commitments had become liabilities to their academics. He decides the next session will be more didactic so he can teach them the importance of good grades.

QUESTIONS

1. In what ways has Tom imposed his values during this group?
2. What could Tom have done differently?
3. Is it possible for Tom to fulfill the purpose of the group (academic improvement of the members) given some students' outside commitments?
4. Instead of lecturing on the importance of good grades, what else could Tom try in future sessions? Describe your reasons for suggesting alternative strategies.

RESPONSE

N. Joan Hornak

Tom has demonstrated a lack of acceptance of group members' perceptions and values both by his direct responses to them and by his inviting other group members to join him in forcing changes that reflect his goals for the group. First, Tom has labeled group members' extracurricular activities and their attention to the emotional needs of friends as *distractions*. He does this by requesting ideas on how to "eliminate or reduce these distractions." Further, he openly agrees with John's goal to spend less time with friends. In the first session, Tom has been critical of some participants' values, has reinforced another's, and has unilaterally determined the desired group outcome is to have students recognize that their "outside commitments had become liabilities." His behavior is contrary to the American Counseling Association *Code of Ethics and Standards of Practice* (ACA, 1995), which states that "Counselors are aware of their own values, attitudes, beliefs, and behaviors and how these apply in a diverse society, and avoid imposing their values on clients" (section A.5.b). He is presenting an either/or situation for culturally different students, which implies they must relinquish their valued activities or they will not be academically successful. These group members respond by defending their values and choices.

Tom would have been wise to first build rapport with group members by accepting their perceptions and values. This could have been done by acknowledging the importance of extracurricular activities and peer/family support and by reflecting on the success group members have had in those areas. The ACA Code of Ethics emphasizes this concept: "Counselors will actively attempt to understand the diverse cultural backgrounds of the clients with whom they work. This includes, but is not limited to, learning how the counselor's own cultural/ethnic/racial identity impacts her/his values and beliefs about the counseling process" (section A.2.b). Supervision might assist Tom in recognizing when his values clash with those of group members. When Tom decided to teach to his goal in future meetings, the group process was changed without group input.

Outcomes for group members cannot be guaranteed or imposed. However, there is the possibility of numerous benefits for this group had members experienced an environment of trust and acceptance. For example, members could have clarified their values, seen consequences of their behaviors and choices, explored alternatives, shared strategies for balancing multiple roles, and built a support network. Because participation in the group is voluntary, members will leave if they feel their values negatively judged and if they are coerced to discard those values.

In future sessions, it may be helpful to explore beyond group members' first responses. When Tom asked members to write about why they are not doing well academically, he essentially invited their excuses. Instead, participants could focus on their academic successes and how those positive experiences were achieved. Group brainstorming and mentoring strategies could facilitate this. In addition, a time management log could give members more accurate insights as to their use of time when not focused on extracurricular activities, friends, or academics. Writing strategies could assist group members in picturing future outcomes of their current actions. Specifically, writing to a significant other a letter about their academic failure could assist participants in poignantly reflecting on the impact of academic failure. Similarly, an essay to be shared with the group could address what successful degree completion will mean to them professionally as well as to their significant others. These several strategies, when woven into the natural group process, will empower members to achieve *their* desired group outcomes without either abandoning their values or assuming those of the group facilitator.

RESPONSE

Carolyn Noël

Tom has imposed his values during this group session by asserting that school should be the number one priority for all of the group members. He fails to take into consideration the importance of outside activities and responsibilities that many of the students in the group have, and instead refers to them as *distractions*. He also neglects to consider the cultural differences that may be impacting the choices the students have made. Tom is quick to assert his opinion and make judgments about the students' commitment to school. He essentially sides with the other White male in the group when discussing where the students' priorities should be.

Although Tom began with an icebreaker, he could have spent more time establishing a rapport within the group. This would have allowed Tom to get to know the members better while developing a greater appreciation of what is important to them. When members participated in the group discussion, Tom could have explored their concerns further instead of immediately jumping into how to "eliminate or reduce these distractions." Exploring cultural differences among group members and what those mean for each person would have been appropriate at this time, as each person's background clearly had an impact on his or her choices. By not looking at these issues or reflecting any of the concerns students put forth about social and family obligations, Tom alienated some of the group members and sent the message that these things are not as important as school.

Given that many of the students in the group have outside obligations that are important to them, Tom could shift the focus from prioritizing to establishing a balance between school and these other commitments. This is a voluntary group, which suggests that the students care about their school performance and are motivated to make changes in order to improve. Tom could provide support to the students while working with them to determine where they are able to make adjustments. With Tom acting as a role model, rather than as a disciplinarian, he is much more likely to help the group members improve their academic performance.

Instead of lecturing on the importance of good grades, Tom could use future sessions to explore some of the resistance he experienced in the first session. Eliciting feedback and addressing these issues early on will prevent members from becoming alienated or dropping out and open up discussion to the issues that have been overlooked. If Tom is able to recognize that he has imposed his values, he can use that information to help him lead the group more effectively by not repeating this mistake during future sessions. Other sessions could be used to brainstorm ideas for improving the students' academic performance without eliminating their other commitments. Finding out what the group members' ideas and goals are will be crucial to the success of this group. Tom could work with these ideas and goals in order to determine how to set up the remaining group sessions. This is, after all, the students' group, and although it is clear that Tom has the best interest of each student in mind, recognizing that his priorities may differ from other peoples' will help him lead this group more effectively.

REFERENCE

American Counseling Association. (1995). *Code of ethics and standards of practice.* Alexandria, VA: Author.

CHAPTER 7

DUAL RELATIONSHIPS: "I THINK I KNOW YOU"

This incident addresses the issue of dual relationships, in this case between a counselor and a group member.

CRITICAL INCIDENT

Kelly L. Wester

Background
Melanie works at a local community mental health agency. She is a Licensed Professional Clinical Counselor who supervises doctoral interns from the local university. She also runs many programs and groups within the agency. Candace began working as a doctoral intern at the community mental health agency 2 months ago. Melanie is her supervisor.

Incident
Melanie and Candace have been seeing many clients individually who have presented with body image concerns, so they decided that it would be beneficial to run a group on body image. They preplanned the group and designed it to explore women's concerns with their body image, shape, size, and weight as well as to explore where negative feelings about their body image arose (i.e., family, media, peers). Melanie and Candace also designed the group so that the group members could learn skills and techniques to combat members' negative feelings about their bodies. The group leaders decided to announce the group to their current clients as well as advertise for the group in the local newspaper. The leaders decided that the group would have a maximum of 10 group members and run for 12 weeks. Both Melanie and Candace understood that many other serious concerns could be related to body image concerns (i.e., eating disorders); therefore, they decided to screen all individuals who inquired about the group in order to make sure that (1) the group was appropriate for the individual and (2) the individuals were not currently under the care of another counselor or physician. They received 28 inquiries from people who were interested in participating in the group. Due to time constraints, Melanie and Candace decided to each take half of the individuals who inquired about the body image group and prescreen them. After prescreening all 28 members, they consulted with each other on the possible group members, only discussing presenting concerns but not discussing demographics. They came to a final conclusion on

10 individuals for the group, with 3 of the group members being individual clients of Melanie, and 1 group member seeing Candace in individual sessions. The following week Melanie and Candace had their first body image group. When she walked into the group, Candace realized that one of the group members was a master's degree student from her university. The master's degree student had been in a couple of her counseling classes over the previous year.

Discussion

After the first group session ended, Candace revealed to Melanie that she knew one of the group members from her counseling program at the university. Both Melanie and Candace realized that the master's degree student had not talked much during the group session and had glanced hesitantly at Candace a couple of times throughout the group. They also realized that three of the group members who were being seen individually by Melanie seemed to dominate the group, taking up the majority of the group time with their body concerns. These three group members also seemed to be way ahead of the other group members in awareness of their body image concerns, while the other group members appeared to shy away from more intimate issues this early in the group. The one group member that Candace saw individually did not seem comfortable in the group and spoke only to Candace when she shared in the group and not to the other group members.

QUESTIONS

1. What important pieces of the prescreening process did the two group leaders overlook?
3. What are the implications of having members in the group that are currently being seen in individual counseling sessions by one of the group leaders?
4. Are there any concerns about the relationship between the doctoral intern and the master's student?
5. What are the next steps that should be taken by Melanie, the supervisor, or Candace, the doctoral intern, before the second body image group takes place?
6. What other ethical issues are important regarding dual relationships in group therapy?

RESPONSE

Barbara R. Herlihy

Melanie and Candace made a sensible decision, given their time constraints and the large number of potential group members, to each interview half of the prospective participants. However, when they met to determine whom to include in the group, their failure to discuss interviewees' demographic information resulted in the inclusion of a group member with whom Candace had a prior relationship. The existence of a dual relationship became apparent when this member, who was a master's degree student, and Candace, a doctoral intern, realized that they had been fellow students in two graduate classes at their university the previous year. Although dual relationships generally are conceptualized as occurring when a counseling professional simultaneously has another relationship with a client, problems can also arise when relationships are sequential. In this case, the prior relationship appears to have made the group member uncomfortable and to have inhibited the member's participation in the initial group session.

Although this group member and Candace do not seem to know each other at all well, the member's discomfort may be arising from a concern over whether her confidentiality will be protected now that a fellow student knows that she has sought mental health services. Also, if doctoral students in the counselor education program at their university provide individual or group supervision to master's students, the group member may be concerned that Candace might supervise her professional work in a future semester. Candace should contact this member before the next scheduled group session to discuss these or any other concerns. If the member wants to remain in the group, Candace should help her weigh the risks and benefits of the decision. Together, they should decide how they want to handle the problem. They need to consider the ramifications of keeping their other relationship secret from the rest of the group and of disclosing that information to the group. They will also want to explore some "what if" scenarios, such as what they will do if they encounter each other on campus or if they need to work together in the future as fellow students or as supervisor and supervisee. If the member wishes to drop out of the group, Candace will need to respect her wishes and assist her in finding alternative services.

Other potential dual relationship problems exist by virtue of the fact that some, but not all, of the group members are being seen in individual counseling by Candace and by Melanie. Although it is not unethical for group leaders to include individual clients in groups they form, in this instance the practice seems to be problematic. The one client whom Candace is seeing individually is uncomfortable in the group. This client, accustomed to having Candace's undivided attention in their individual sessions, may resent having to share Candace's attention with other members. She may be concerned that Candace may say something during group that could inadvertently reveal information she has shared with Candace privately. Candace will need to constantly self-monitor to ensure that this does not happen.

The inclusion of the three group members who are individual clients of Melanie appears to have created a problem with group member compatibility. These three members seem to be far ahead of the other members in their awareness of body image concerns and thus to have dominated the group. Melanie and Candace will need to meet and discuss how to handle this situation before the dominance of the group by these three members becomes normative for the group's functioning. If dealt with skillfully, the advanced awareness of these three members can become an asset to the group process as they can serve as role models for the others.

It is imperative that Melanie and Candace meet to discuss these issues before the next group meeting. They may also want to consult with a fellow professional who has expertise and experience in group work. This incident underscores how important it is for co-leaders to screen very carefully and to consider any potential dual relationships between members and leaders.

RESPONSE

Perry C. Francis

This case illustrates two different types of dual relationships that can exist in the group counseling process, the importance of having a clear understanding of the group's goals and purpose, and the need for a comprehensive prescreening process.

The process of screening clients for any group begins before the first prescreening interview, with the conceptualization of the purpose of the group. Having a clear understanding of the purpose of the group will help in the selection of members. In this case it is clear that although Candace and Melanie had a good idea about the purpose of their group, they did not take into account the potential group members' developmental awareness or experience in regards to their body image. The members are clearly at different stages concerning their feelings about their body image. Although it is important to have a variety of people in the group, people from extremely different levels of emotional development may inhibit group process and cohesion.

Part of the prescreening process includes a review of the facilitators' names and credentials. If this information had been made available to the master's degree student prior to the beginning of the group, the student could have made a more informed decision about participation. The facilitators would have also had the chance to decide if the relationship between Candace and the student was too problematic to allow the student to join the group. Generally, dual relationships are to be avoided in any counseling relationship. At times they cannot be avoided, especially in underserved areas. When a dual relationship cannot be prevented, the counselor is to inform the client about the nature of the dual relationship and the impact it may have on the counseling process. The counselor is also to take steps to ensure that his or her judgment is not impaired and that no exploitation occurs. This was not allowed to take place in this particular situation.

Related to this issue are the implications of working with the same client in both individual and group sessions. It is not uncommon for a counselor to see a client in both settings. In that instance, the counselor sets appropriate boundaries for the client concerning the different objectives that are dealt with in individual and group sessions. Should a client bring up a group issue during an individual session (e.g., a conflict with another group member), the counselor generally needs to redirect the client to the group. If this same individual session focuses on issues of personal learning from group sessions that are impacting the individual sessions, the counselor may want to process that within the individual sessions, as appropriate. The client also needs to be made aware of the different roles the counselor will take in the individual session verses the group session. A client may expect the counselor to take his or her side during a conflict in group rather than understanding the role of the counselor as a process facilitator.

Another related issue that may arise is the perception of an unintentional alliance between the counselor and the client who is seen individually. This may inhibit other group members from participating because they feel alienated. The counselor is to provide equitable treatment for all members of the group, regardless of their current or prior relationship with individuals in the group.

As previously stated, group counselors are to avoid dual relationships that might impair their objectivity or professional judgment or that might impair a client's ability to participate fully in the group. Generally those relationships could be screened out in the prescreening process. In this case, the previous relationship between Candace and the student was missed, and now the client may feel apprehensive about participating in the group process. This will need to be addressed with the student individually before the group can continue. This may include several steps.

First, both Melanie and Candace need to review the goals and purpose of the group to ensure that the members match the objectives. If it is decided that the differences in the members' developmental awareness of their body images match the objectives of the group and that this difference can be worked through appropriately, then the group can continue. The differences will need to be addressed in the group as both Melanie and Candace review with the group the purposes and objectives. Should the difference be too much to overcome within the group, than an offer to split the group into two different groups can be made.

Second, Melanie needs to meet with the master's degree student outside of group for a second screening. This will allow the student the opportunity to decide if she wishes to continue in the group. As part of that conversation, Melanie can review with the student the ethical requirement that Candace must maintain confidentiality about this student's (or any member's) participation in the group. Melanie can also work with both the student and Candace to identify any possible common classes or assignments that may arise at the university and cause conflict or discomfort for either person and thus impair the group process.

Dual relationships within group counseling are to be avoided whenever possible. Yet it is common that counseling students participate in a group experience as part of their education. Ethical guidelines point out that those instructors who participate in group leadership take steps to separate course grades from participation in group by allowing the student to decide what issues to explore and when to stop.

RESPONSE

David M. Kaplan

I have become convinced over the years that most ethical dilemmas boil down to a specific issue: informed consent. It may appear that a quandary focuses on dual relationships, confidentiality, competency, or another ethical area. However, upon closer inspection, one realizes that the counselor could have avoided the problem by emphasizing informed consent when counseling was first initiated.

Therefore, I reframe this critical incident (as I do most ethical dilemmas) as a problem with informed consent. What is informed consent? It refers to the right of a client to know what they are getting into before they get into it. The American Counseling Association speaks to the importance of obtaining informed consent in its *Code of Ethics and Standards of Practice* (ACA, 1995):

> When counseling is initiated, and throughout the counseling process as necessary, counselors inform clients of the purposes, goals, techniques, procedures, limitations, potential risks and benefits of services to be performed, and other pertinent information. Counselors take steps to ensure that clients understand the implications of diagnosis, the intended use of tests and reports, fees, and billing arrangements. Clients have the right to expect confidentiality and to be provided with an explanation of its limitations... (section A.3.a)

The Association for Specialists in Group Work *Best Practice Guidelines* (ASGW, 1998) points out the need for informed consent in group counseling:

> Group Workers facilitate informed consent. Group Workers provide in oral and written form to prospective members...: the professional disclosure statement; group purpose and goals; group participation expectations including voluntary and involuntary membership; role expectations of members and leader(s); policies related to entering and exiting the group; policies governing substance abuse; policies and procedures governing mandated groups (where relevant); documentation requirements; disclosure of information to others; implications of out-of-group contact or involvement among members; procedures for consultation between group leader(s) and group member(s); fees and time parameters; and potential impacts of group participation. (section A.7.b)

One of the major purposes of obtaining informed consent is to avoid surprising clients. Counselors never want to hear the dreaded words, "But you never told me that..." Unfortunately, that is what happened to Melanie and Candace. They did not emphasize informed consent either during their pre-screening or at the first session. They did not construct an informed consent brochure as specified in the ASGW *Best Practice Guidelines* that covered the areas listed in the preceding ACA and ASGW quotes. They did not review important statements in the informed consent brochure with the group members. As a result, the group members did not know enough about what they were getting into. They did not know that they might recognize another group member. They did not know that a leader might be in their graduate department. What they *did* know was that they did not like being surprised with these facts.

So what should Melanie and Candace do at this point? My suggestion is to immediately construct a written informed consent brochure that covers all points mentioned in section A.3.a of the ACA Code of Ethics and section A.7.b of the ASGW *Best Practices Guidelines*. It should be stated in the brochure that there is a possibility that group members may recognize or know other group members or the group leader(s) from social, business, academic, or other settings and that group members may also be receiving individual counseling from the leaders.

The brochure should be distributed to all group members and reviewed verbally. I suggest that Melanie and Candace first review the brochure individually with each group member. This will provide the opportunity to see how specific group members feel about recognizing a leader from their academic program or being a participant in individual counseling. Any necessary adjustments, accommodations, or referrals can then be made. The brochure should then be reviewed in the next group session so that everyone is on the same wavelength about the group rules.

In closing, I want to take the opportunity of speaking to the issue of providing both individual and group counseling to the same person. I have met some group counselors who feel that it is a dual relationship to provide both individual and group counseling to a client. In my opinion, this is a misinterpretation of the concept of dual relationships. *Dual relationship* has a very specific meaning. It refers to a counselor who has both a counseling and a noncounseling (e.g., romantic, business, or academic) relationship with a client. Providing both individual and group counseling to the same client does not fit this definition, and I know of no ethical code (including the ACA and ASGW documents) that prohibits or even cautions against this practice. A counselor may very well decide in a given situation not to provide both individual and group counseling to the same person. However, that is a practice issue, not an ethical issue of dual relationships.

REFERENCES

American Counseling Association. (1995). *Code of ethics and standards of practice.* Alexandria, VA: Author.

Association for Specialists in Group Work. (1998). Best practice guidelines. *Journal for Specialists in Group Work, 23*(3), 237–244.

CHAPTER 8

TERMINATION: "WE'LL TELL YOU HOW IT'S DONE"

A critical variable in the preparation of group counselors is the termination process.

CRITICAL INCIDENT

Linwood G. Vereen

Background

Trey and Janice are both second-year graduate students who are co-leading a personal growth group for undergraduates as a part of their practical experience. For each co-leader this has been their first experience in leading a group (they have completed 7 of 10 scheduled group sessions). To date both Trey and Janice feel that the group has progressed well and has made a number of important strides throughout the semester.

Incident

While in supervision, Trey and Janice each expressed their concerns about co-leading the group through the termination process. Trey expressed concern that group members should be pushed to talk about how the group has impacted their life, how they have grown because of the group experience, and how they will maintain the progress they have made because of their participation in the group experience. Janice expressed her belief that the termination process should focus on positive things that have happened within the group. Janice felt that the group members should avoid conflict in the last 3 weeks of the group experience to ensure that they have a positive experience.

Following the supervision session, Trey and Janice agreed that the group members should not be pushed or coerced into sharing feelings about the group experience. The leaders agreed that they should try to present what they feel has been pervasive throughout the semester: an atmosphere in which the group members feel comfortable saying what they feel and what comes naturally to them and are not pushed to say more than they feel.

During the next 2 weeks of the growth group, the co-leaders actively discussed the need for each group member to focus on and detail what was important to him or her about participation in the group and how important it is to be an active participant in the termination process. During the 2 weeks prior to the final meeting, the co-leaders spent a great deal of time explaining the termination process and the benefits of participation versus the downside of choosing to remain quiet about the process of the group.

Discussion

Prior to the final group meeting the co-leaders met to discuss and plan the final group meeting and to evaluate the progress of the past few weeks' sessions. Although the co-leaders agreed they had done a fair job of explaining the termination process and its potential benefits, they realized that they left little time for group members to take part in the process. The co-leaders realized they faced a dilemma: with only one group session left, how would they actually allow for termination to occur? During the final meeting, the group members confirmed the leaders' beliefs that they had left little room for members to participate in the process of termination.

QUESTIONS

1. What factor/factors about the termination process did the counselors neglect?
2. What learning outcomes could be gained as a result of the dilemma created by the counselors in this incident?
3. What are some of the specific issues that were not addressed as a result of the dilemma created by the counselors?
4. By avoiding the termination process, did the counselors contribute to premature termination? Why or why not?
5. Why would it or why would it not be appropriate for the leaders to discuss (in group) how they have taken away from the termination process?

RESPONSE

Valerie L. Guay

When preparing and running a group, beginning counselors often neglect the termination stage, second only in importance to the working stage of the group. The termination experience gives the group members the chance to deal with unfinished business, discuss how they will use what they learned in the group, and share their experiences of being in the group. Depending on the type of group, the termination stage can last from 10 to 15 minutes to one to two full sessions; the general rule is the longer and more intense the group experience, the longer the termination stage needs to be.

The termination phase of the group process has many different factors that need to be taken into consideration. In the case study presented, the first factor Trey and Janice seem to have neglected involves telling the group members well in advance that the group will be terminating. Usually this is done 3 to 5 weeks before the final session to remind the group members that termination will occur soon and to allow the counselors time to explain the termination process. Although Trey and Janice did explain the termination process, it seems that they overexplained the process to the group members, taking up too much valuable group time and effectively cutting the members of the group out of the termination process. Janice also took valuable working time away from the members of the group when she attempted to eliminate any conflicts during the final 3 weeks of the group to "ensure that they have a positive experience." It seems that Trey and Janice unconsciously tried to ensure that they themselves had a positive experience with the termination process and simply did not meet the needs of the group members, a mistake of many beginning counselors.

According to Jacobs, Masson, and Harvill (2002), there are seven goals in the termination stage of a group: reviewing and summarizing the group experience, assessing members' growth and change, finishing business, applying change to everyday life, providing feedback, handling good-byes, and planning for continued problem resolution. Unfortunately, with their emphasis on explaining what the termination process would be like instead of letting it happen, Trey and Janice did not leave any time for these specific goals to be met by the group members, thereby contributing to premature termination. It will be appropriate for Trey and Janice to discuss their missteps with the group so the group members can understand that Trey and Janice did not take away from the termination process intentionally, but rather from a lack of experience in leading groups.

The termination stage also has other considerations that Trey and Janice seem to have neglected during their termination process. Members of the group may be feeling anxiety over separating from the group, especially a personal growth group like the one that Trey and Janice are leading. These feelings need to be dealt with in the group atmosphere along with other strong emotional feelings. By restricting the final three sessions to focusing only on the positive experiences of the group, the leaders also stumbled a bit; members of the group may have had issues they would have liked to have discussed but felt they could not because of the leaders' emphasis on only the positive aspects of the group experience. By working through the dilemma they created for themselves, Trey and Janice hopefully will learn to focus more on these goals for future groups they will lead and focus less on explaining the termination process in exacting detail.

RESPONSE

Beverly A. Burnell

Termination of a personal growth group requires some advance preparation. Unlike a therapy or counseling group, however, preparation for termination of a personal growth group does not need to be a lengthy process. Identification of the overall length of a group, in this case 10 sessions, at the outset of the group is the first step in preparing members for termination. Depending on the structure of the group, leaders might acknowledge when the group has progressed about halfway (in this case five sessions), often catalyzing the work of the members, particularly if the group members have not fully advanced to the working stage and progress is not being made. Again, as the end of the group nears, at the end of session 8 or beginning of session 9 in a 10-session group, it is sufficient to announce the impending termination and explain, briefly, the anticipated process and content of termination. An earlier introduction of termination may or may not be needed if members are to be included in the design of the termination process. What is most important, however, is that leaders understand and are able to convey to group members the importance of attending to the ending of the group.

In preparing their group members for upcoming termination, Trey and Janice appear to have identified the process and content of termination as having members actively summarize their own learning and outcomes as well as the means to transfer this learning from the group to life outside the group. This incident does not mention whether other termination issues were addressed, such as providing feedback, saying good-byes, or planning for follow-up as needed. It appears from the description of this incident that Janice and Trey spent almost the entirety of the two sessions prior to the final session preparing the members for termination, much more time than was necessary. If this was the case, then the group became leader-focused in these two sessions, resulting in premature termination for the members. For the leaders to then spend time in the final session to discuss how they have taken away from the termination process would continue this leader focus and would continue to take away from the termination process. The co-leaders addressed, in supervision, some leader-focused concerns about the termination process, yet they do not seem to have been provided guidance for addressing these concerns.

The criticism that the members were provided "little room" to participate in the termination process is unclear. How is "participate in the process of termination" to be understood? Was there an expectation that the members would take part in designing the termination process? If so, it is obvious they were not included in this way. If not, to use the final session for the members to focus on and identify what was important to them about their participation in the group seems sufficient time. If in sessions eight and nine, the leaders had spent only *some* time on termination preparation but *most* of the time on the ongoing work of the group, the group would then have been ready to use the final session for the termination activities and process. However, by using "a great deal of time" in sessions eight and nine to prepare the group members for termination, the co-leaders essentially interrupted the successful personal growth process in which members had been participating.

The incident does not explain how Trey and Janice dealt with the criticism from the members about how the termination process occurred. The incident also does not state whether, in the final session, the group attended to the stated goals of termination, that is, "what was important to them about participation in the group," in addition to the discussion about member nonparticipation in the termination process. If this was accomplished, and if Trey and Janice were able to acknowledge (but not spend group time analyzing) their role in impeding the work of the group, then the members are likely to have left the final group with some sense of their own growth and the value of the group process in that growth.

REFERENCE

Jacobs, E.E., Masson, R.L., & Harvill, R.L. (2002). *Group counseling strategies and skills* (4th ed.). Pacific Grove, CA: Brooks/Cole.

CHAPTER 9

INVOLUNTARY MEMBERSHIP:
"DO I REALLY HAVE TO GO?"

This incident explores some of the issues that confront school counselors who lead groups that consist of involuntary members.

CRITICAL INCIDENT

Stephanie Rogers Howard

Background

Ms. Jackson, school counselor, frequently conducts small group counseling sessions on varying topics at Washington Middle School. The topics are generally derived from parent, student, and teacher needs assessments at the beginning of the school year. Other topical groups are formed based on needs indicated through individual counseling sessions. Groups are advertised, and students express their interest in joining the groups to the counselor. However, on occasion, a parent, teacher, or administrator may request that a student participate in a particular group.

Incident

Ms. Jackson has recently advertised that she will conduct a small group on anger management. Several students have indicated their interest in attending the group, and one teacher has sent two names of students who may benefit from participating in this group. Ms. Jackson talks to the students who have been referred by the teachers for the group. Both students are willing to participate.

After the formalities of beginning the group have been completed, Ms. Jackson is ready to start her group. Participants have been notified of the first session of the group. Two hours before the group is to begin, the principal, Mr. Tang, tells Ms. Jackson that he wants two more students to participate in the anger management group. The students, Jeff and Dante, have had several disciplinary referrals that involved a lack of self-control. He tells the students to participate as a part of their consequences for the disciplinary referrals that he has recently received. Neither student wants to participate in the group.

Ms. Jackson agrees to allow Jeff and Dante to participate in the group. Aware that parental permission is necessary for minors to participate in the group, Ms. Jackson calls Jeff and Dante's parents. She is unable to reach them and leaves a message for them to return her call as soon as possible.

Having had previous contact with the boys' parents and cognizant of her principal's directive, Ms. Jackson is pretty sure that the parents will agree to the boys' participation in the group. Consequently, she decides to include the boys in the initial session of the group anyway and makes a mental note to send home the permission papers today. She notifies their fourth period teacher that they will not be in class today. Furthermore, right before the group is about to begin, Mr. Tang calls Ms. Jackson into his office. He informs her that if Jeff and Dante do not actively participate in the group, they will be suspended.

Ms. Jackson begins the initial session by telling the group the nature and goals of the group as well as the procedures to be used in the group. However, she does not inform Jeff and Dante of the consequences to them of not participating in the group. Jeff interrupts Ms. Jackson while she is talking to tell her that he is not interested in participating in the group. He asks her why they have to participate in the group since they did not sign up for the group. Frustrated, Ms. Jackson tells the students that since they are in the group, they may as well make the best of it. Dante responds that he does not want to go to class anyway. Brushing past this subject, Ms. Jackson begins her formal presentation as planned in her initial address of anger management.

Discussion

After the group, Mr. Tang asks the counselor about Jeff and Dante's participation in the group. Ms. Jackson responds that the two were present and participated. The principal reminds her to keep him informed about the boys' participation in order to avoid suspension from school.

QUESTIONS

1. Can involuntary members of a group benefit from the group experience? Why or why not?
2. What strategy might the leader have used to gain more participation and relieve some of the tension at the beginning of the group?
3. Because the principal mandated the participation of Jeff and Dante, what important issue needs to be addressed?
4. Should group members be informed about the consequences of the quality of their participation in a group?
5. What other important information should Ms. Jackson have given to the group members?

RESPONSE

Mary Ni

Involuntary membership in groups raises the fundamental question of whether a person can benefit from a situation that they do not want to be party to. Is it true that "you can lead a horse to water, but you can't make him drink"?

In some groups, involuntary members can and do benefit. A good example is when unwilling participants are drawn into a group, and are able to find something of interest in the group despite their initial resistance. Involuntary members can benefit if they are able to come to some kind of understanding (tacit or explicit) that the group actually has something to offer them.

The leader of involuntary group members must be skilled enough to build a positive rapport with these members in order to help them transcend initial unwillingness. Membership issues must be satisfactorily addressed, or there is strong probability that negativity will arise in later group sessions, potentially sabotaging forward movement of the whole group.

In this situation, although Ms. Jackson agreed to allow two involuntary participants to join her group at the last moment, she did not speak with either of the boys about their group membership before the opening session. This was an important missed opportunity. However, Jeff and Dante both knew that their lack of self-control (and anger?) had gotten them into trouble. Although the counselor did not talk to them about their group membership, Jeff and Dante knew about their mandatory attendance from their principal.

Jeff interrupted Ms. Jackson's opening statements to tell her that he was not interested in the group and asked why he had to be there. This was a perfect moment for Ms. Jackson to retreat from her formal presentation to respond with some "here and now" information. Rather than be frustrated with the question, Ms. Jackson might have welcomed Jeff's comments with a more receptive reply. (For example, "I can see that you don't want to be here. But I had a brief conversation with Mr. Tang about you earlier today, and he felt that it was important for you to come and participate. Can you think of any reasons why he would think this way?") If she had been able to hook him in with some kind of engaging response, it might have given Jeff an opportunity to reflect more seriously about his participation and opened up any number of responses that related to the relevance of anger management in his life.

When Ms. Jackson remarked that the two involuntary participants should just make the best of the group since they were there, Dante responded that he did not want to go to class anyway. This was a somewhat hopeful reply and might have been reinforced by Ms. Jackson, rather than brushed past. (For example, "I'm glad that you'd rather be here than in class. I think that you have a lot to offer this group... And I also think that you could learn from others here and even have a good time, too.") An engaging response to Dante might have helped build some prerequisite rapport to offset his initial unwillingness.

Mr. Tang, the principal, did well to assure that Ms. Jackson had the time, space, and administrative support to lead these types of important groups. One thing he could improve in his practice would be to give her more adequate notice in the future. Asking Ms. Jackson to take in two unwilling group members at the last minute was disorienting, and left Ms. Jackson off-centered and probably less effective than she might have been had she more prepared to receive them.

Dante and Jeff should be fully informed participants in this group. They need to clearly know

- what the principal's expectations of them are (to participate or be suspended);
- that these expectations have been conveyed to Ms. Jackson;
- exactly what kind of participation is expected of them (for example, will nonverbal participation be satisfactory? Will negative participation still count?); and
- that Ms. Jackson will be telling the principal of their behavior and performance in the group.

Moreover, Ms. Jackson should clarify joint expectations for the whole group, including such matters as

- whether the group will be open or closed to new members;
- how many times they will meet;
- when and where they will meet;
- what results she and the participants hope to gain from the experience;
- how the meetings will be run;
- what kind of confidentiality she and the participants could assure each other;
- what the grounds rules will be; and
- how breaches in conduct will be dealt with.

RESPONSE

J. Kelly Coker

There are certainly circumstances in a school setting under which involuntary participation in individual or group counseling may occur. Counseling may be mandated by an administrator, a parent, a teacher, or the courts. Reasons can include concern for behavior, concern for adjustment, and concern for learning. Although involuntary participation is not optimal for students, by laying a proper foundation, involuntary members can still benefit. According to Greenberg (2003), it is important to inform involuntary members of a group that participation in the group is not a punishment. When possible, participation in group should be voluntary, or at least presented as a choice between two outcomes. Even if the choice is the lesser of two evils (e.g., participate in this group or be suspended), at least the student has been given an option. This may help create more buy-in for the group process.

If the two students mandated to the group had been given the choice to either attend group or be suspended, they could be reminded that they chose to participate. The counselor could also spend some time normalizing their frustration and resistance and allow the two students some time to vent about having to be there. Dealing with their angry feelings about being made to participate openly could help to create some buy-in. Members should also be given some freedom in determining how they will spend their time in the group. This could be difficult given the principal's condition of active participation, but these students may need a session or two before they will feel free to talk.

A primary issue in this incident is one of confidentiality. According to the American School Counselor Association's *Ethical Standards for School Counselors* (ASCA, 1998), counselors strive to protect student confidentiality in regard to information received in the counseling relationship, and the information should only be revealed to others with the express consent of the counselee, except in certain specific situations such as clear and imminent danger (standard A.2). The counselor should clarify the nature of the mandate and what the principal specifically expects. The counselor should not feel obligated to share details of the two students' quality of participation in the group process.

Another issue based on this mandate is one of parental consent. The counselor made a judgment call in allowing the two students to participate in the first meeting without the parents' knowledge. The nature of the parental consent is different in this case as well because the two students are not voluntarily participating. Parents should have been informed by both the principal and the counselor regarding Jeff and Dante's participation in the group. According to the ASCA Ethical Standards, school counselors respect "the inherent rights and responsibilities of parents for their children" (standard B.1).

Further, all members of the group should have the same rights as everyone else in the group. If there are different rules and expectations set up for different participants, a dynamic of inequality is created. The two boys mandated to the group are already at a disadvantage because their attendance is not optional. They should at least be given the same opportunities to participate or not participate as the other members.

According to the ASCA Ethical Standards, the school counselor "informs the counselee of the purposes, goals, techniques, and rules of procedures under which she/he may receive counseling at or before the time when the counseling relationship is entered" (standard A.2.a). The student participants in the group do have a right to know the consequences of the quality of their participation in a group. That being said, the school counselor might be more cautious about agreeing to the principal's condition that quality of participation is tied to possible suspension. This association blurs the boundaries between counseling and discipline and can impact the degree to which the students actually benefit from the group. The principal may have the power to mandate attendance to the group, but he should stop short of mandating quality participation. Participation should be a norm set by the group for all members of the group, not just a select few. Further, more detailed informed consent including limits to confidentiality, group members' rights and responsibilities in the group, and the conditions set forth by the principal concerning participation should have been shared.

REFERENCES

American School Counselor Association. (1998). *Ethical standards for school counselors*. Alexandria, VA: Author.

Greenberg, K. R. (2003). *Group counseling in K-12 schools: A handbook for school counselors*. Boston, MA: Allyn & Bacon.

CHAPTER 10

INAPPROPRIATE GROUP ACTIVITIES: "THESE WILL WORK!"

This incident addresses some of the issues associated with group leaders choosing group activities that are inappropriate for the time and place of a group.

CRITICAL INCIDENT

Seth Olson

Background

Joe is the leader of an adolescent anger management group at a juvenile detention center. Even though Joe has facilitated these groups twice in the past, he has not received any formal training in group work other than one course in his master's program. The policy of the center in which Joe works dictates that all residents need to participate in the anger management group. Due to the large number of residents at the center, Joe tends to focus on the psychoeducational aspects of the group rather than the therapeutic power of the group to facilitate change in the group members' angry behaviors.

Incident

Toward the end of a group session, one of the members became argumentative with Joe regarding the purpose and relevance of the group. The group member refused to participate, and stated, "This group is stupid and cuts into my free time." Joe became angry with the member and said, "You need to respect me and this group. Your participation is mandatory and that is final!" The group member fell silent and slumped in his chair. Other members began mumbling things under their breath and sending glares Joe's way. Shortly after Joe's words, the group session was required to end, and as a result, the conflict was never resolved.

Joe felt uneasy about the unresolved conflict that occurred at the end of the last session. Joe had limited group experience and was uncertain how to manage the conflict that had arisen. A situation like this one had never happened to him before, and he did not know who would be able to help him at the detention center. During the week, he thought it might be helpful to start the next group session with a conversation about the conflict that had occurred at the end of the previous session. However, he then realized that there was a lot of information to cover in a short amount of time, and he would not have time to cover all of it if he dealt with the conflict. Guided imagery and other relaxation techniques were planned for the next session, and Joe thought that those activities were essential for the group members. After mulling the choices over, he decided to go ahead with his plans and devote the next session to a relaxation exercise. In that session, Joe asked members to close their eyes and take a few deep breaths and relax. He then began to guide them through steps in muscle relaxation. During the session, he asked group participants to talk out loud about heaviness and warmth in their arms, legs, and overall body.

Discussion

At the end of the session, one of the members exclaimed that they had to talk because they felt unsettled about the last group session. As it turned out, this group member was still angry about some things Joe had said during the conflict in the last group session. Other members voiced their concerns, stating that they also had similar feelings and wanted to discuss the previous week's conflict.

QUESTIONS

1. What are some important considerations regarding activities?
2. What are potential drawbacks to the use of activities with a group?
3. What was this activity trying to accomplish?
4. How important is the leader's training in administering activities or techniques? Are there any ethical concerns that should be brought to Joe's attention?
5. What are the leader's issues in this incident that may interfere with the success of this group? What could Joe have done differently regarding the conflict?

RESPONSE

Janice L. DeLucia-Waack

There are two considerations when using activities in group work. The first is whether the activity addresses an important theme or issue in the group, either a content issue (i.e., one of the goals of the group) or a process issue (i.e., some aspect of the interpersonal dynamics in the group). The activity must always work toward meeting the goals of the group, whether to teach new skills particularly in psychoeducational groups, or to promote honest communication and feedback among members. Even icebreaker activities should work toward the goal of having members self-disclose something about themselves that is related to group (i.e., how they deal with new situations, what personal characteristics they bring to group) and interacting with other group members.

The second consideration is the effective processing of the activity. Particularly in psychoeducational groups, leaders often hurry through the activity because of time constraints and give little or no time to the processing of this activity. Members often comment that the activity was great, real fun, but when asked what they learned, they do not know. Processing questions must be provided to help members apply what they have done and learned, as part of the activity for changing their behavior. For example, how can you apply this new skill outside of group? Who is one person you could talk to about this concern? What is one thing you can do when you are angry to cool off?

There are several drawbacks to using activities in group. One is that the group becomes dependent on the activity and the leader. The activities become the structure for the group members; they wait for the leader to tell them what to talk about and how to interact. Thus the interactions become prescribed, not free-flowing. It is important, then, for the leader to decide to use an activity that aids in getting to the important issues and that teaches needed skills for the group members, rather than to just use an activity because it is expected or because it is prescribed by a treatment manual. Another potential drawback is that leaders often use activities when they are anxious about what will happen in group. For instance, if they think the group is not safe for all members, they might do an activity to promote trust, typically a trust walk or a trust fall. Yet if the lack of trust is based on the interpersonal dynamics among group members, blindfolding members and leading them around is not going to make them trust the group with their secrets any more than before.

The goal of Joe's relaxation activity seems to fit with the goals of the anger management group. However, this activity also seems to be a way for Joe to deal with the anger of the last session indirectly and perhaps to relax the members enough so that they will not bring up the issue again.

My concern is not so much that Joe is trained in every activity or technique that he uses, but rather that he understands (and agrees with) the theoretical framework of the technique. Specifically in this example, relaxation and guided imagery techniques typically fall within a cognitive-behavioral orientation. Does Joe understand and believe that changing one's beliefs and perceptions and reactions to a situation is effective? And more importantly, does Joe believe such interventions are appropriate and will be effective in changing his group members' approaches to anger? Or is he simply following a treatment manual that has been given to him?

Joe is a novice group leader. Most novice group leaders, along with many experienced leaders, have difficulty dealing with conflict. Resolution of conflict is acknowledged as an integral task of counseling and therapy groups, and thus is openly addressed when it arises. As a corollary, I often suggest to beginning group leaders that an implicit goal of all groups, whether they are psychoeducational, counseling, or therapy groups, is to teach good communication and interpersonal skills. Within that goal are listening, asking for help, expressing feelings, and resolving conflict.

Leaders of psychoeducational groups have a more difficult task as they must balance the content of the group, typically structured activities each week, with the interpersonal dynamics of the group. Members must feel safe, and be willing to give feedback and disclose; yet often in psychoeducational groups, little time is spent building cohesion and emphasizing the importance of giving feedback. In addition, there is pressure in psychoeducational groups to cover the content, and most of the time the content is very ambitious. Thus Joe needs to work on paying attention to the process of the group, initially to make sure that cohesion is building and later on to ensure that accurate and honest feedback is being given among members and that the resolution of conflict is modeled within the group.

Joe probably should have done several things differently. First, Joe should have noted where they were in group time and realized that this essentially was a hit and run and that there was not enough time in this group session to effectively deal with the "This group is stupid" comment. Based on this, Joe might have acknowledged the anger, suggested that it is important to talk about, but gone on to state that such an important topic would have to wait until the next session. He might also have added as a statement to the other group members that they should think about what was helpful and what was not helpful so far in this group in preparation for the following session. Another strategy might have been for Joe to use the member's comment as a teachable moment in an anger management group. Joe might have acknowledged the anger but then asked the member to be more specific about what was making him angry and what needed to be different for him not to be angry anymore. If the group had already discussed ways to express anger, another group member might be asked to review the techniques before the group member responded.

In hindsight, there might also have been some things that Joe could have done in earlier sessions to prevent such a confrontation. In a mandatory group, it is often helpful to acknowledge this in the beginning of the group, to recognize the anger and frustration about this, and then ask members to set their own goals about what they want to get out of the group. Another suggestion is to use a check-in technique at the end of each session to assess what group members are learning from the group and how helpful it is. Setting aside 3 to 5 minutes at the end of the group for members to answer questions—such as, What did you learn today? How helpful was this session? What will you do differently?—can provide continual feedback about the usefulness of the group.

RESPONSE

Gail Mears

Group leaders need to consider the composition of the group, group norms, the stage of development of the group, the purpose of the activity, and the immediate group climate before introducing activities. Activities that are poorly timed, or not relevant to the current group concerns, may actually reduce the overall effectiveness of group interventions.

Relaxation exercises are frequently taught in anger management programs. Such activities are designed to help group members learn to recognize and reduce emotional arousal and to acquire strategies to lower their overall stress levels. The assumption is that these strategies will aid in effectively managing anger. Activities can facilitate the work of the group when their introduction is timed to take into account the current needs and receptivity of the group members. The relaxation exercise that Joe introduced did not respond to the issue of conflict in the group and therefore did not match the current group needs. The conflict from the previous group meeting needed to be processed before moving on to a different agenda. Joe used his authority to thwart a potentially useful opportunity to engage the group in a discussion of the members' feelings about being in this group, their commitment to the group, and their commitment to change, as well as missing an opportunity to model effective conflict management. The use of the relaxation activity, in the absence of addressing the group conflict, probably interfered with the process of group members learning anger management strategies.

Counselors are required to practice within their boundaries of competence (American Counseling Association *Code of Ethics and Standards of Practice*, 1995, section C.2). Joe has no group training beyond one graduate group course. Although such a course is an important step in building competence as a group leader, this course alone does not provide Joe with the requisite knowledge and skills needed to run this anger management group. In addition to participating in supervised group training, Joe needs specialized training working with adolescents who are struggling with significant anger management problems. He needs to be current on the literature regarding effective interventions for this population, and he needs to be engaged in ongoing continuing education and professional consultation regarding his group work with this population.

A counselor's primary responsibility is to the welfare of his client (ACA Code of Ethics, section A.1). It appears that Joe developed his model of group intervention based on the number of residents he is asked to serve rather than the needs of the adolescents in the group. Joe's first obligation is to the welfare of the group members rather than to the detention center. With the appropriate education, supervised training, and consultation, Joe will be able to help the detention center develop models of group counseling that meet the emotional needs of the group members as well as the objectives of the detention center.

Joe's behavior in the group indicates that he does not understand group dynamics. He seemed to overlook important aspects of group development, including developing agreements among the group members regarding their participation, the establishment of therapeutic group norms regarding emotional expression, and the identification of the relevance of this anger management group to the members' lives. Joe did not recognize that conflict is a normal and useful stage of group development, and he had no strategies to deal effectively with anger when it arose in the group. Rather than using expressions of anger as an opportunity to engage members in the group process, he used an authoritarian statement, "Your participation is mandatory and that is final," followed by an activity that did not address the apparent group conflict. This modeled ineffective conflict resolution, and Joe missed a wonderful opportunity to help group members develop more effective anger management strategies.

If Joe had more skill as a group leader, he could have reflected the group member's sense of frustration with this group experience. He also could have invited group members into a discussion of the relevance of this group to their lives and how anger management skills might be helpful to them. By modeling good listening skills, Joe could have demonstrated the important role of listening in effective conflict management and in the development of meaningful relationships.

Competent, skilled counselors know when to seek consultation and supervision. Joe should have sought supervision when he realized that he did not know how to handle the situation that arose in the group. This group situation has hopefully helped Joe recognize his group leadership shortcomings and motivated him to take the steps needed to competently lead this and other groups.

REFERENCE

American Counseling Association. (1995). *Code of ethics and standards of practice.* Alexandria, VA: Author.

IMPAIRED GROUP LEADER: "DO WE HAVE TO TALK ABOUT IT?"

This incident explores some of the issues that may arise when a counseling professional encounters a peer who seems to exhibit signs and symptoms of impairment.

CRITICAL INCIDENT

Suzanne M. Hedstrom

Background
Karen is a recent doctoral graduate of a counselor education program and is excited to join the counseling center staff at a state university. One of Karen's colleagues is Alan, a counselor who has been at the present work setting for all of the 20 years since he received his doctoral degree. Alan typically leads a personal growth group each semester, along with one of his female colleagues. This semester Karen is co-leading the group with Alan.

Incident
In planning for the group, Alan told Karen that because he has run this sort of group many times, it made sense for the group to be set up the way he has always done it in the past. Karen, being the new staff member and the new graduate, agreed to abide by his directives. The two of them also agreed to meet after each session to discuss the group.

The group has completed 4 of the 10 scheduled sessions. During the group sessions Alan has assumed primary leadership. He begins and ends each session, jumps in to be the first responder to member disclosures, and guides the group in directions he sees as most helpful. When Karen has offered reflections or made connections among members in the group, Alan has usually talked over her or made subsequent comments that negated her contributions. Karen has come to feel discounted and not respected. She notices that certain members of the group receive this same treatment from Alan if they do not contribute the way he thinks they should. Karen has seen the surprise on the faces of members when their perspective is dismissed or diminished. She also notes that only 6 of the original 10 members have maintained membership through session four.

In their postgroup meetings Karen has attempted to share her perspective with Alan. She told him that she feels as though there is little room for her to participate in the leadership of the group and that when she does make an intervention, Alan negates it. Alan's response to this sort of discourse is to deflect it by saying it is unfortunate that she feels this way, but his experience is what guides the group, and the point of their postgroup meetings is to talk about the group and group members, not about each other. On the way out of Alan's office after their session three postgroup meeting, Karen catches a whiff of what might be alcohol, but she is not sure. She asks Alan; he gives her a puzzled look and shakes his head "no." Their next postgroup session did not take place; Alan told Karen that he was not available.

Session five begins with only five members present. As usual, Alan takes control of the group. Today the sharing is primarily focused on the difficulties and fears the group members have in establishing romantic relationships. Toward the end of the session Alan interrupts with vehemence, saying with a slightly slurred loud voice, "Relationships aren't all they are cracked up to be. You think someone is committed to you and loves you and then she screws you. You're left all alone and worse than you were before she ever came into your life. You know you screwed up, too, but now you're getting the giant shaft. So if you know what's good for you, don't even mess with relationships. You always get burned." Group members look wide-eyed at Alan, and then at Karen. Alan seems to have lost his steam and slumps in his chair, head down. Karen manages to bring some closure to the discussion of the day (without directly commenting on Alan's statement) and then ends the group.

Discussion

As Karen and Alan move toward Alan's office for their postgroup meeting, Alan asks to have a couple of minutes before they begin. Karen agrees, checks her voice mail, and returns to Alan's office. As she walks in, she sees him putting a bottle into his bottom desk drawer. Karen asks, "What's going on here, Alan? I see the bottle, and I can smell your breath. And what happened to you in the group? It sounded to me as though you were talking about you, not helping the group with its work." At this point Alan breaks down, sobbing to Karen that his life is a mess. His wife threw him out of the house during the summer and is keeping the kids away from him. He lives in an apartment now with basically no furniture. He has not told anyone at work about what is happening. The only thing he has going for him is work. He knows that things are not quite what they should be, but he knows he will get a handle on it, especially if Karen will help him. Alan tells her that surely together they can keep the group going in a good direction. He begs Karen to not tell anyone what has happened. He swears that he will mend his ways. In fact, he states that he has scheduled a counseling appointment for himself for next week. Surely this will help.

QUESTIONS

1. What signs of impairment are present in this case?
2. What ethical issues are involved? What are Karen's responsibilities to Alan? To her place of employment? To the profession? To the public?

3. What options does Karen have at this point in responding to what she has observed in Alan's behavior? Which of these courses of action is recommended? What might she have done earlier in the life of the group?
4. What are Karen's responsibilities to the group? How can she see to it that the group's needs are met?
5. Should Karen or Alan bring up his statement at the next session of the group? How? If Alan does not continue co-leading the group, what does Karen say about this to the group?

RESPONSE

Charleen Alderfer

Co-leading a group is a complex relationship between the two facilitators. It takes time to develop an understanding of and respect for each person's work. In this case, Alan and Karen are colleagues but they are not peers. Alan has been with the counseling center for 20 years, and he has more years of experience than does Karen. Therefore, he is hierarchically above Karen and has the responsibility of facilitating the development of a colleague who is young in the profession.

Signs of impairment are evident in Alan's relationship with Karen and in his relationship to the group. In regard to Karen, the behavior consistent with effective co-leadership is not occurring. That absence is an early warning of some disturbances in Alan's approach to co-leading the group with Karen. Another indication of difficulty is his inability to allow Karen to add input to planning of the group process. Subsequently, he is controlling in the group sessions and keeps Karen from fully contributing as a co-leader. Karen's unsuccessful attempts to express her concerns to Alan are indications of serious breakdown between the facilitators. Other potent symptoms of Alan's impaired behavior in relation to Karen include the lack of a postgroup meeting after a difficult meeting, his apparent use of alcohol (which is denied), and his personal revelations with no further explanation to the group.

There are also signs of difficulty in his relationship to the group members. By ignoring members with opinions different from his own and, further, by ignoring Karen's attempts to raise this issue, he is setting the stage for scapegoating individuals and negating opportunities for them to learn and grow. The group is losing members and neither facilitator is addressing this phenomenon. A well-functioning group does not lose members, and if it does, the leaders are responsible for addressing that loss.

All codes of ethics for mental health practitioners include the injunction to "do no harm." It is likely that harm to participants occurs in relation to negative qualities of group leadership. The loss of members is an indication that they do not feel safe in the group, and safety is the responsibility of the leaders. Alan's behavior also violates the ethical practice of senior counselors in facilitating the development of junior counselors. Karen is not free of all responsibility and should persist in speaking to Alan about her difficulties with him. By allowing Alan's behavior to continue, she is hindering his opportunity to change, especially when alcohol becomes complicit in the problems. If his behavior continues, the reputation of the counseling center may be compromised, as is the profession's, by tolerating potentially harmful behavior on the part of one of its members. Students who use the center may choose to seek help elsewhere if Alan's problems become known to the community.

Because Alan continues to be unresponsive to Karen's expressions of concern, she has the option of going above Alan and talking to her supervisor. It will be important to let Alan know that she plans to do so. She could also bring the concerns to the group by asking members about their experiences with the leaders, which addresses the pattern of scapegoating. She also needs to ask about the loss of members, which is due in part to the split in the leadership.

Karen has the responsibility to meet the goals of the group and to provide a safe learning environment to the members. If this is not happening, she needs to take proactive steps toward that end. The most effective way to find out if the needs of the group members are being met is to make that issue an item of discussion. Because of Alan's behavior, it may be difficult to get honest feedback, but it is Karen's responsibility to open the door for group members to speak.

The session following Alan's leadership breakdown is likely to be difficult and should be carefully planned by the co-leaders. In the best situation, Alan should give an honest disclosure of his difficulties without going into great detail. He can serve as a positive role of self-disclosure for the group. In that session, he may also decide to stop as a group leader, and this can be a topic of discussion in the group, offering a way of dealing with endings and closure. In the worst situation, Alan will not participate in the session, and Karen will have to handle the group alone. In this case, she needs to recognize Alan's absence and offer some explanation. Without going into detail, she needs to be direct about the existence of personal problems in Alan's life. It is important that she guide the process toward an expression of the members' own feelings about Alan's situation and not to a discussion of Alan as leader. They must then focus on how they plan to continue as a group and what the effect of Alan's absence will be on the group process, on each member, and on Karen's role as single leader.

RESPONSE

Ford Brooks

Due to the number of ethical breaches needing immediate attention, this case can best be addressed by applying the American Counseling Association's *Code of Ethics and Standards of Practice* (ACA, 1995). Applying the code and the standards will help the counselors, Karen and Alan, identify the ethical breaches and develop action steps to protect their group members as well as other clients in the process.

A first ethical breach of the ACA Code of Ethics relates to professional competence and impairment:

> Counselors refrain from offering or accepting professional services when their physical, mental, or emotional problems are likely to harm a client or others. They are alert to the signs of impairment, seek assistance for problems, and, if necessary, limit, suspend, or terminate their professional responsibilities. (section C.2.g)

It is clear from Alan's behavior that he is not only impaired emotionally and mentally by his recent separation, but he is also physically impaired by his use of alcohol prior to group as evidenced by the smell of alcohol on his breath and slurring of words on numerous occasions.

A second ethical breach concerns negative conditions: "Counselors alert their employers to conditions that may be potentially disruptive or damaging to the counselor's professional responsibilities or that may limit their effectiveness" (section D.1.c). In this case Karen could utilize this section to report to her supervisor the conditions in which she is working with Alan. Or Karen could talk with Alan first about her concerns, and he could self-report to their supervisor with Karen present.

A third ethical breach of the Code of Ethics relates to professional conduct: "Counselors have a responsibility both to clients and to the agency or institution within which services are performed to maintain high standards of professional conduct" (section D.1.j). Again, Alan has a responsibility to his clients and is required to maintain a high standard of professional conduct. At this point he is obligated to take responsible measures in getting help for his impairment, which it appears he has started.

There are also two items in the Standards of Practice that focus on impairment and expected ethical behaviors. SP-19, Impairment of Professionals, states that "Counselors must refrain from offering professional services when their personal problems or conflicts may cause harm to a client or others," and SP-49, Ethical Behavior Expected, states that "Counselors must take appropriate action when they possesses reasonable cause that raises doubts as to whether counselors or other mental health professionals are acting in an ethical manner." SP-19 asks for counselors to refrain from work with clients when there is a potential for harm; SP-49 indicates that counselors need to take appropriate action with regards to counselors that are impaired.

Also to be addressed, in addition to Alan's drinking and relationship issues and ethics, is his condescending behavior toward Karen both in and out of group. Should they run a group together in the future, this issue will need to be addressed by Karen. What makes this a sensitive situation is Karen's position as a junior counselor and her potentially making a report to her director on a 20-year veteran counselor at the center. If this is a tenure track faculty position, it will make it even more challenging for her. Additionally, if the counseling center staff is primarily male, they may not support her reporting of Alan's drinking and relationship impairment, although it is clear from the description that Alan drinks alcohol before group and during work hours (as evidenced by the bottle hidden in his desk drawer). His slurred speech and intoxicated manner indicate his impairment. In addition to his use of alcohol is his behavior that demonstrates how closed he is to feedback from Karen. Further, his self-centeredness and all-knowing approach to group excludes not only Karen but also other group members that do not share in the manner he deems important. Alan is putting his needs and agenda before the group's needs by projecting his own situation into the group discussion.

A first recommendation for Karen is to speak with Alan about her concern surrounding his drinking and his comments in the last group session. Other recommendations for Karen are to support Alan in his pursuit of obtaining counseling/treatment and to realize that it is her responsibility, not only to the group members but also other clients he may be seeing, to report this to the counseling center director. It will be best if both Alan and Karen meet with the director so as to support Alan in obtaining help. It is also important for Karen to document this and place the concern with the presiding supervisor of the clinic. Alan is attempting to quash Karen's voice and keep his secret, although chances are this has occurred before and no one else has made a report. Thus, another recommendation is for Alan to meet with Karen and the counseling center director to talk about what has transpired, how Alan has agreed to seek counseling, and how Alan will pull himself out of the group as a facilitator.

Karen has a responsibility to the group and to the presiding supervisor of the clinic to address Alan's behavior. She can help the group by processing the previous group comments, Alan's absence, and the group's feelings, and by allowing time for exploration. Starting the group with reflecting back on the previous group meeting, and on how Alan's comment may have impacted them both individually and as a group, is suggested. Alan should be pulled out of group immediately and not return until he has satisfactorily begun to address his drinking and separation problems. A leave of absence or time off could enable him to return to the workplace. Karen could state to the group that Alan is taking time off and will be returning in a number of months and briefly cover that it was evident from last group he was wrestling with some personal issues, which at this time need support.

REFERENCE

American Counseling Association. (1995). *Code of ethics and standards of practice.* Alexandria, VA: Author.

CHAPTER 12

GOAL DEVELOPMENT: "LET'S JUST TALK AND SEE WHERE WE GO"

This incident explores creation of a support group and discusses the development of goals for the group.

CRITICAL INCIDENT

Linda H. Foster

Background

Ty and Cindy, both experienced licensed counselors, have recently opened a private practice office. Both of these counselors are experienced in conducting group therapy for individuals in drug and alcohol treatment facilities, residential treatment facilities, and psychiatric hospitals. Their private practice offers counseling for a broader clientele, and focuses on interpersonal relationships and personal problems such as grief, anxiety, and/or depression.

Incident

Ty and Cindy decided to offer a weekly Monday morning parents' support group. Although Ty and Cindy both had a great deal of experience in leading counseling and therapy groups, the support group area is a new experience for them. The co-leaders appropriately planned the logistics of the group meetings, including advertising, screening of members, time limits, and length and duration of the sessions to be held over an 8-week time period. The co-leaders then moved into the specifics of planning for each session and each stage of the group process. The co-leaders developed plans for a counseling and therapy group, anticipating that members would bring problems to the group and utilize other members as resources with the leaders providing assistance.

The first two sessions went as the co-leaders had planned. The co-leaders used the first session to focus on getting the members acquainted with each other, beginning with a warm-up introduction exercise and a brief discussion of ground rules for the group process. The first session also included a discussion of problems perceived by the co-leaders and suggested possible behavioral changes to alleviate problems. The second session focused on explaining the co-leaders' role and clarifying the logistics in regard to how the group meetings would be conducted. Also included in the second session was the opportunity for the members to verbalize their expectations of this support group.

After the second session, Ty and Cindy met to evaluate and discuss the progress of the Monday morning parents' group. They were surprised at the responses of the members. The membership conveyed to the leaders their disappointment concerning the environment of the group meetings. Ty and Cindy believed the group process was on track and progressing nicely; however, the membership had communicated this was not the case.

After their discussion of the first two meetings, Ty and Cindy realized that goal development for the group had been overlooked. Due to their own lack of experience in conducting support groups, and perhaps relying on their expertise in counseling and therapy groups, they had failed to provide the opportunity for members to discuss and establish goals for the group. Both process goals and outcome goals had not been included in preplanning or in the initial sessions with the members.

Discussion

One of the main tasks of group leaders is to identify, clarify, and develop meaningful goals for the group. Ty and Cindy failed to include in the initial sessions exploration of group goals. Ty and Cindy also failed to consider that outcome goals pertaining to specific behavioral changes in each member's life needed to be included in the initial sessions and early stages of the group development.

QUESTIONS

1. During the planning stages what should the co-leaders have done to incorporate goal development in the group process?
2. In planning to conduct support groups, what could these co-leaders have done to overcome their lack of experience in conducting such groups?
3. Are there any ethical concerns regarding the co-leaders' training and experience in conducting group therapy?
4. Which goals are more appropriate for a support group—process goals or outcome goals?
5. How will process goals assist support groups? How will outcome goals assist support groups?

RESPONSE

Shannon D. Smith

Ty and Cindy unfortunately have made a critical mistake in the Monday morning parents' support group, in part due to their vast experience in conducting regular therapy groups. Too often similar mistakes occur in the field setting due to what I call *careless familiarity*. Careless familiarity is simply overlooking important details due to one's previous knowledge and experience with a topic or subject, which includes the belief that previous knowledge and experience prepare one to be competent in a variety of situations. Often these incidents of careless familiarity involve only minor details and go unnoticed or result in minor mishaps; however, there are times when such instances lead to critical mistakes as in the case of Ty and Cindy.

In the Monday morning parents' support group, careless familiarity led to the members' disappointment concerning the environment of the group meetings. This mistake could have been avoided during the planning stages if the co-leaders had clearly considered the purpose of the group (group support) rather than operating out of their familiar paradigm of traditional group therapy. Considering this paradigm shift would have alerted Ty and Cindy to group member goals (rather than group therapy goals) and subsequently would have allowed for members to discuss problems from their own individual perspectives, rather than discuss problems as perceived by the co-leaders and possible behavioral changes to alleviate problems

Based on their inexperience with conducting support groups, Ty and Cindy should have both acknowledged their lack of experience and taken steps to prepare themselves for this new role. For example, they should have conducted a review of the literature to increase their knowledge and understanding of the methods/procedures for conducting a parents' support group. In addition, they could have consulted with other professional counselors who possess the experience and expertise in conducting this particular type of group. Also, Ty and Cindy could have contracted for professional supervision of the support group throughout its duration; this would have limited the potential for mistakes of careless familiarity and would have also limited their legal liability.

One of the major ethical violations found in this incident is practicing therapy outside of the area of expertise/competence. The American Counseling Association *Code of Ethics and Standards of Practice* (ACA, 1995) clearly states that "Counselors practice only within the boundaries of their competence, based on their education, training, supervised experience, state and national professional credentials, and appropriate professional experience" (section C.2.a). Although Ty and Cindy have extensive experience conducting therapy groups, their lack of experience in conducting parent support groups is a potential cause for violation of the Code of Ethics. This particular situation highlights the importance of acknowledging one's limitations and ensuring that the highest level of assistance is offered in a counseling environment.

One of the main tasks of a group leader(s) is to identify, clarify, and develop meaningful goals for the group. In this particular incident, both process and outcome goals are necessary considerations for Ty and Cindy. As previously noted, outcome goals are to be developed during the initial session so as to provide the members with an opportunity to clearly state their support needs and group goals. It is essential to remember that outcome goals will vary according to the unique needs of each member and each group. Again, this fact highlights the notion that outcome goals must be established by each individual member and the group in an effort to meet the various and diversified needs of the members and various groups. Process goals are an equally important consideration for a parental support group. The very nature of a support group presumes that through its duration/course members will offer or provide support to each other. Therefore, it is imperative for group leaders to facilitate group processes among group members. For example, Ty and Cindy could have taken a less directive leadership role by participating as process consultants to the group. A process consultant simply provides group feedback in the form of observations/reflections regarding the overall dynamics and processes of a group, rather than directing interactions or participating in discussions or providing behavioral solutions.

Both process- and outcome-oriented groups may be important to support group members. However, by its very nature, a support group constitutes the facilitation of member support by group members. In this case, support can be facilitated by encouraging particular sequences of group interactions (particularly those deemed supportive). Outcome-oriented therapy may not be necessary to facilitate group members' support for one another even though there are inherent goals that may emerge from both a goal-oriented or ongoing support group.

RESPONSE

Linwood G. Vereen

Goal development is a central element in group counseling. The co-leaders might have done a few things differently to ensure that goals were incorporated early in the group process. For one, during the planning stages, the co-leaders could have worked from a checklist to ensure that all elements of the initial group sessions would be met. The co-leaders could also have worked through the planning stages, shared planning notes, and requested feedback in consultation with a colleague. By not allowing group members to develop concrete goals, the co-leaders took the focus and direction away from the group process and negated the work they had already accomplished in the initial sessions. The co-leaders' failure to include goal development contributed to poor group work.

Their lack of experience in support group facilitation could have been overcome through professional development activities, practice with supervision, and consultation. There is no substitute for professional development in enhancing the skills and techniques used in the therapeutic setting. Without proper training and development, it is difficult to gain skills no matter how long one has practiced.

Another important aspect in this incident is the obligation of counselors to practice within the scope of their education, training, and expertise. Some of the ethical concerns raised in this case study are encompassed within professional responsibility (see section C in the ACA Code of Ethics), especially in relation to boundaries of competence, new specialty areas of practice, and continuing education. The group leaders stretch the boundaries of their competence, given their lack of practical experience, training, and education in this specialty. One could question whether the leaders have provided for the protection of the group. This type of incident can lead to harm to the clients by not providing the best possible treatment. The leaders in this incident need to recognize their limitations and take steps to overcome them.

The use of process goals has a unique function in a support group, in which working with group members who are seeking help with similar issues is likely. Group leaders need to facilitate supportive responses and actions of group members in order for all members to reach their own outcome goals. Process goals assist support groups in that they help to build group cohesion, trust, and feelings of being valued and respected within the group setting. Process goals set the tone for group members taking risks and developing autonomy and responsibility, and for increasing group members' individual growth in areas of self-confidence, self-knowledge, self-respect, self-acceptance, self-direction, self-awareness, and self-esteem. Process goals are a critical element of early stage development in group work. These goals increase awareness and interaction with other group members and aid in defining a group purpose. Process goals lead to the development of outcome goals.

Although outcome goals appear to be a good fit for groups that focus on a change of behavior and task completion, they are inherent to all groups. The fact remains that both types of goals are essential elements of group work, and a progression from process to outcome goals exists in functional groups.

REFERENCE

American Counseling Association. (1995). *Code of ethics and standards of practice.* Alexandria, VA: Author.

CHAPTER 13

LEADER PROFESSIONAL DEVELOPMENT: "THERE IS NOTHING NEW ABOUT GROUPS"

This incident addresses the experienced group leader's inability to learn and benefit from new research and training opportunities that affect the learning experiences of groups and their members.

CRITICAL INCIDENT

Charleen Alderfer

Background

Jack has been in the counseling profession for over 25 years. His training was excellent, and he has frequently attended training for conducting groups in a variety of theoretical modalities. Jack has run the group counseling classes at the college for most of those years. The students are very fond of him and always report beneficial outcomes from the group and from the learning experience. In the past few years, the chair of the department has offered him opportunities to attend training to update his understanding of specific group modalities. He has refused to attend, always citing more pressing work in his academic schedule.

Incident

In a recent group class, students have asked Jack to teach them about some specific kinds of group work. In light of their proximity to an area where terrorist attacks had occurred, they are particularly interested in learning about trauma. Jack has not availed himself of the many trauma trainings that have been offered to counselors even when the chair was highly supportive of his doing so.

In the class, he used the standard group work practices, which were adequate but lacked the specific new information about trauma that was being discovered in response to the terrorist attacks. Not wanting to show his lack of training in the area, Jack resorted to his early group dynamics training and told the students all they needed to know were the basic fundamentals of group work. Some students' frustration increased when they were asked to run trauma groups in their internship placements. They began to feel that their training and preparation in this area were inadequate, and at the same time, they did not want Jack to come under scrutiny as he was a very respected professor. They felt caught between their loyalty to him and their professional responsibility.

When two students who were co-leading an adult trauma group in their placement found themselves unable to cope with the difficult emotional issues they were facing, they decided to speak to the chair about Jack's reluctance to teach the necessary material. The chair thanked them for coming forward and listened to their concerns. As they were preparing to leave his office, he began to ask questions about other aspects of Jack's work in the class. Their responses about Jack's teaching were favorable, but they were very concerned about what the chair would do with any additional inferences he might take from their answers. All they wanted to do was get the training they needed to do their work, not create problems for Jack.

Discussion

After leaving the meeting with the chair, the two students felt extremely uncomfortable. They began to regret their decision to speak up and thought perhaps they had made a mistake by not speaking more directly to Jack. They also had some concerns about having gotten into the middle of department politics that might harm the faculty and even themselves in the process. They began to question the trustworthiness of the faculty and were uncertain about in whom they could place their trust when they had a learning issue. If only Jack had gotten the needed training, none of this would have happened.

QUESTIONS

1. What might the chair have done to be more attuned to Jack's reluctance to go for further training?
2. What are Jack's responsibilities to his students in terms of his leadership examples, the content of his teaching, and ethical perspectives?
3. What other options were available to the students in light of their discontent?
4. How might the chair have dealt differently with the students?
5. What are the best possible outcomes of this situation?

RESPONSE

Jeri L. Goodman

Each leader's unique capacities or incapacities either enhance or deter the group process, making it a priority for leaders to engage in a routine introspective process of self-awareness. Though his fundamental knowledge and confidence enabled Jack to prepare his students for most group leadership opportunities, his lack of continuing education and experience with specific group modalities demonstrated an attitude of complacency on his part. The chair might have sensed this given his repeated attempts to send Jack for training.

The Association for Specialists in Group Work *Best Practice Guidelines* (ASGW, 1998) point out the need for ongoing and continuous professional development, an ethical standard with which Jack and the chair would be familiar. Resistance to change on Jack's part may also indicate an internal conflict of some sort, which falls within the realm of the chair's responsibility to his faculty for consideration. A collaborative decision about continuing education possibilities with the chair could have provided Jack some incentive to attend training, which would have benefited him, the program, and this new group of students. In light of recent terrorist attacks, the call for trauma training may be expected. Not only would it add strength to the counseling program's content, but it would also demonstrate the program's interest in staying current with professional training to meet shifting clients' needs.

The leader's influence on the nature of the group becomes apparent to members, and in this case Jack communicated neither openness nor flexibility in his teaching over the years. His lack of openness, and lack of flexibility and sensitivity to the needs of his students, prevented Jack from simply admitting his lack of specialization in trauma work. He chose to rest on his laurels in providing solid core fundamentals in group training, but he withheld the direction and leadership the students needed to procure necessary resources.

Jack could have created an opportunity for the students to research the training they desired, or to seek supervision in their area of interest, providing an example of leadership and problem solving. Ethically, he needed to state his area of competency and expertise, as he would in a professional disclosure statement, rather than downplay the need for specialization that the students may have desired for themselves.

Students are encouraged to participate in professional organizations, through which they receive information about training opportunities. Practicing specialty group work without proper training and supervision is unethical and unprofessional. Their desire to specialize in trauma work was beyond the scope of the group course context. Awareness of the societal context after terrorist attacks is commendable on the part of the students who could be further prompted to seek training and supervision in this specialty area. This would be an excellent topic to bring up in their internship group for processing, as well as in supervision with faculty such as Jack.

The fact that the students felt respect for Jack was not enough to keep them from going directly to the chair. This should instead have been an option after they had first tried a more direct approach with Jack. The two students who met with the chair needed supervision about their process rather than an opportunity to vent their frustration about an issue that reflected on one instructor. The chair demonstrated poor leadership by including inquiries to the two students about other aspects of Jack's work in class. The students' sense of mistrust was enhanced by such exploration on his part.

The chair has a responsibility to oversee the program and its various components. As an authority figure his perceived power by the students over courses and faculty may be out of line with realistic expectations. Just as a group leader demonstrates a certain leadership style, faculty have leadership styles as well. In an authoritative role the chair listened and gleaned information from the students without providing the emotional relief they wanted. In a laissez-faire style, the chair might have instead listened and thanked the students for coming and gone back to work, or just directed them to Jack himself. Leaders are faced with deciding whether to intervene on behalf of the group (the program), the individual (Jack), or a subgroup (the students). The chair could have invited Jack in to the meeting and modeled effective communication skills for the students as well as a more democratic leadership style.

The best possible outcomes of this situation are directed toward the students who will benefit from an increase in trust and observation of professional conduct by meeting with the chair and Jack to clear the air. Jack can emphasize the *Best Practice Guidelines* to reinforce the need to obtain specialization training and, most importantly, supervision prior to the leadership of a group for which the students are not trained. Perhaps they missed the class on assertiveness training, when the students learned that they could turn down a leadership role in the internship placement for which they are not qualified. Jack may now be motivated to seek additional training, and the chair is supportive of the process of resolving conflicts while considering the needs of all concerned.

RESPONSE

Nicole R. Hill

The critical incident related to leader professional development challenges us to explore our responsibilities as counselor trainees and our professional responsibilities as educators and mentors in the field. Counseling is an evolving field in which new trends and applications emerge. Counselor trainees, counselors, counselor educators, and supervisors have an ethical responsibility to remain competent by engaging in ongoing professional development. Section C.2.f of the American Counseling Association *Code of Ethics and Standards of Practice* (ACA, 1995) asserts that counselors actively engage in continuing education to remain current in the field and to learn about new information.

The chair of Jack's department has a responsibility to facilitate the professional development and competence of the faculty in the department. The chair has offered on numerous occasions throughout the last few years to support Jack in his professional development. The chair could have been more active in exploring the reasons behind Jack's reluctance to attend any training. The initial offer of support for ongoing training could have been coupled with an open discussion of how Jack was meeting his ethical responsibility of maintaining and expanding competence related to group work. This active dialogue with Jack would have shown support for his professional development and would have provided the chair with information related to Jack's openness to remain current in the field. It is unclear how much involvement the chair had with Jack prior to the students approaching him. A supportive professional relationship between the chair and Jack might permit a more timely resolution of the issue.

Jack, as a counselor educator, acts as a professional role model of appropriate and ethical behavior. The ACA Code of Ethics is clear about expectations of counselor educators in sharing with students' ethical responsibilities and professional standards (section F.2.d) and in being competent and knowledgeable as practitioners (section F.1.a). Jack is the primary educator in group work in the program. His students have requested on numerous occasions that Jack respond to recent developments in group work and prepare them to facilitate trauma groups. Jack chooses not to prepare students in this area due to his lack of training. Jack, then, has an ethical and professional responsibility to seek out opportunities to gain training in this area. Jack acknowledges his lack of training and yet does not engage in available training opportunities. Furthermore, the Council for Accreditation of Counseling and Related Educational Programs (*CACREP) Accreditation Standards and Procedures Manual* (2001) and the Association for Specialists in Group Work *Best Practice Guidelines* (1998) underline the importance of faculty members who are active in the development and renewal of their training. As a counselor educator and group work specialist, Jack has an ethical and accreditation responsibility to remain current in the field of group work and to role model this process to his students.

In regards to teaching content, CACREP Accreditation Standards indicate that course work on group encompasses basic fundamentals as well as approaches used for other types of group work. Jack is providing a limited foundation of content in his group counseling course. Jack could be more active in teaching content that encompasses the areas highlighted in the CACREP Accreditation Standards. Jack is responsible for covering much material within the span of one course. If he feels that trauma-specific material could not be integrated into the present course and taught by him, then he could seek other methods of ensuring that students are prepared in this area. For example, Jack could utilize the local chapter of Chi Sigma Iota to present some workshops on this topic, bring in some guest speakers who are facilitating trauma groups in the community, integrate an assignment that permitted the students to explore the group development process with a population of interest, or assign specific readings that address the issues related to trauma groups. Jack is faced with the responsibility of ensuring that his students are prepared to handle the experiences in their placement sites. He could seek out creative methods for responding to this need before he had another opportunity to gain some training.

The students who felt frustrated and unprepared could have sought assistance in other areas. Students at their placement sites have an ethical responsibility to practice within the parameters of their knowledge, training, and competence (ACA Code of Ethics, section C.2.a). Prior to discussing the issue with the chair, the students could have scheduled a meeting with Jack and expressed their discontent and feelings of inadequacy. This might have generated some brainstorming about how Jack and the students could gain the knowledge and training necessary to lead trauma groups. It is not clear if the students approached Jack once they began co-leading trauma groups at their placements. A more detailed explanation of what skills they felt they were lacking might have prompted a more active response from Jack.

Furthermore, the students could have sought training on-site. The on-site supervisors of counselor trainees also have an ethical obligation to ensure that clients are receiving appropriate services from competent practitioners. Sharing their frustration and feelings of incompetence with on-site supervisors might have prompted the placement to provide a workshop and training specific to trauma groups.

The students in the group counseling course do have the right to file grievances and to express their frustration with training provided by the program. Seeking out the chair is an appropriate step once the students have actively presented their case to Jack. The chair responded to the meeting by seeking out more information about Jack. The chair could have focused on the issue at hand and thanked the students for sharing their concerns. The chair could then approach Jack and discuss some opportunities for training. If Jack continued to be reluctant, the chair could share the concerns of the students. Furthermore, the chair could have discussed with students other avenues for gaining knowledge and competence in the area of trauma groups. The chair might have encouraged them to seek out workshops in the community and to request that Chi Sigma Iota host a training on this topic.

The best outcome for this situation is that Jack and the students receive adequate training in facilitating trauma groups. Jack has an ethical and professional responsibility to further his understanding of new developments in group work. The students also have a responsibility to practice within the parameters of their professional competence. Both parties need to seek out resources that provide the knowledge and skills to facilitate trauma groups. The best outcome will be for Jack to attend some workshops and to integrate trauma groups into his group counseling courses. The best outcome for the current students will be to attain training and supervision in this area because they are leading a trauma group in their placements.

REFERENCES

American Counseling Association. (1995). *Code of ethics and standards of practice*. Alexandria, VA: Author.

Association for Specialists in Group Work. (1998). Best practice guidelines. *Journal for Specialists in Group Work, 23*(3), 237–244.

Council for Accreditation of Counseling and Related Educational Programs. (2001). *CACREP accreditation standards and procedures manual*. Alexandria, VA: Author.

CHAPTER 14

CHALLENGING THE LEADER: "I KNOW WHO I AM!"

This incident focuses on issues that may surface when a group counselor is challenged by members of the group. The incident comes alive for me, as it is one that I personally experienced in the past.

CRITICAL INCIDENT

Kurt L. Kraus

Background
"What do you know about me? I hate people like you, Kyle."

"What is it that Kyle just did that you hate, Lenny, why don't you tell him?"

"There you go, Mr. Counselor, always telling us what to do in here! You are worse than Kyle! Everybody is sick of you in here! Why don't you just shut the hell up? Give us a break," Lenny said.

I remember the feeling that I had in that very instant. It was one of realization. I realized that my fears of lurking incompetence were proving true. I remember thinking that Lenny is probably correct; others in the group are tired of my relentless attempts to have the group establish norms that will eventually lead to an effective group experience. Given this group, six boys ages 12 to 15 who were referred for counseling by their middle-school principal, I realized that nothing I had learned in graduate school was working here. All that supervision and instruction was not helping me now. Lenny was not angry with Kyle; he was angry with me. This was some sort of attack on me! I felt my defenses soar into view. I felt my desire to lash out and crush Lenny — Lenny and his anger — Lenny and his painful truthfulness — Lenny, this troubled, angry adolescent. Lenny was giving me his rough-hewn version of corrective feedback, and he was telling me that I did not know what I was doing.

I did not let my feelings show. I did not lash out. I did not retreat from my position as the leader of this group. Instead, I found some inner resolve not to collapse under the weight of an accusation hurled by this 14-year-old, despite the fact that at that moment I believed he knew more about this group than I did!

Incident

I was a new school counselor. I had taken the rather unenviable position of replacing a beloved middle-school counselor who had moved the previous summer. The vacancy was one I initially thought was close to ideal if not perfect. The middle school was well respected in the region with an emphasis on educating the whole child. Services provided through the counseling office were well integrated into the life of the school. The previous school counselor had a recognized and respected voice in much of what went on in the school. Developmental guidance classes, weekly consultation with administration and faculty, numerous parent contacts, and individual and group counseling were all expectations of the administration and teachers. I was thrilled to be hired. Then, it seemed without fair warning, I was given many students with whom the last counselor had worked. My principal, in a note asking me to resume seeing some of these children, wrote, "Here is a list of kids that Fred had been working pretty successfully with last year in one way or another. Several of them, being eighth graders, have lots to lose if their behavior this year doesn't turn around for the better. But most of them have huge problems (lots of them home-related) and will not be easy! Don't spend too much time on any one of them. There are lots of kids here in school, as I know you know, who really would benefit and appreciate your time...." Thus began my experience with this group, including Lenny.

My decision to see these boys in a group seemed like a good one. After all, each boy had a similar history. Each was currently experiencing difficulty in his classrooms largely due to behavioral problems. Their teachers described them with words such as *belligerent, oppositional, antagonistic, lazy,* and *rude.* Some added *insecure* and *hopeless* in their obvious disdain of several boys in particular. And one teacher, who had Lenny as a student the year before, referred to him as "a loser." I felt that if I could bring them together, structure them with activities and dialogue around their feelings relating to school, and get them to open up with one another about their current difficulties in school and at home, we might see a decrease in their acting out in classes. The consequence would be that they would thrive and be viewed as successful students.

I decided that I should see the boys individually first, to be sure that they would be acceptable in the group, just as I had been taught to do — screening. Each boy offered pretty good reasons as to why he should be in a group. I described the group as an opportunity to meet once a week with other boys, some of whom they might know well and others of whom they might not know very well at all. I told everyone that the members of the group all had several things in common in that they were all struggling in school academically and they had all been sent to the principal for misbehavior of one sort or another. Each of the boys had the potential to be successful in the middle school, which was a prerequisite to promotion to the high school and ninth grade.

In addition, I asked each boy if he could think of several goals that he would be willing to share out loud with the other members, goals that he would be willing to work on through the group. I told each boy how excited I was for the group to begin. I reviewed some basics about how the group would run as well as the ethical issues of confidentiality, duty to warn, and safety. I told each boy that he would have a very special role in the success of the group, that I would expect him to be honest, to take risks, and to trust that the group would help him reach the goals that he had set for himself.

The first session was wonderful, as the boys seemed to connect with one another. They knew each other, and it felt as if I was the only new guy in the group. The boys acted out with insider snickers, occasional profanity, and challenging remarks. Wendell said to Juan, "Hey, are you going to feel okay in this group without any other of your kind in here?" When Juan jumped up my heart sank, but they both looked at me, and burst into big laughter. I guess it was Wendell's way of seeing what kind of reaction he could get from me. The joke (in poor taste) was on me. I let it slide.

In that first meeting most boys were willing to share some appropriate personal goals. "I want to pass math," Mark said. "I want to work on my anger issues," Kyle said jokingly, but went on to add, "Seriously, I do have a bad temper and it gets me in lots of trouble!" Others said, "I want to get to ninth grade." "I can't stand it here. I want to get out of school, but can't quit until I'm 16." "I have to pass or my parents told me that they would send me to military school for high school." And then there was Lenny. He told the group that they were losers, and he did not "want sh - -" from them. To my surprise, instead of evoking any angry outburst, the other boys laughed and said that Lenny's remark was "cool." I let that slide too.

At the end of the first session I asked the boys to simply close by stating one thing that they hoped they would gain from the other members of the group or that they had gained by being in the group today. It was great listening to these "difficult" boys as they responded.

"I'm glad that we are doing this."
"I was nervous about coming here today, but I'm glad that I did."
"It wasn't so bad. Maybe this group will help. It can't hurt, I suppose"
"I like you, Mr. X, you're alright."

The second session was different. The dialogue seemed to bounce around aimlessly. One boy would share something and the others would nod, chuckle, or offer some advice. Advice was common, and I made an effort to discourage giving advice and instead helped several boys make meaningful connections with their own behaviors and feelings that seemed to be shared by others in the group. I worked hard during this session, but during the closing round the boys seemed less able to offer anything profound. It seemed as if for the final 15 minutes of the 55-minute session, the boys were all stealing glimpses of the clock on my desk.

I planned the third session to begin with an activity. I thought that an activity could help the boys focus and be more present. Most of the boys shuffled in rather passively, and Kyle was the last one to arrive. He stormed in and immediately accused someone in the group of breaking confidentiality! "I want to know who the f- - - told Coach McGrath that I was in this stupid group for losers? And I want to know if I have to stay in this stupid g - - d - - - group, because it isn't going to help me to be with these f- - - ing a - - h - - - -."

I asked Kyle to please sit down and then we could talk about how angry he was. I reflected how furious he obviously was and added that I hoped he could keep his voice down and watch his language. I did not want him or anyone else in the group to get in trouble by people overhearing as they passed by the office. Kyle sat down. He folded his arms across his chest and seethed. He looked as if he was going to cry, but the tears would have been of rage had he let them come to the surface. I turned to the others in the group and encouraged them to hear what Kyle was saying. One or two seemed to be amused. Others seemed to be hiding behind feigned, nervous smiles. Not Lenny though, as he looked at Kyle incredulously. His disbelief did not seem to be about Kyle's anger or his language. It was in response to Kyle's accusation.

Being accused was something that Lenny had grown used to in many areas of his life. It seemed that Kyle's accusation was more than Lenny could stand. I said, "Lenny, you seem to me to be feeling some pretty strong feelings right now. I wonder if you can tell others what that is all about." Lenny appeared to have reached his limit as he responded. "What do you know about me?" Lenny snarled. "I hate people like you, Kyle." "What is it that Kyle just did that you hate, Lenny, why don't you tell him," I said. "There you go, Mr. Counselor, always telling us what to do in here! You are worse than Kyle! Everybody is sick of you in here! Why don't you just shut the hell up? Give us a break."

Discussion

No one moved as Lenny snarled his accusation as much as he spoke it. I just sat. No one disagreed with Lenny, not even Kyle. This situation did not appear to involve the confrontations I had learned about in school or discussed in supervision. This was not about whether to confront something that a member had said. None of this was my decision. This was an attack, an attack by a 14-year-old group member that struck my most vulnerable place: my confidence. I remember the feeling of realization that I had in that very instant.

QUESTIONS

1. What are you feeling about the way this counselor inherited these boys as well as others upon his arrival to his new position?
2. How do you feel about the counselor's decision to see these boys in a group? What do you see as potential strengths and weaknesses of his decision?

3. What feelings did you have when the counselor exclaimed, "nothing I had learned in graduate school was working here"?
4. What do you think of the counselor's response to Kyle's accusations about a break in confidentiality?
5. What do you think about the counselor's reaction to Lenny's attack?
6. As a counselor, what might you do differently if faced with this incident?
7. What would you specifically recommend that this new counselor bring to supervision regarding this incident?

RESPONSE

Jody J. Fiorini

I was first struck, as I read this critical incident, by the courage this author showed in sharing a part of his own experience with us. The clarity with which he recalled the events surrounding this group illustrates the powerful impact this experience had on his psyche and development as a counselor. The fact that this was a real case helps novice group counselors understand that it is not unusual to have strong trepidations and feelings of inadequacy when beginning one's journey in becoming a group facilitator. So I begin this critique by thanking the author for his honesty and forthrightness.

Several aspects of this case led to the counselor's heightened sense of insecurity. First, the counselor was both new to the profession and replacing a much beloved veteran counselor at his new workplace. Seeing students, especially troubled students, who had been inherited from the previous counselor was bound to lead to issues that may not have been adequately foreseen by the counselor or the administrator. In this case the counselor not only had to deal with getting to know the students but in a sense was also competing with the ghost of the previous counselor. One might expect resistance to the new interloper who was trying to replace their former counselor. Students might feel a sense of being disloyal to the former counselor by developing a relationship with the new counselor. Students are savvy enough to be aware of any new counselor's sense of inadequacy and fear. It could be expected that students with known behavior problems might try to exploit these feelings to gain a sense of control over the situation, much as they might in a classroom setting with a substitute teacher. If the counselor had foreseen these possible interactions, or if he had been prepared for them through supervision, it is likely that he would not have personalized the attack in the way that he did.

In terms of whether this set of students was suitable for a group setting, I agree with the counselor in his decision to see the students in a group counseling format. First, he had been instructed by the principal not to spend too much time on any one of these students. Therefore, seeing them in a group was the most efficient means of seeing them all. Second, as the author points out, the students had similar issues, which would allow for more focused interventions. It is difficult, if not impossible, to acquire prosocial skills in isolation, so a group was the modality of choice in this situation. However, given the nature of the students, it was incumbent on the group leader to expect some problem behaviors among the group members. I do not take issue with the counselor's choice to see students in a group setting; however, I feel that his goals and expectations might have been unrealistic. At one point the author implies that he felt that if the group intervention was successful, "The consequence would be that they would thrive and be viewed as successful students." This goal, although noble, may be unrealistic and only add to the pressure that the counselor already feels. The counselor appears to have set himself up for failure. Better to start with more realistic, manageable goals: fewer referrals over the next marking period, grades raised by a half letter grade, or, not to be overlooked, an increased level of trust and ability to empathize with fellow students.

With regard to the counselor's response to Kyle's accusations about a break in confidentiality, this might have been a time when more direct leadership was necessary. It might have been an appropriate time to reiterate the ground rules and seriousness of breaching confidentiality. It also might have been an excellent time to get at the heart of a shared underlying issue that had finally surfaced in the group. This might have been the time to reflect the hurt, embarrassment, and stigma felt by members of the group. This was one of several times that the group members referred to themselves as *losers*. Interestingly, one of the referring teachers referred to Lenny as a loser. It would not be surprising if this message was received and interjected by Lenny and the other group members at various times in numerous milieus. I would have pursued the feelings surrounding having others know that they were attending this group.

With regard to the counselor's response to Lenny's attack, once again I feel that a teachable moment was lost here. It seems as though the counselor was so absorbed in his own feelings of inadequacy that he personalized Lenny's response as an attack on himself. I suggest that Lenny's reaction was therapeutic. He was sharing with the leader how incensed he feels about being wrongfully accused, an event that happens quite often in his life. In a sense the counselor strongly identified with Lenny's feelings, so much so that a countertransference reaction took place with the counselor feeling attacked and wrongfully accused. Instead of enhancing his sense of understanding and empathy for Lenny, the counselor's own sense of fear and inadequacy prevented him from seeing the interaction from an objective perspective. I suggest that some good stuff went on in this session that could be used to help all of the group members explore their feelings around being identified as losers and the frustration inherent in continually being pegged as troublemakers. The group itself serves as a reminder of this designated loser status in the eyes of the members. What an eye-opener it was for the well-meaning counselor.

When reading the counselor's comments noting that "nothing I had learned in graduate school was working here," I chuckled to myself and thought, "I think you forgot to read a chapter in your group text." It is well documented that turning on the leader is an expected stage in group counseling. Tuckman (1965) referred to this as the storming stage, Corey and Corey (2002), the transition stage. This is the stage when the leader can expect to encounter resistance and to be challenged. Once again, I argue that the counselor's own feelings of anxiety and inadequacy clouded his ability to recognize this incident as a normal stage in the group process. In fact, this incident is an indication that the group is moving toward the working stage.

It is important to note that this incident is not all that unusual for novice counselors and is certainly not insurmountable. It is incumbent upon the counselor to receive supervision both to recognize the underlying issues and opportunities presented in the group and to work through the feelings of insecurity that are interfering with his ability to be there for the group. In addition, he needs to be reminded of how many things he is doing right with these boys. He is well prepared, takes his responsibilities as group facilitator seriously, has the best interests of the boys at heart, and has high expectations that they can make it. With some supervision he has the makings of a terrific group counselor. I bet he already is!

RESPONSE

Edward Neukrug

This counselor was clearly elated about his new position at the middle school and looked forward to putting into practice many of the skills he learned in graduate school. However, a bit of naivety on the part of this counselor is present. His statement that he was given "without fair warning...many students with whom the last counselor had worked" certainly shows this inexperienced side. After all, could one expect when entering a new system as a counselor to receive only the healthy children for counseling? In fact, in many ways one should expect the opposite, that is, to be given those children who are exhibiting problem behaviors. And a good number of those children will be the same children with whom the previous counselor had worked.

So this counselor is walking into a situation with unrealistic expectations, and this may be an indication that he is worried about how he will fare as compared with the previous "recognized and respected" counselor. A new counselor will most likely be concerned with his or her performance, and then to be worried about being compared with a past counselor who was good raises the stakes. Now, to put gasoline on the fire, the principal is placing this new counselor in a precarious situation with the multiple messages in his note, which can be translated by the new counselor as follows:

> Here are some very difficult kids with whom the former counselor worked successfully. They have huge problems. They have much to lose if they do not turn around. But do not spend too much time with them. There are other kids here too!

The new counselor's reactions to this translation are, "Am I going to be as good as the former counselor? The principal and others are watching. And I must show everyone that I can work successfully with these students in a relatively short amount of time." The new counselor is walking into a loaded situation. If the students do not improve, he has failed them and the principal; but if he spends too much time with them, he may be seen as inadequate, as not being able to accomplish the entire job that is required of him.

Thus on the surface, a group counseling experience for these students seems like a good quick fix. The counselor can attend to all of these students' needs in a shorter amount of time. After all, this is one of the advantages of running a group. The rationale that they all have similar problems and might do well in a group seems to make sense. And it is good that he met with the boys individually at first. However, the basic decision to see the boys in group may be flawed.

Group process theory tells us that all groups go through a period in which members begin to feel threatened because they are being asked to share increasingly intimate parts of themselves. This stage in group development often leads to hostility, sometimes directed at the group leader, in an effort to redirect the individual's fears about self-disclosure. With a group of students already known for being belligerent and defensive, it is almost a given that there will be hostility directed at the leader at some point. Thus the group leader must be prepared to deal with this possibility and to seriously consider whether group counseling is the way to proceed. At the very least, it would have been prudent for the counselor to spend additional time building individual relationships with these boys, which could have tempered the amount of hostility likely to come his way during the group experience.

When a confrontation does arise, the counselor states, "This was not like the confrontations I had learned about in school or discussed in supervision." This remark by the counselor reflects his anxiety, feelings of inadequacy, and sense of helplessness, and may be masking hostility toward his graduate program. It is likely to be an example of parallel process. That is, hostility within the group is being expressed toward the leader, and now the leader has hostility toward his leader (graduate school). This is an excellent opportunity for the counselor to explore, in supervision, his feelings, including any feelings of hostility. This exploration is likely to lead to his feelings of incompetence, inadequacy, and helplessness, and perhaps to some unfinished business from his past. Uncovering these feelings may give the counselor some insight into the feelings of both Kyle and Lenny and be an opportunity for him to have greater empathy toward them. Perhaps they, too, feel incompetent, inadequate, and helpless.

The counselor notes that he explained "ethical issues of confidentiality, duty to warn, and safety." However, he may not have fully explained the limits of confidentiality to the group. If this is the case, the counselor may even be in violation of the American Counseling Association *Code of Ethics and Standards of Practice* (ACA, 1995) concerning confidentiality in groups, which says in section B.2.a that

> In group work, counselors clearly define confidentiality and the parameters for the specific group being entered, explain its importance, and discuss the difficulties related to confidentiality involved in group work. The fact that confidentiality cannot be guaranteed is clearly communicated to group members.

Within any group it is critical that group members understand that although confidentiality is essential for a successful group experience, it cannot be guaranteed. This must be particularly stressed when running a group such as this in which problems with impulsivity are likely.

The counselor's response to Lenny may be fueling the fire. Lenny is clearly enraged at Kyle, and to ask Lenny to direct his anger at Kyle could escalate the situation. Silence, an empathic response, or taking the focus away from a direct confrontation between Kyle and Lenny (e.g., asking other group members to discuss what they think is going on with Lenny and Kyle and in the group) might be a better response. In either case, one needs to keep in mind that Lenny's response is a reflection of group process, and the counselor should take a wider view of Lenny's attack. In fact, Lenny's attack can be seen as a sign of progress in the group. If the group is allowing the expression of anger, the members are likely to be beginning to get close to underlying feelings.

As a counselor I would have done a number of things differently with the group. First, I would have spent a longer time developing individual relationships with the group members in order to create a firmer foundation for a group of potentially difficult group members. Second, I would clearly explain the limits of confidentiality, as noted in the ACA Code of Ethics. Third, I would view Kyle and Lenny's anger as a sign of progress in the group. Underlying issues are being churned up, and the hostility is a reflection of this. Fourth, I would accept Kyle and Lenny's feelings, but I would be careful not to escalate the anger between these two group members. I, as the leader, can work with the anger, but I do not want the anger to get out of control between the group members.

Supervision could afford this counselor a number of opportunities. It could allow him to examine whether or not he has fully prepared the group members for this experience (e.g., issues related to cohesion, explanation of confidentiality). It could give the counselor the opportunity to examine his fears about the group succeeding, about being compared with the past counselor, and about his ability in general. It could allow the counselor to examine parallel process issues. Finally, it could provide the counselor the ability to examine any historical issues and unfinished business that might be interfering with his ability to successfully run this group.

REFERENCES

American Counseling Association. (1995).   *Code of ethics and standards of practice.* Alexandria, VA: Author.

Corey, M.S., & Corey, G. (2002).   *Groups: Process and practice* (6th ed.). Pacific Grove, CA: Brooks/Cole.

Tuckman, B. W. (1965).   Developmental sequence in small groups. *Psychological Bulletin, 63*(6), 384–399.

CHAPTER 15

SELF-ASSESSMENT: "WHAT ARE WE DOING HERE?"

This incident explores issues related to training for group leader-ship in substance abuse treatment.

CRITICAL INCIDENT

John A. Bayerl

Background
Two practicing school counselors in a small, rural school district called their former professor to discuss their concerns about an assignment given by their instructor for a course in substance abuse treatment in which they were enrolled. The assignment was to attend at least four meetings of an Alcoholics Anonymous (AA) group in order to become familiar with it as part of a substance abuse treatment referral.

The schools in which the counselors worked had a high incidence of alcoholism in students' homes, and the counselors were anxious to become more proficient at working with students from such homes, including conducting support groups for them. Their school counselor preparation program had included a review of group counseling theories, techniques, and procedures, but they had had no specific training in substance abuse treatment.

Incident
The concerns that the counselors raised with their professor were related to the requirement that they attend meetings of AA. Because they lived and worked in a small town, they anticipated possibly seeing family members of their students at the AA meeting. They were anxious to complete the assignment in order to be better able to help their students. However, they were weighing the benefits of completing the assignment and attending the meetings versus complications that could arise if they were to encounter people they knew at the meetings.

These counselors had already paid tuition for the class, attended three sessions, and found it to be a meaningful learning experience thus far. They had discussed their concern with their instructor, but she was adamant about enforcing the requirement that they attend the AA meetings as part of the class assignment.

Discussion

In addition to the personal/professional issues raised by the two counselors, this incident provokes legal and ethical issues. The personal/professional issues have to do with how the attendance of the counselors at AA meetings could be interpreted. They were concerned with possibly encountering members of their school community at the meeting, thereby compromising their anonymity. Noteworthy is that there are open meetings of AA to which guests and observers are invited, but it is not clear at the meetings which of those present are guests/observers and which are participants. The counselors were concerned about how their attendance at the meetings could be interpreted by community members in attendance. That is, could their attendance at the meetings be seen as evidence that they were in treatment for substance abuse?

The counselors were also fearful about possible legal and ethical concerns that might arise as a result of information they were exposed to at the meetings. What, for example, would be their legal responsibility if they heard the father of one of their students talk at a meeting about abusing his children? Would other information they became privy to at the meetings create additional ethical dilemmas?

QUESTIONS

1. How do you see the concerns of the two counselors about being seen in attendance at an AA meeting as the concerns relate to their awareness of the disease of alcoholism?
2. If the counselors were to attend an AA meeting and hear a participant discuss abusing his or her children, what would their legal obligation to report be?
3. What good could accrue as a result of their attendance at the AA meetings as opposed to any possible bad that could happen?
4. What alternative ways might the counselors suggest to satisfy their instructor's requirement?

RESPONSE

Thomas E. Davis

The case presented here is a common one for those who teach chemical dependency issues in counselor education. It presents the challenge of drawing the line between what is important for a counselor to know, and how best to learn it, versus protection of individuals' rights to privacy. In cases such as this, the counselor must consider the moral, ethical, and legal aspects and ramifications of attending open Alcoholics Anonymous or other step/support group meetings.

A fundamental question in this case deals with the value gained by the counselors from the experience of attending an AA meeting. When it comes to addressing addiction, it has been said that there is no single intervention or counseling modality that is as effective as AA. The school counselor who works with students (or their significant others) who abuse or are dependent on any form of drugs must possess accurate and outcome-driven methods of intervention.

Two primary questions are posed in this case, and both have merit. First, there is the counselors' concern that by attending the open AA meetings they may encounter "members of the school community at the meeting, thereby compromising their anonymity," and further, it may "not be clear at the meeting which of those present are guest/observers and which are participants." It is critical to weigh the rights of all concerned in training professional school counselors. Supervisors have an obligation to assure that the counselor in training "does no harm." In this case the individual with the supervisory responsibility for the student is the course instructor. It is important that the individuals taking such a course have an understanding of the various types of AA meetings that exist, including open meetings that are open to any member of the public who chooses to attend. Alcoholics and nonalcoholics alike routinely attend open meetings. Those attending an open meeting might include family, friends, interested community members, and helping professionals. The intent of the open meeting is to allow anyone interested in learning about AA to do so without disclosing his or her own personal reasons for attending other than wanting to learn about AA.

In the current case, it is important to understand that all should be aware of the purpose of an open meeting. It is fair to say that most members of AA understand the purpose of such meetings, and welcome visitors. It is also important to recognize that many first-time attendees, including students, find it difficult to attend AA open meetings. They often are self-conscious about attending themselves, and worry that someone might think they are alcoholics. Such resistance is common, and should be recognized and addressed by the instructor.

The second question posed in this case suggests that counselors may be "fearful about possible legal and ethical concerns that might arise as a result of information they were exposed to at the meetings," such as child abuse. This issue is more complex in nature. Counselors must be aware of the possible legal and ethical issues that might arise as a result of information they are exposed to at the open meetings. The school counselors attending the meeting have no professional duty as counselors to those attending the meetings, unless they are their own clients. This in no way suggests that the anonymity of those attending AA meetings should be compromised without compelling justification.

The example used in this case addresses the potential of child abuse expressed by an individual attending an AA meeting. The American Counseling Association *Code of Ethics and Standards of Practice* (ACA, 1995) states that the counselor's confidentiality requirement "does not apply when disclosure is required to prevent clear and imminent danger to the client or others" (section B.1.c). Reporting suspected physical, sexual, or emotional child abuse or neglect is a legal requirement as well. The burden in a situation such as this is squarely on the counselor and his or her clinical judgment. Because the ethical questions posed in this case are complex but not directly addressed in the ACA Code of Ethics, it seems appropriate for the school counselors to consider using a structured format such as the multistep decision-making model for making sound ethical decisions posed by Forester-Miller and Davis (1995). The seven steps included in this model are to

1. identify the problem and examine from several perspectives;
2. apply the ACA Code of Ethics;
3. determine the nature and dimensions of the dilemma;
4. generate potential courses of action;
5. consider the potential consequences of all options and determine a course of action;
6. evaluate the selected course of action; and
7. implement the course of action.

Employing this type of decision-making model can aid all counselors in grappling with challenging situations such as the one posed in this case.

RESPONSE

Howard B. Smith

There are two levels of concern presented in this incident. The first level is personal. The two counselors' concerns about being seen at an open meeting of Alcoholics Anonymous, and being mistaken by a parent who is attending as someone who is in treatment for substance abuse themselves, is a personal issue as opposed to a professional issue. It may cause them some embarrassment but would in no case be seen as a professional, legal, or ethical issue. If the two counselors are concerned about that happening, the worst imaginable consequence is that the school principal might find out about it. That consequence can be alleviated by discussing the assignment with the principal in advance and explaining the benefits they expect to gain toward serving their students more effectively. If the counselors are concerned about their public image and the fallout of the rumors that could result from this mistaken identity, that could take a while to settle down; but if they respond honestly and openly that they were there as a part of the assignment to learn how to better serve their students, again the damage will be minimal. Further, the counselors must give some credit to the fact that anonymity is and always has been the basis of the AA program. Although this cannot be guaranteed at a 100% level, it certainly reduces the likelihood of any loss of personal profile.

The more serious level of concern is obviously the issue of being a mandated reporter should they hear a parent disclosing that he or she has abused his or her child while under the influence. In such a case, a wise course of action would be to discuss this with the school principal, who is aware of school law and subject to the same reporting law as the counselors, or perhaps with the school's attorney who could help them come to understand their legal obligations given the circumstances described in this critical incident. Yet another avenue would be to discuss it with the state board of counselor examiners (licensure board) to get a different perspective. The question to be asked is, "Under these circumstances, in which I am not acting as a school counselor nor am I in any way attending this meeting as a job-related assignment, and given that the 12-Step program addresses the issue of admitting wrongdoings and attempting to make amends with those who have been harmed, am I obligated to report this confession?" The safest interpretation of the concept of mandated reporter is to report everything, but there is some small room for judgment, or at the very least when reporting suspicions of abuse, an obligation to provide all the facts, that is, where this was heard and under what circumstances, and a description of any evidence they had seen in the discharge of their responsibilities as a school counselor.

There is no doubt that firsthand exposure to this population could enhance the counselors' understanding of and appreciation for substance abuse issues. However, I urge the instructor to provide some information or assign the counselors to go on the Web to learn about AA prior to attending the meetings. The counselors will then know the meaning and history of AA and be prepared for what they will experience.

The risk discussed earlier in this response, at the personal level, is not sufficient to warrant canceling the assignment. Being known in our society as a mental health professional affords certain privileges (e.g., being with people who are in need and not being seen as one of those in need). Assuming that the counselors had discussed the assignment with the principal prior to attending the AA meetings, and that they conducted themselves with professional decorum and demeanor in aspiring to becoming mental health professionals, there is nothing about which to be concerned.

I suggest that the counselors could get the same benefit without any of the potential inherent risks by simply driving to another town to fulfill the assignment. The AA group will offer them the same experience, and their concerns will be ameliorated.

REFERENCES

American Counseling Association. (1995). *Code of ethics and standards of practice.* Alexandria, VA: Author.

Forester-Miller, H., & Davis, T.E. (1995). *A practitioner's guide to ethical decision making.* Alexandria, VA: American Counseling Association.

CHAPTER 16

INFORMED CONSENT FOR MINORS: "WHY DO YOU HAVE MY SON IN THERAPY?"

This incident addresses the issue of assuring informed consent for minor clients in counseling and explores some of the practical, legal, and ethical considerations the school counselor confronts in conducting group counseling with children and adolescents.

CRITICAL INCIDENT

James J. Bergin

Background

It is January, and Paula is beginning her internship in school counseling at Meadow Elementary School. Her university supervisor, Dr. Johns, made special arrangements for her to intern at Meadow under the site supervision of Mr. George, one of Dr. Johns' favorite graduates and the only male elementary school counselor in the school system. Ms. Starr, the school principal, is proud to have the only male elementary school counselor working in her school, and regularly seeks his counsel in making administrative decisions. She considers Paula fortunate to have Mr. George as an internship supervisor and advises her to pay close attention to him and "follow his suggestions and example."

Paula decides that she wants to conduct a counseling group with elementary students because she has never done so. She consults with Mr. George, and together they decide that Paula should create a counseling group for boys in third grade whose parents have divorced within the last 2 years. In addition, they decide that Paula will focus the sessions on helping the group members manage the changes in their responsibilities at home and school that have resulted from the family's new situation. Paula conducted a counseling group using this theme with eighth-grade students during her practicum experience, so she requested that she be allowed to adapt her group organization plan to elementary students rather than creating a new theme and group plan.

Mr. George felt confident that the group procedures and activities could easily be adapted to the third-grade boys and encouraged Paula to begin her group as soon as possible. Accordingly, Paula began the tasks of redesigning the group plan, soliciting recommendations for the group from third-grade teachers and the counselor, scheduling the time and place for the sessions, interviewing prospective group members, and getting their consent to join the group. By the last week in January, Paula had completed all her group preparations and selected the sixth and final student, Lance Smith, following her interview with him on the Friday prior to the week the group was scheduled to hold its first meeting.

Incident

Before arriving at school the following Monday morning, Paula received a telephone message at home from the school secretary informing her that Ms. Starr wanted to see her "immediately." When Paula entered Ms. Starr's office she noted that Mr. George was already present. Ms. Starr stated that Dr. Johns was expected to arrive shortly to participate in their discussion, but that the first order of business was for Paula to cancel her group counseling sessions "until further notice." Mr. George immediately assured the principal that her directive would be followed. Ms. Starr then explained that she had received a telephone call Sunday evening from the father of Lance Smith. She said that Mr. Smith was extremely upset and quoted him as wanting to know, "Who gave you permission to put my son in therapy?" Mr. Smith conveyed to Ms. Starr that Lance had told him about being selected by "Ms. Paula" to be in her group with some other boys so they could all talk "about divorce and stuff." Mr. Smith consulted with his ex-wife about the group when he returned Lance to her home Sunday afternoon. Mr. and Mrs. Smith have joint custody of Lance. Mrs. Smith has custody during the week while Mr. Smith has custody on weekends.

Upon discovering that Mrs. Smith had no knowledge of Lance's participation in the group, or of the existence of a "Ms. Paula," Mr. Smith called the principal and insisted that Lance be withdrawn from the group and any other "psychotherapeutic" activities without first obtaining the expressed written consent of both himself and his ex-wife. Moreover, upon hearing from the principal that "Ms. Paula" was only an intern, Mr. Smith stated that even in the event that he and his ex-wife would consent to Lance participating in counseling they would certainly only do so if the counselor were fully credentialed.

Ms. Starr asked Mr. George and Paula for their advice on how to respond to Mr. Smith. Paula stated that his classroom teacher had referred Lance because he was not acting responsibly toward his work in the classroom and keeping his desk and materials orderly. Although a capable student academically, his performance was erratic and his assignments often sloppy or incomplete. During parent conferences in December, his mother indicated she was having similar problems with Lance at home regarding his room and household chores. Therefore, the teacher felt Lance might benefit from the counseling group. Paula checked with Mr. George before inviting Lance to join the group to be sure the parents had given permission for their child to participate. Mr. George checked his files and told Paula that there was no letter from the parents stating that Lance could not participate in group counseling. It was noted that the counselor keeps a record of all letters from parents stating that they do not want their child to participate in counseling activities. The school counseling program and curriculum is approved for all students by the Board of Education. Meadow Elementary School sends a letter to the parents of each child at the beginning of the school year informing them of this fact and stating that unless the parents request in writing that their child not participate in counseling activities, the school will assume that their consent for participation has been given. Therefore, Paula assumed that Lance's verbal agreement to join the group was sufficient. The same was true for the five other students Paula had selected for the group.

Discussion

Mr. George reiterated Paula's description of the procedures she followed and added that he had led a counseling group the previous semester in which Lance's sister, Lori Jones, participated without parental complaint. Mr. George noted that school records indicate that Lori Jones is Mrs. Smith's daughter by a previous marriage and that Mrs. Smith has sole custody of Lori. Mr. and Mrs. Smith divorced last summer, and Mrs. Smith moved into the school district in late September. When she registered Lori and Lance at Meadow she was given the packet of new-school information that contained the letter informing parents about the school counseling program and consent for their child's participation in counseling activities. Paula considers all these facts in consideration of determining an appropriate course of action.

QUESTIONS

1. How should the school respond to Mr. Smith's complaint and his insistence on acquiring "expressed written consent of both parents" for Lance to participate in the counseling group?
2. What additional actions should Paula take before continuing with the formation of her counseling group so that her behavior is in accordance with the American School Counselor Association *Ethical Standards for School Counselors* (1998) or the American Counseling Association *Code of Ethics and Standards of Practice* (1995)?
3. How would you describe the school's implied consent policy in terms of being ethical and legal?
4. What would be the ethical response Paula should make to Mr. Smith should he ask her the question, "What are you going to talk about with my son that you don't want me to know?"

RESPONSE

Trish Hatch

How should the school respond to Mr. Smith's complaint and his insistence on acquiring "expressed consent of both parents" for Lance to participate in the counseling group? The school should ensure that permission is received from the parents or guardians before counseling groups take place on sensitive topic areas such as familial relationships. If Mrs. Smith had full custody, then she certainly could have provided permission for the student to obtain counseling services at the school. However, in this situation, there was joint custody, and especially if the parents notified the school that they are to be informed about all activities pertaining to the student (often accomplished through a legal notification), permission from both parents was appropriate.

What additional actions should Paula take before continuing with the formation of her counseling group? Paula should call all of the parents of the students in the group counseling session, disclose that she has enlisted their child in group counseling, and seek their verbal (followed by written) permission. This is vital to the success of her counseling group because counselors (especially elementary counselors) must enlist family understanding and involvement as a positive resource (ACA, 1995, section A.1.d). Further, it is important to establish a collaborative relationship with the parents to enhance the effectiveness of the group process (ASCA, 1998, section B.1.a).

How would you describe the school's implied consent policy in terms of being ethical and legal? In 1994, a court decision upheld the right for a school district to have a child see a school counselor (in this case for peer relationship issues) without securing his parents' consent. In that case, *Newkirk v. East Lansing Public Schools* (1995), the school district did not violate the rights of the parents under the Hatch Amendment. The Hatch Amendment, enacted in 1978, retains parents' rights to review material in programs and requires parental support for students who participate in psychiatric or psychological examination, testing, or treatment designed to elicit information in sensitive topic areas such as personal beliefs and family relationships (Hatch Amendment Coalition, 1985). It could be argued that group counseling is psychological in nature and will reveal sensitive topics on familial relationships. Further, the Parental Rights and Responsibilities Act (1995) requires compelling justification to interfere with the fundamental rights of parents to direct their child's upbringing.

School counselors are responsible to disclose to clients the nature and purpose of the counseling group. Clients are offered the freedom to choose whether to enter the group (ACA, 1995, section A.3.b). This voluntary consent on the clients behalf is afforded to the parent when clients to be counseled are minors as they are unable to give voluntary consent (section B.3) unless allowed by law (as in California ED Code 49602 [1987], which provides that a child may enter into a confidential relationship with a school counselor at the age of 12). The schools' informed consent policy may protect school counselors from the counselor performing guidance lessons in the classroom, individual counseling, or small-group sessions, such as self-esteem, anger management, or attendance groups. These are typical groups that any student could attend, and the goal of these groups is to assist the student in academic achievement. Divorce groups and, for example, alcoholic or incarcerated parent groups and incest victim groups are particularly sensitive in nature and should always have the support of the family. The ACA Code of Ethics (1995) states that "counselors must adequately inform clients, preferably in writing, regarding the counseling process and counseling relationship at or before the time it begins and throughout the relationship" (SP-2). Another point to be noted is that although adhering to local laws and guidelines is important, honoring the wishes of the parent, so long as they do not violate the rights of the students, is appropriate from an ethical standpoint (ASCA, 1998, sections B.1.b, B.2.c).

What would be the ethical response Paula should make to Mr. Smith should he ask her the question, "What are you going to talk about with my son that you don't want me to know?" Paula has an obligation to inform the parent as to the nature and purpose of the group counseling session. She should explain that school counselors do not provide therapy, but rather that group counseling services assist the student in coping with whatever personal/social issues are interfering with the student's ability to learn or be successful in school. The purpose of school counseling programs is to enhance and promote the learning process. In this case, it is inferred that the student's academic success seems to be affected by the parents' divorce. If this is true, then Paula should share with Mr. Smith all materials that may be used during the group sessions. Further, she should explain that although these materials may be used to elicit discussion and conversation in the group, the nature of the conversation (as well as that of other members in the group) is confidential unless disclosure is required to prevent clear and eminent danger, and that therefore any information given to the parent should be with the consent of the counselee(s) (ASCA, 1998, sections A.2.b, A.2.f).

Other issues to be addressed in this case. Group work requires the protection of the members through screening prospective members for appropriateness. In this case, the students' behavior may not have constituted a reaction to the divorce, but rather something else, such as attention deficit disorder. Certainly before beginning the group process, Paula should have taken reasonable precaution by consulting the parent and teacher as well as the student's cumulative records to ensure that these behaviors were not present before the divorce. Otherwise, by simply placing the student in group counseling and attributing his or her actions to the divorce, the student's needs and goals could be incompatible with that of the group (ASCA, 1998, section A.9.a).

Additionally, it is of some concern that Paula (as an intern), with the permission of her lead counselor (Mr. George), was using curriculum designed for eighth graders. Curriculum should always be designed as developmentally appropriate. Further, Paula's area of competence was with eighth graders, and until she demonstrated competence with third graders, Mr. George should be co-leading the group (ACA, 1995, sections C.2.a, C.2.b). As an experienced site supervisor, Mr. George is responsible to ensure that Paula's (and his) behavior is held to the highest ethical standard (sections F.3.e, H.1). As Mr. George was remiss in appropriately supervising Paula,

Dr. Johns should serve in a more active role to ensure that Mr. George clearly understands his role as a site supervisor or find another site for his student interns.

RESPONSE

Mary A. Hermann

The policy of the school regarding the provision of school counseling services is ethically and legally valid. Generally, minors can only exercise their legal rights through their parents, and thus from a legal perspective minors are unable to give informed consent for counseling services. However, in school settings, counseling services are an implicit component of educational programming. Thus, though a parent probably has a legal right to request that a student not participate in counseling activities, it is a legally and ethically acceptable practice to have students participate in counseling services unless a parent has requested otherwise.

The ethical documents that relate to group counseling in school settings are the American Counseling Association *Code of Ethics and Standards of Practice* (1995), the American School Counselor Association *Ethical Standards for School Counselors* (1998), and the Association for Specialists in Group Work *Best Practice Guidelines* (1998). All three of these documents acknowledge minors' lack of legal capacity to provide informed consent. Additionally, the ACA Code of Ethics directs counselors who are working with minors to act in the best interest of these clients (section A.3.c). The ASCA Ethical Standards reiterate that both custodial and noncustodial parents have legal rights related to the welfare of their children (section B.1.c). The ASGW *Best Practice Guidelines* provide that group workers are to obtain the appropriate consent forms when working with minors (section A.7.c). However, some legal and ethical dictates, including this ASGW guideline, take on different dimensions in a school setting because counseling services are implicit in the services school personnel provide to students. Neither the law nor any code of ethics obligates schools to obtain written consent from parents to provide counseling services to students.

The school's policy of sending parents notification of the existence of the school counseling program and asking parents to make a request in writing if they do not want their child to participate in counseling activities is a reasonable policy. The policy affords parents their legal right to discontinue the counseling services being received by their children. From a practical standpoint, the policy provides the counselors in the school with a quick and accessible record of which parents do not want their children to participate in counseling, and the counselors at the school comply with the policy and refer to the records before working with a student.

According to this hypothetical situation, Lance's mother had been given the letter informing parents of school procedure related to counseling services. Thus she had constructive knowledge of the procedure. Written, informed consent of the parent was not legally or ethically required before providing Lance with school counseling services. Yet when responding to Mr. Smith's complaint, the school counselor should remain cognizant that school counselors are to respect the rights of parents and work to facilitate student development by establishing a collaborative relationship with parents (ASCA, 1998, section B.1.a).

It is important to note that from an ethical perspective establishing a collaborative relationship with parents does not involve breaching counselor/student confidentiality. However, the issue of confidentiality is one area in which ethics and the law do not exactly coincide. Though confidentiality is a critical component of the counseling relationship, legally Mr. Smith probably has the right to know what was discussed in his son's counseling sessions. From an ethical standpoint, if Mr. Smith wanted to know what Paula and Lance talked about in counseling sessions, ASCA ethical standards direct Paula to inform Mr. Smith of the school counselor's role placing particular emphasis on the confidential nature of the counseling relationship (ASCA, 1998, section B.2.a). Paula could explain that ethical principles require her to keep information received through the counseling relationship confidential unless a student poses a clear and imminent danger to self or others (section A.2.b). She could assure Mr. Smith that if she felt that Lance were a danger to himself or others she would contact him.

Remley and Herlihy (2001) have provided an excellent framework for dealing with parents who demand to know the contents of counseling sessions. Noting that some minors do not object to counselor/parent dialogue about counseling sessions, these authors have suggested that the counselor ask the child if he or she is opposed to the counselor discussing the content of the counseling sessions with the parent. If the child does not want the counselor to discuss this information, Remley and Herlihy have recommended attempting to persuade the parent that confidentiality is in the best interest of the child. However, these authors have reiterated that the parent may have a legal right to the information. Thus, if the parent is still insistent about having information about counseling sessions, Remley and Herlihy have advised scheduling a joint session with the child and the parent, thereby providing the child an opportunity to participate in any disclosures about information revealed in counseling activities.

REFERENCES

American Counseling Association. (1995). *Code of ethics and standards of practice*. Alexandria, VA: Author.

American School Counselor Association. (1998). *Ethical standards for school counselors*. Alexandria, VA: Author.

Association for Specialists in Group Work. (1998). Best practice guidelines. *Journal for Specialists in Group Work, 23*(3), 237–244.

California ED Code 49602. (1987). Retrieved October 1, 2003, from http://www.leginfo.ca.gov/cgi-bin/

Hatch Amendment Coalition & American Educational Research Association (AERA). (1985). *The Hatch Amendment regulations: A guidelines document.* Washington, DC: AERA.

Newkirk v. East Lansing Public Schools, No 91-00563, 1993 U.S. Dist. LEXIS 131194 (W.D.Mich) aff'd mem, 57 F. 3d 1070 (6th Cir, 1995) cert denied, 116 S. Ct. 380 (1995).

Parental Rights and Responsibilities Act, H.R. 1956, S. 984, 104th Cong. 1st sess., 1995.

Remley, T. P., Jr., & Herlihy, B. (2001). *Ethical, legal, and professional issues in counseling.* Upper Saddle River, NJ: Prentice Hall.

CHAPTER 17

MAINTAINING RECORDS: "IT'S ALL UP HERE!"

The focus of this incident is on the issue of maintaining records on clients who are members of a required parent training group through the Department of Social Services.

CRITICAL INCIDENT

Michael LeBlanc

Background

Jerry works for a community mental health center that provides services for a rural county. He is a Licensed Professional Counselor and is well respected in the community. Jerry was asked by the center to run a parent training group for parents referred through the Department of Social Services (DSS). He had facilitated this type of group several times in the past and had attended special training to run parenting groups. Jerry was told by the DSS to keep records of attendance and participation by the group members and to submit them to the DSS at the conclusion of the group sessions. These records would be used to document that referred members followed through with their required participation in the group. The group met weekly for 6 weeks. At the initial group meeting, Jerry told all of the participants that he was going to "submit verification of attendance to the Department of Social Services" at the conclusion of the 6 weeks. Jerry then passed an attendance checklist to the members and repeated this message about attendance at subsequent meetings.

Incident

At the end of the 6 weeks of group meetings, Jerry collected his attendance sheets and wrote a summary of the group members' participation. One of the members, Tom, had disclosed during the course of the group that one of the reasons he was required to attend the group was because he had been accused of abusing his wife in front of his children. Tom was an imposing man who often appeared angry although he was usually reserved during the group meetings. Jerry wrote extensively about Tom in his group summary. Although he had not made separate notes at the end of each group session, Tom prided himself on his ability to remember past sessions. Jerry wrote about Tom that he appeared hostile and resistant throughout the group and that his mannerisms throughout the group were "intimidating."

Jerry concluded that based on these observations, it was likely that Tom was continuing to be abusive in the home. Soon after Jerry submitted this information to the Department of Social Services, Tom's children were removed from the home.

Discussion

This incident raises certain ethical questions as well as possible legal concerns. Consideration should be given to Jerry's education, training, experience, credentials, and the ethical guidelines that may apply. Jerry's ability to implement and maintain appropriate records is questioned.

QUESTIONS

1. What ethical concerns are raised by Jerry's handling of note taking?
2. As a professional counselor, how do you feel about the appropriateness of Jerry's impressions of Tom's abusive behavior?
3. What concerns about informed consent exist in this incident?

RESPONSE

Tommie R. Radd

Jerry has a professional and ethical responsibility to maintain precise records of every group meeting. It is impossible to recall all essential details of a group's dialogue. Records need to be maintained for each group member and his or her issues and interactions, plus the dynamics of the group process. Record keeping is the professional and ethical way to keep objective notes and observations of each group member and their interactions during the group session (American Counseling Association [ACA] *Code of Ethics and Standards of Practice,* 1995). Plans for the next week's group session need to be based on information from records of that week's group meeting.

Jerry informed the group members that he was going to submit verification of attendance to the DSS. Jerry did not discuss informed consent with the group and have them sign an informed consent statement. Informed consent is a document clients sign acknowledging that they have been informed of the activity they are about to participate in and are entering it voluntarily. Because the participants were referred by the DSS, informed consent as well as confidentiality should have been discussed with the group members before beginning the group process (ACA, 1995).

In addition, Jerry did not inform the group that he was going to state to the DSS details of group conversations. A group needs to be a safe place in which group members can trust the facilitator to protect their information so that they can learn ways to handle the issues that brought them to the group. Tom stated his reasons for referral to the group in what he believed to be a confidential, therapeutic setting. It is appropriate for a person with Tom's issues to behave in a group as described in this incident. Jerry made a huge leap to assume that Tom was being abusive at home based on his recall of Tom's behavior. The appropriate course of action would have been to privately discuss with Tom the concerns that Jerry had and then make the necessary referrals for continued individual, family, or group counseling.

Because Jerry is a well-respected, experienced professional counselor in the rural county where he lives, he knows his report will be accepted as credible by the DSS. He has facilitated groups for DSS in the past and is held in high regard. DSS will assume Jerry has acted in a professional and ethical manner and will therefore take action on his report. Jerry's professional power impacted Tom's life to the degree that Tom's children were removed from the home.

If Tom learns that his children were removed from his home based on Jerry's report, he may decide to seek legal counsel and enter into a lawsuit against Jerry and the community mental health center where he works. If that were to occur, Jerry has no record that documents his ongoing work with all group members. This puts both Jerry and the mental health center at risk. According to Gladding (2003), the group worker needs to "document for third parties, such as courts and managed care agencies, information that may be relevant to any ethical or legal issue that may arise" (p. 233). Jerry would need to provide a report that includes specific statements given by Tom during the group sessions and that documents other recommendations made to Tom privately.

Jerry disregarded his ethical and professional responsibilities when he took the actions outlined in this incident. Over time Jerry and his clients may suffer. At this point Jerry is relying on his community reputation, experience, and training to carry him professionally. Training and experience, based on strong ethical and professional practices, are essential to building and maintaining the skills to help clients. These skills include conscientious and accurate record keeping and appropriate use of informed consent and confidentiality. Communication with any appropriate third party needs to be based on counselor records that are not only secure but also made with care.

RESPONSE

Jim Whitledge

Section B.4.a, Requirement of Records, of the ACA *Code of Ethics and Standards of Practice* (1995) emphasizes that counselors maintain those records that are required to render appropriate professional service to their clients. In this incident, Jerry was charged by the DSS to maintain a record of and to report attendance and participation by each group member. The law, regulations, or institutional policies may impact what he does as a counselor in terms of record keeping and reporting as well.

Jerry went above and beyond what the DSS required, which was to report on attendance in the required group sessions and participation in the sessions, when he reported his conclusion that Tom's abusive behavior was continuing. Although Jerry had an obligation to maintain his notes on a session-to-session basis, he waited until the 6 weeks of group meetings were over before writing summaries of members' participation. It is not considered a sound ethical practice to let even several sessions go by and then attempt to recall what took place in order to provide accurate notes. Further, it is good practice in facilitating a group to maintain notes on what occurred at each session in order to plan effectively for the group session that follows.

A professional counselor point of view disputes Jerry's handling of his impressions and reporting of Tom's abusive behavior. Section B.1.a in the ACA Code of Ethics states that "Counselors respect their clients' right to privacy and avoid illegal and unwarranted disclosures of confidential information." Although Jerry was correct in informing his clients in the group that he was required to report their attendance and participation, he apparently did not inform them about confidentiality and other aspects of informed consent.

Tom disclosed in the group the specific reason he was referred by DSS, which implied that he should work on this area of his life. Jerry appeared to add to this information his own conjecture, which had no foundation, that Tom was a danger to his family. This action indicated that Jerry was not protecting the rights of his client, and that both he and his agency might be vulnerable to future legal action. It could be that Jerry was judging and reporting Tom on the basis of his own values, attitudes, and beliefs. If this was the case, Jerry is in conflict with sections A.5.a and A.5.b of the ACA Code of Ethics, which states that counselors do not impose their own values, or take any action that, at the expense of the client, meets their own needs.

As already indicated, Jerry carried out only part of his responsibility to Tom and others in the group in regard to informed consent. Section A.3.a in the ACA Code of Ethics clearly indicates that the counselor has an initial responsibility, when the counseling begins, and then through other sessions as necessary, to "inform clients of the purposes, goals, techniques, procedures, limitations, potential risks, and benefits of services to be performed, and other pertinent information." As a professional counselor, Jerry has a responsibility to ensure that his clients understand and have an opportunity to ask questions about the counseling process as well.

Another factor that may be considered here is that Jerry could have followed good group work practice and screened the group participants individually prior to the first session, in accordance with section A.9.a. Even though this was an involuntary group, Jerry could have explained the benefits to them as individuals, as well as the limitations. The benefits and limitations could have been processed as a group in the first session.

Jerry had, in addition, a responsibility to explain that confidentiality cannot be guaranteed in group work, but that there are clearly defined parameters for the group even though there are some difficulties related to group work in general. This is consistent with section B.2.a in the ACA Code of Ethics. There is also the possibility that Jerry could have consulted with a colleague or supervisor if he was in doubt about what to do in handling the reporting to DSS. Consulting section B.6.a could have contributed to an appropriate course of action for Jerry in this incident.

In conclusion, this incident points out the importance of Jerry, as the professional counselor, being aware of the important aspects of the standards of practice, laws, institutional policies and procedures, and ethical guidelines as they relate to maintaining records and facilitating groups. Jerry was considered competent in his field, but he still had a responsibility to follow the ethical guidelines of the counseling profession, as stated in section C.1.a of the ACA Code of Ethics.

REFERENCES

American Counseling Association (1995). *Code of ethics and standards of practice.* Alexandria, VA: Author.

Gladding, S. T. (2003). *Group work: A counseling specialty* (4th ed.). Upper Saddle River, NJ: Merrill Prentice Hall.

CHAPTER 18

ADVERTISING GROUPS IN A SCHOOL SETTING: "WHO SAID I WAS?"

This incident explores some of the issues that accompany novice group leaders who negate the preplanning details involved with advertising a successful group experience.

CRITICAL INCIDENT

Shelley A. Jackson

Background
Kelly recently began her first job as an elementary school counselor. She completed her counseling practicum and internship for her master's program at a local summer youth camp for disadvantaged adolescents run by the school system. She believed this placement would give her the appropriate experience in working with children in individual and group situations to become a successful school counselor. At the summer youth camp Kelly had the opportunity to co-lead an adolescent relationship group. In addition, she had experience leading a personal growth group as part of her group counseling class.

Incident
After Kelly attends the annual state fall counseling conference, she returns to work excited about beginning a group for children who have a parent who is abusing drugs or alcohol. At the conference, Kelly attended a 90-minute presentation about working with children of alcoholics, and she wants to replicate the small group activities that were presented in the session at her own school. She solicits referrals from teachers using the following letter:

Dear Teachers:

I will be starting a small group for children who live with someone who abuses drugs or alcohol. If any of your students fit into this category please let me know so that they might be included in the group.

Thank you,

Your School Counselor

In addition, Kelly reviews her case notes and identifies three students who she has been working with individually that might benefit from the group.

As Kelly prepares for the group and collects names from teachers of students who live with someone who abuses drugs or alcohol, she decides that she will name the group "The Sunshine Club." In order to avoid having to explain that the group will deal with issues concerning the fact that the person with whom the child lives abuses drugs or alcohol, she states in the parent permission letter that the group will deal with issues concerning getting along with others.

Six fourth- and fifth-grade students return signed parent permission forms, and Kelly begins meeting with the students on a weekly basis. Kelly's principal calls her into a parent conference after the second week of the group to meet with a parent who is very upset about his child's involvement in the group. He demands to know who has identified him as an alcoholic and threatens the school and Kelly with a lawsuit. He tells Kelly not to speak with his son ever again.

Discussion

After the meeting in the principal's office with the parent, Kelly wonders about the boy in her group and what had happened at home to upset the father. Her principal told her to withdraw the boy from the group and not to have any further contact with him. She decides she has to meet with him individually to make sure that he is okay and to process the termination of the group with him.

QUESTIONS

1. How would you describe the ethical implications for Kelly in advertising the group as being one for children who have trouble getting along with others?
2. How might the counselor handle the meeting with the parent differently?
3. What appropriate steps should a school counselor take when obtaining parent permission for group counseling?
4. How could the counselor advertise the group differently?
5. How would you describe the appropriateness of this group in school settings?
6. What are your feelings about the appropriateness of the counselor meeting with the student one final time?

RESPONSE

Trish Hatch

How could the counselor advertise the group differently? It is inappropriate for Kelly to obtain students for her group by asking teachers to refer students who live with someone who abuses drugs or alcohol. First, how could the teacher know which students these are? An inexperienced or naïve teacher could ask students to raise their hands if they have an alcoholic in their home, thus breaching any form of confidentiality and labeling the student unnecessarily. It is far more appropriate for the school counselors to notify the students when she visits classrooms, perhaps after a guidance lesson on drug or alcohol abuse, that she is available to counsel them if they believe they would like this assistance for themselves or a friend. This should become a normal statement made after all guidance lessons (e.g., anger management, student skills).

Fourth and fifth graders are capable of referring themselves for assistance. In doing so, they maintain their confidentiality regarding the issue, and the teacher need never know why the student is seeing the school counselor. For Kelly to presume that children who have parents whom the teacher thinks are abusing alcohol need guidance is creating a problem where none may exist. Her decision to allow the teacher to determine which children have parents who abuse alcohol is unethical and presumptuous. Not every child living in a family with a crisis requires group counseling. Referrals to the counselors should come from teachers who are concerned that a student's ability to learn is impacted by an immediate or chronic personal/social crisis. Instead Kelly took it upon herself to decide that all children whom the teacher thinks have parents who use alcohol or other drugs require group counseling. This is simply not the case.

How would you describe the ethical implications for Kelly in advertising the group as being one for children who have trouble getting along with others? Stating that the group was for children who "have trouble getting along with others" was erroneous and unethical. Kelly's advertisement was false, misleading, and deceptive (American Counseling Association [ACA], *Code of Ethics and Standards of Practice*, 1995, section C.3.a). School counselors must recognize that families are important in children's lives and should make every effort to enlist family understanding (section A.1.d). When counseling minors, school counselors must act in their clients' best interest (section A.3.c). It is not in the child's best interest to lie to the parent. Kelly should have met with the child and gained the child's consent, and then talked with the parent regarding the group, its goals, and confidentiality.

What appropriate steps should a school counselor take when obtaining parent permission for group counseling? First, the counselor should screen the students to ensure that this is the appropriate group for them. Then the counselor should send home a permission slip that clearly identifies the nature, content, and goals of the group for the parent. If it is a sensitive topic, as in this case, it may be more appropriate to call or have a conference with the parent so that there are no misunderstandings. As stated in the ACA Code of Ethics, when counseling minor clients, "parents or guardians may be included in the process as appropriate" (section B.3).

How might the counselor handle the meeting with the parent differently? Kelly should have admitted her error to the parent immediately and apologized for any misrepresentation that may have inadvertently occurred as a result of her mistake. It is always best to be honest and forthright when an error in judgment is made. It would have then been appropriate to explain the specific goals of the group, and to politely inquire whether the parent believed the child might benefit from it.

What are your feelings about the appropriateness of the counselor meeting with the student one final time? This depends on the nature of the parent's threat. Did Kelly have reason to believe that this child was in danger or would be harmed by this parent? If so, then she had an ethical obligation to inform the student that she was available to the student should a need arise. However, the counselor, after being requested by the parent to cease contact, should heed this request. It serves no purpose for the school counselor to come between a parent and student. The counselor should agree to not seek out the student, but should inform the parent and the administrator that if the student should seek out the school counselor with a serious issue or concern, the counselor is ethically obligated to provide counsel. In the same way, if the school counselor becomes aware of any concerns regarding the safety or well-being of the student, she will provide the counsel necessary to ensure the student's safety. It is important to protect the student from believing he was at fault in this situation. Therefore, instead of meeting with the student covertly, Kelly might recommend a meeting with the parent, administrator, and student during which Kelly admits her mistake and explains to the child that the parent has the right to provide permission for their continuing in the group, and that it is the parent's decision that the student not continue at this time. In this way, the student will understand that he is not being abandoned and has done nothing wrong. Lastly, if the parent agrees that the child might benefit from counseling by someone other than Kelly, she should make every effort to obtain the appropriate referral (ACA Code of Ethics, sections A.11.a, A.11.b).

How would you describe the appropriateness of this group in school settings? At the secondary level, these types of counseling and support groups are far more common than at the elementary level. This is partly due to the nature of the topic: the older the students, the more likely they are to know someone (friend or relative) who is abusing alcohol or other drugs. At the elementary level, this type of group counseling is often run outside the school setting by an outside agency using referrals by the school counselor. The purpose of school counseling programs is to enhance and promote the learning process. School counselors will often create a group with students when they have a significant number of students referred who have the same concerns or issues that are serving as barriers to learning. But to advertise a group and seek out members presumes a problem where one may not exist. Further, it detracts from other activities the school counselors should be providing to the entire school population. Remembering that school counselors' caseloads are high, especially at the elementary level, and considering what constitutes the best use of school counselors' time— weekly groups for a few students or school-wide activities to benefit all— is important.

Finally, it is inappropriate for Kelly to assume that a 90-minute presentation at a conference on working with children of alcoholics is enough to provide her the appropriate training to lead this group. Rather, it was more likely to have been enough training to understand when it is appropriate to refer a student (and parents) with these issues to a mental health professional who is specifically trained to provide the group or individual counseling this student and her or his family requires. As clearly stated in the ACA Code of Ethics, counselors should only practice "within the boundaries of their competence" (section C.2.a). Further, counselors should only practice in areas of specialty if they have "appropriate education, training, and supervised experience" (section C.2.b).

RESPONSE

Vivian V. Lee

How would you describe the ethical implications for Kelly in advertising the group as being one for children who have trouble in getting along with others? There are several ethical implications that arise from Kelly's decision to advertise this group as one for children who have trouble getting along with others. First, Kelly's actions do not reflect truth in advertising. The ACA *Code of Ethics and Standards of Practice* (1995) states that "There are no restrictions on advertising by counselors except those that can be specifically justified to protect the public from deceptive practices" (section C.3.a). Kelly uses a deceptive group name to avoid explaining to parents the true nature of the group. This deceptive advertising leads to a second ethical issue as it negates the possibility of the parents/guardians giving true informed consent. The Code of Ethics states that "counselors inform clients of the purpose, goals, techniques, procedures, limitations, potential risks, and benefits of services to be preformed" (section A.3.a). Because Kelly is working in a school with minors and must secure parent/guardian permission, she has a responsibility to provide them with accurate information that avoids jargon and uses language that they can understand. This empowers parents in their decisions regarding counseling services for their children and allows them to give informed consent. Additionally, these types of practices support the American School Counselor Association *Ethical Standards for School Counselors* (ASCA,1998), which in section B.1.a addresses the inherent rights and responsibilities of parents for their children. This section also addresses the counselor's responsibility to establish as appropriate a collaborative relationship to facilitate the maximum development of students.

How might the counselor handle the meeting with the parent differently? During the parent meeting Kelly needed to openly acknowledge and validate the parent's feelings. She needed to tell the parent the truth about the group and apologize for her errors in practice, including deceptive advertising, disrespecting the rights of the parent/guardian to make an informed decision regarding the welfare of their child, labeling the parent, and creating dissension between the parent and child. She needed to indicate to the parent and the principal that she will respect their directive and have no further contact with the student. Additionally, she needed to assure the parent and the principal that she will revise her practices so that this type of incident did not happen again.

What appropriate steps should a counselor take when obtaining parent permission for group counseling? When obtaining parent permission for group participation, information as to the nature of the specific group should be clearly and accurately provided. The permission form should include the nature of the group, when the group will be offered, the duration of the group, exactly who the group leader(s) will be and how to contact them, the nature of confidentiality in groups, and how students will make up missed work if the group is offered during class time. Additionally, the form should have a space for parents/guardians to respond in either an affirmative or negative manner to their child's participation. Parents/guardians need to know school counselors are interested in what they have to say even if they do not grant permission. Respect for parent/guardian rights can open a door to dialogue on sensitive areas such as the topic of this group.

An outline of the topics to be covered and the goals and objectives of the counseling group should be attached to the permission form. These goals should be part of an approved developmental school counseling program. Counselor openness can demystify the counseling process, and assure the parent/guardian that services follow established policies and procedures. These steps can serve to engender parent/guardian trust, and promote involvement in counseling services.

How could the counselor advertise the group differently? There are several things Kelly could have done differently in advertising this group. First, when advertising any type of group, counselors need to be accurate in their descriptions, and exercise sensitivity regarding the nature of the group and the language they use to describe the group. It is understandable that parents/guardians as well as teachers may be offended by the language Kelly used to describe issues of substance use and abuse. It may be more appropriate to advertise the group as one to help students cope with the challenges of having a family member or loved one who struggles with alcohol/drug use. In this way Kelly could accurately describe the nature of the group and use language that is less derogatory and more inviting to parents/guardians.

Second, Kelly's advertising procedures do not provide access and equity of service to all students. When advertising the services available within a comprehensive school counseling program, counselors need to ensure access and equity for all students. To do this, Kelly could make arrangements with all of the fourth- and fifth-grade teachers to visit their classrooms and conduct a short presentation and needs assessment to all of the children. A letter with an assessment form should be mailed to all parents/guardians that outlines services available to students and invites them to refer their children to counseling groups. Parents are often more open to counseling than is sometimes expected if they feel they are accurately informed about services to assist their children.

At the elementary level, teachers are often active in referring students for counseling services. This is a practice that school counselors need to encourage. However, for this practice to be established and maintained in a manner that protects the rights, privacy, and confidentiality of students, it is essential for school counselors to educate the faculty. This can be facilitated during an in-service orientation program at the beginning of each year (Ripley & Goodnough, 2001). This will familiarize them with the need for group services, the associated policies such as confidentiality and its limitations, and the benefits students may gain from participating in counseling groups. In this way, school counselors can assist teachers in becoming active participants in referring students to groups in a manner that maintains their privacy and confidentiality.

How would you describe the appropriateness of this group in school settings? Despite the highly sensitive nature of the group, it is appropriate in the school setting as part of a developmental school counseling program. Group counseling services can assist children with family issues that disrupt their ability to function effectively and achieve academic success in school. Children facing the issues and challenges that result from family members and loved ones who struggle with substance abuse may feel isolated and alone. Group counseling can offer a forum for children to begin to reduce their feelings of isolation and experience a different response from adults and peers in a safe environment. However, because of the highly sensitive nature of the group and potential stigma attached to a child's participation, school counselors must be aware of the culture and climate of the community. This sensitivity allows counselors to develop practices that respect a community's unique mores yet offer a venue to address issues of concern such as substance use and abuse. This enables school counselors to offer services that address the needs of students and create a bridge of understanding between schools, parents/guardians, and students.

What are your feelings about the appropriateness of the counselor meeting with the student one final time? According to the ACA Code of Ethics, counselors discontinue counseling services "when it is…clear that the client is no longer benefiting" (section A.11.c). Kelly's insistence on seeing the child one last time seems to be driven by her own needs rather than the needs of the child. Additionally, it violates the directive of the parent and the principal. Seeing the child one last time will only serve to exacerbate the situation and has potentially negative consequences for the child and Kelly.

Two additional issues. Important to this incident are two additional issues. The first focuses on counselor competence. As the ACA Code of Ethics makes clear (in section C.2.a), counselors need to possess the self-awareness to accurately assess their level of skill competence before offering counseling services. Kelly's inexperience as a school counselor is evidenced in her inability to accurately assess the depth and complexity of skill required to appropriately advertise and lead a group for children who face the challenges of substance use in the home. Further, as the ACA Code of Ethics also states, "Counselors practice in specialty areas new to them only after appropriate education, training, and supervised experience. While developing skills in new specialty areas, counselors take steps to ensure the competence of their work and to protect others from possible harm" (section C.2.b). When translating this section of the Code of Ethics into practice in the school setting, it may be advisable for new school counselors like Kelly to co-lead this type of group with an experienced drug and alcohol counselor before attempting to lead it on their own. Thereafter, seeking out regular supervision and consultation from a more experienced peer or community-based colleague is advisable. Although these practices are especially advisable for new counselors, both new and experienced counselors need to engage in this type of ongoing professional development to meet the changing needs of the students they serve.

The second additional issue focuses on the policies and practices that govern a comprehensive school counseling program. Despite the obvious ethical implications of Kelly's behavior, the responsibility of the institution in this incident cannot be overlooked. Schools have a responsibility to develop policies and practices that govern school counseling services. These institutionally approved policies and procedures are essential to ensure that counselors offer consistent and ethically appropriate experiences for all students (Ripley & Goodnough, 2001). To accomplish this goal, appropriate orientation and mentoring of new school counselors is necessary to acquaint them with the policies and practices that govern their work with students and the school community.

REFERENCES

American Counseling Association. (1995). *Code of ethics and standards of practice.* Alexandria, VA: Author.

American School Counselor Association. (1998). *Ethical standards for school counselors.* Alexandria, VA: Author.

Ripley, V. V., & Goodnough, G. E. (2001). Planning and implementing group counseling in a high school. *Professional School Counseling, 5,* 62–65.

CHAPTER 19

SUPERVISION ISSUES: "I'LL PROTECT YOU"

This incident explores moral development and ethical decision making within the context of a peer supervision group.

CRITICAL INCIDENT

Stephanie G. Puleo

Background

Sophia is a novice counselor who has joined a peer supervision group in the community where she works. Sophia counsels women who are homeless, whereas other members of the group work in settings such as substance abuse treatment centers, employee assistance programs, pastoral counseling facilities, and private practice. All of the group's 11 members hold master's degrees in counseling and are pursuing licensure. Some of the group members earned their degrees a year or two before Sophia earned hers. The group, which has been together for about 2 months, meets weekly and is facilitated by a Licensed Mental Health Counselor.

Incident

Typically, the peer supervision group session begins with a check-in, in which each group member shares something about the previous week. Following the check-in, an individual group member may ask for time to discuss a client case with which help is needed. In this particular session, Sophia asked for time to discuss a client with whom she had been working for several months.

The group began in the usual way. During the check-in, group members compared their workloads and traded stories about their clients and counseling experiences. Few questions were asked during this time, and group members directed few comments or suggestions toward one another. One group member disclosed a personal issue that she feared might be impacting her counseling relationships. She provided the group with a detailed description of her situation, and freely shared her resultant feelings. She continued by asking the group for help in determining if the situation might be affecting her professional work. In response, one group member provided a suggestion for dealing with the personal situation, whereas others simply responded that she seemed to be strong, courageous, and "doing the right thing." Sophia listened to the exchange, but did not comment.

Sophia began to talk about her client. She disclosed some of her client's background; the client was homeless and eligible for a number of community social services. Sophia continued to say that recent counseling sessions focused on issues of self-worth. Although services were being provided for her, the client felt angry and disappointed in herself for not living up to her potential. Although she was grateful that she had been helped in securing a job, she was disappointed that the job was neither challenging nor satisfying. Sophia felt a great deal of empathy and compassion for this client. She understood the client's desire to utilize her talent and her embarrassment at having to settle for an unfulfilling job. Sophia asked the group for suggestions for helping the client come to terms with her feelings.

In response to Sophia's presentation, group members emphasized the client's homeless situation and need for public services. One group member stated, "She's homeless. She needs to recognize reality." Another said, "She's getting services, what more does she want?" As the group members fired off such comments, Sophia found herself withdrawing and withholding further information about the client. Although she had brought several recordings of her counseling sessions with the client to the group, she did not share them. She concluded her presentation by saying that she felt inadequate and unworthy of the trust the client had placed with her. Group members did not respond verbally to this last remark.

Discussion

After the supervision group session, Sophia went for a long walk and reflected on her reaction during the group. She found that she felt an overwhelming need to protect her client. When group members seemed to be defining the client by her homelessness, Sophia attempted to characterize her as more human. Although the client had given written consent for Sophia to disclose information about her with the supervision group, Sophia eventually began to feel uncomfortable sharing her story with this group of counselors. She felt that the group was in some way violating the client, and that the more she disclosed, the more she was a participant in this violation. Sophia noticed that her own attitude was in conflict with what she perceived to be the group's attitude about the client she was presenting. She thought that the group members were judgmental, purposefully disengaged, and not invested in helping her or her client.

QUESTIONS

1. How do you describe the appropriateness of Sophia's behavioral response during the group?
2. What dynamics were operating in this group?
3. How might Sophia have utilized the group more effectively?
4. What role should the group facilitator have taken?
5. Given the group member's responses, what ethical issues were involved? Was anyone being harmed?
6. What should happen the next time the group meets?

RESPONSE

Mary L. Anderson

When considering Sophia's response during the group, several factors need to be addressed. Appropriate behavior in the group depends on the group norms and goals that have been established, along with Sophia's own goals for personal and professional growth. However, as a supervisee, a central ethical concern for Sophia is getting the feedback and supervision she needs in order to meet the needs of her client. It seems her desire to protect her client gets in her way. By withholding information and not sharing her tapes, she sabotages her own professional growth as well as her client's best interest. Sophia's discomfort in the group and unwillingness to risk are evident in her pattern of silence within the group. By blaming the group members for not being "invested in helping her or her client" she is projecting her own withdrawal back onto the group. This type of behavior could indicate some fears or resistance to being a group member. This may be a reflection of a general lack of trust operating in the group.

Although trust issues often relate to the initial stage of a group's development, this group seems to be in the transition stage of the process. Characteristics of this stage include anxiety, defensiveness, and resistance from group members (Corey & Corey, 2002). The members of this group resist exploring problems presented during this session in any significant depth. Feelings are ignored with advice giving, general dismissive statements, or pseudosupport. These types of behaviors exemplify the transition stage of a group's development. An interesting dynamic is the lack of challenge and support from the group leader. Sophia, however, could have better utilized the group by eliciting more specific feedback, and by sharing her own reactions to what was said and not said by group members. The implicit conflict she was experiencing in the group could have been made explicit through direct sharing and processing. In this way, Sophia could possibly work through the conflict and further her own development as a clinician.

This group, by definition, is a supervision group, which puts responsibility on the leader to act in a supervisory capacity. Bernard and Goodyear (1998) have provided a working definition of a supervision group as

> the regular meeting of a group of supervisees with a designated supervisor, for the purpose of furthering their understanding of themselves as clinicians, of the clients with whom they work, and/or of service delivery in general, and who are aided in this endeavor by their interaction with each other in the context of group process. (p. 111)

This definition makes clear that a central focus for the group supervisor is to facilitate further understanding of the counselors, both of themselves and their clients. A related professional function is overseeing the clinical aspects of the counselors' caseloads. The group leader has an ethical responsibility to fulfill the supervisory role by monitoring client welfare along with the clinical performance and professional development of the supervisees. Another inherent ethical responsibility for the supervisor is compliance with all relevant ethical and professional standards for practice (Association for Counselor Education and Supervision [ACES], 1993). According to Corey and Corey (2002), most professional organizations affirm that practitioners are expected to be aware of the prevailing standards of practice, and of the possible impact on their own deviation from these standards.

According to Holloway and Johnston (1985), three group supervision foci are important for group supervision: didactic, case conceptualization, and interpersonal process. Each of these areas could be incorporated in assisting the group members in furthering their understanding of the client and counselor issues presented. The supervisor did not respond to the material presented in any of these supervisory capacities, and no interventions were implemented during this session. Key aspects of the supervisory role include the utilization of appropriate methods and techniques to promote the supervisees' professional development and case management strategies.

This incident is filled with rich material that could be responded to in a constructive manner. It is important to remember that although groups have immense power for positive change, there is also the potential for the group to be more damaging than beneficial (Corey & Corey, 2002). It is imperative that group issues be addressed in order to promote both the interpersonal and the professional functioning of the participants. Facilitating a supportive and interpersonally effective group requires addressing the process issues directly. The lack of supervisory intervention has implications on many levels. The interpersonal group issues are not resolved and the issues impacting practice are not addressed, leaving no meaningful exploration or feedback for the participants.

The leader might challenge Sophia and the group to explore the dynamics operating within the group, bringing the implicit to explicit clarity. It is important, as well, to heighten the members' awareness around the ethical and multicultural issues presented in this particular session. The supervisor could implement a variety of methods to bring the ethical issues to the foreground and facilitate further awareness. The members could be challenged in a caring and respectful way. Perhaps some educating might take place regarding the ethical standards and guidelines of the counseling profession. Group members could be asked to process their feelings about possible roadblocks to their own effectiveness as clinicians. The leader could use modeling to exemplify respect for diversity, giving and receiving appropriate feedback, and involvement in the group process. Linking could be employed to increase the cohesiveness of the group (Corey & Corey, 2002). Methods, such as role-play and role reversal, could have been utilized as well. The leader could provide structure for the group by working through an ethical decision-making model. A combination of these types of interventions is effective in facilitating further exploration of the issues presented, heightened awareness of the multicultural and ethical concerns, and effective case conceptualization and treatment planning.

The main focus of the supervision group is the professional development of competence, especially in that these supervisees are not licensed. An ethical concern for this group is that the supervisor is not a Licensed Professional Counselor, yet the members are seeking licensure as counselors. Additionally, the leader does not respond according to the standards for supervisors in the counseling profession. More specifically, this supervisor does nothing to demonstrate conceptual knowledge of supervision methods and techniques or skill in using this knowledge to promote counselor development (ACES, 1990). This issue of the development of competence of these new professionals is a central ethical concern. Another equally important ethical concern is client welfare. According to Sherry (1991), attending to the best interests of both client and supervisee is simultaneously the greatest clinical and ethical challenge of supervision. The issues presented in this group session suggest that multicultural issues are key. These factors have become more important as the field of counseling has developed, and experts in ethical issues have included competence in cultural matters as a significant area to be monitored by supervisors (Sherry, 1991; Vasques, 1992). The supervisor in this incident neglects the responsibility to address multicultural competencies with these supervisees, thus providing a disservice to both the new professionals' development and the welfare of the clients they serve.

Ideally, in the next session, the supervisor will provide a format to address both the ethical and process issues of this group. In the transition stage it is crucial to manage conflict effectively in order to promote trust. Thus a primary focus for the leader will be working through the conflicts constructively (Corey & Corey, 2002). Dealing with the resistance operating in this group requires a great deal of sensitivity on the part of the supervisor, as well as the use of an appropriate balance of support and challenge. The leader could share her observations and invite members to discuss how they are being affected in the group, thus bringing conflicts to light. Unproductive behaviors could be explored in depth, with the ultimate goal of increased member awareness and resolution of conflict. A proactive stance regarding the ethical issues for these practitioners is also imperative. Ultimately, the members come away with an increased awareness of the multicultural issues, along with some guidelines for ethical problem solving and case management. Through addressing the issues directly, the group will most likely move to a more productive working stage.

Although supervising and leading a group presents a unique combination of challenges, the group format provides a vital format for identifying solutions, techniques, and responses to ethical situations. This group will most likely move to some meaningful work, yet much of this is dependent on a competent leader/supervisor. For this group's development, it may be vital to include a co-leader who is a Licensed Professional Counselor, especially with a group of 11 members. Most importantly, the requirements for appropriate supervision for licensure will then be met, and the further professional development of the supervisees will be provided.

RESPONSE

S. Lenoir Gillam

Sophia's response to the group was certainly understandable, although she could have taken some different actions. She initially provided appropriate background information on the client when she presented her case to the group, and her level of disclosure in sharing her concerns about how to help the client was appropriate and relevant to her thoughts and feelings related to her professional work. That is, the personalization of her issues with this client was presented to the group in terms of asking for feedback about how to use herself as a vehicle to help the client, not for the purpose of seeking therapy from the group to meet her own needs. As the process progressed, what she did not do was challenge group members directly about their inappropriate responses, although she did attempt to diffuse the negative comments made about her client by describing her as "more human" than the characterizations made by group members. Her decision not to share the recording of the counseling session after hearing insensitive remarks from group members was justified at that time based on her concern for the welfare of the client, and her withdrawal from the process did not challenge members to act more professional.

Ultimately, a group that leads a supervisee to withhold samples of her work and refrain from full participation will be detrimental to the supervisee's development and the best interest of clients. It was interesting to note, however, that she acknowledged her own feelings of inadequacy in working with the client. This disclosure was quite bold, based on the lack of sensitivity of the group members, and she received no response to this admission. Given her assessment that her attitudes about counseling and supervision seem to conflict with other members' attitudes, she appears to recognize that what she wants from supervision cannot be realized within the current structure of this group.

Various dynamics are evident in this supervision group. In general, there appears to be a loose structure in terms of how the group functions. This is different from a group that is purposefully unstructured. Supervisors, for reasons related to supervisee development or their own leadership style, may often decide to impose little structure on the content of the group in order to let the members assume responsibility for the group's agenda. Nonetheless, there will be clearly defined ground rules and expectations about how the group will function and member responsibilities. Sophia's group is similar to many groups that are structured to involve check-in, that have member-driven agendas for that meeting, and then case presentations. However, the lack of supervisor involvement in this group seems to be leading to ineffective and unethical practices.

Harmful patterns of behavior are present, probably restricting the development of healthy norms. For example, member feedback seems to be inappropriate or, at best, absent. That is, insensitive comments about Sophia's client seem to fuel other inappropriate remarks, as if this kind of communication is acceptable among members. Other times, supervisees will ask for feedback and receive no response at all from members, or their personal issues will be explored without linking them to their work with clients. Failure to acknowledge someone's thoughts or feelings can impact group process as much as harmful remarks. Either way, an unsafe environment exists, one in which client worth is devalued, and supervisee appeals for support may be ignored. Therefore, expecting that supervisees will use the process to enhance their professional development is not reasonable. Neither the supervisor nor other members address supervisees' verbals or nonverbals, and in general, the lack of leader intervention perpetuates the harmful communication processes. It is interesting to consider the roles members assume and the stage of this group's development. Although conflict is certainly present in this group, the nature of it seems to be more reflective of poor group forming as opposed to a natural period of storming.

Another factor worth noting, and related to the preceding discussion, involves an apparent imbalance between task and relationship variables. Members are likely to stay somewhat topic focused, although they need to be refocused on conceptualization and personalization issues that promote client well-being and supervisee development. However, there is limited exploration of group process. In other words, how members' interactions drive the process is virtually unexplored.

Further, another dynamic suggests that there is a parallel process occurring related to Sophia's presentation of her client. She describes her client as "disappointed in herself for not living up to her potential," and she, too, acknowledges in group that she feels inadequate in helping her client. Focusing on this dynamic could be a useful supervision intervention.

Sophia does, however, possess some control over her experiences in this group; she just needs to utilize the process differently. She could have tried to generate greater structure for her own presentation by being more specific about her needs for processing this particular client in group. Asking the group "for suggestions for helping the client come to terms with her feelings" is a fairly general request. Instead, she could ask members to address questions such as the following:

- What emotions does the client express during the session?
- What are some examples of times when I miss opportunities to deepen the affective focus by reflecting the client's thought processes instead of her feelings?
- What is an example of how I could respond more reflectively on feelings than on thoughts?

Specific questions such as these examples are designed to assist Sophia in soliciting the kind of feedback she is seeking. They give members a more focused idea of how to respond to her needs.

Similarly, Sophia could assign roles to each group member to elicit certain feedback. She could ask someone to provide feedback from the role of the client, from a theoretical perspective, or with a certain metaphor in mind (Borders, 1991). She could also be more concrete about the things she has tried, successfully and unsuccessfully, and invite other input. Adding this bit of structure may tend to help set more appropriate boundaries for the type of feedback she is seeking.

It is difficult to know what happened in preplanning for this group or how much structure was put into place in earlier sessions. Ultimately, the supervisor needs to be aware of her concerns. There probably will be no changes unless the issues are addressed directly in the group. If the environment does not change for the better, members may drop out without explaining to the group why they are leaving. This should be prevented because losing a group member with no explanation can have a strong impact on the dynamics of any group. In addition, subgrouping may take on a stronger presence if the environment does not change.

Sophia needs to be encouraged and supported to raise her concerns in the group, although this type of challenge is likely to feel risky. Another risky alternative could be to employ a process observer (if members are trained to participate in this way). However, a group this ill-formed will probably be resistant to this process.

The supervisor needs to be much more involved in facilitating the group. It is difficult to imagine that much structure took place in the forming stage of the group. Regardless of counselors' prior training and experience, group supervisors cannot assume that all supervisees will necessarily be good group members. Helping people make connections, reviewing confidentiality and other ground rules, establishing boundaries related to giving feedback, and providing better structure for case presentations are only some examples of the kinds of interventions the supervisor could have made initially.

The supervisor needs to be a better process observer and facilitate the group around those issues, as well. Although conflict is an inherent part of any successful group, there are likely to be times when the supervisor may need to challenge the appropriateness of member feedback or cut off insensitive comments or monopolizing. There are occasions when the leader may need to redirect the group to task, as in the case of the feedback around the member's personal issues, or redirect the group to focus on the supervisee rather than on the client. The process could stand a better balance of roles and functions related to supervisee development (e.g., not focusing only on case conceptualization). There is nothing wrong with being a nondirective group leader and letting the members assume leadership and drive the process if the group can handle it. This does not just happen. It must be facilitated.

The group supervisor failed to address ethical violations. As a result, this supervisor was not practicing ethical behavior. The supervisor, as a Licensed Mental Health Counselor, should at least recognize infractions that violate promotion of client welfare, as described in the Association for Counselor Education and Supervision *Ethical Guidelines for Counseling Supervisors*

(1993) in section 1.01. Although the insensitive comments made by group members about Sophia's client were not being heard by the client, they did devalue her worth and impact the quality of the supervision Sophia received. Given the hostility of the remarks, both the client's and Sophia's welfare were being compromised. The supervisor had the responsibility to address these ethical infractions and make supervisees aware of the ethical standards, in general (section 2.03).

This case raises questions about the presence or lack of the supervisor's training in group work (section 2.01) and supervision process and practice. If the supervisor had been trained in group work, observation of this supervision group could be expected not to reveal so many missed opportunities to facilitate purposeful benefits of group participation. In terms of supervisory responsibilities, the supervisor is in violation of a number of standards outlined in the ACES Ethical Guidelines. For example, no feedback appears to be given to supervisees (section 2.08). In addition, personal issues that surface within the context of supervision should be relevant to the supervisee's clinical work and professional practice (section 2.11). Supervision should not be a substitute for therapy. The supervisor may also need to rethink the size of future groups. Although professionals may debate what number constitutes the right size of a group, a larger group might be even more unmanageable than a small group for a supervisor with limited training and experience in group work and supervision. Furthermore, even if the supervisor is prepared to facilitate groups effectively, it is important to note that as the number of group members increases, the complexity of dynamics will increase, as well. Supervisees may be better served in smaller groups.

Although the supervisor may have missed some ethical considerations, Sophia does demonstrate evidence of ethical practice. She acquires appropriate consent from her client to share her work in supervision (section 1.04), and she prepares samples of her work for feedback in supervision (section 2.06).

Assuming that the supervisor becomes aware of the group's limitations and is able to spring into action, perhaps the first appropriate step will be for the supervisor to consult with a peer. When the group meets again, suggestions to influence change include the following:

- Process the group's experience to this point. Group work can be facilitated by ongoing assessment of both the content and process of supervision.
- Revisit the ground rules as part of that discussion.
- Address concerns about unethical behavior. The supervisor must attend to the infractions and facilitate support of corrective experiences.
- In the event that these discussions reveal conflicts between individual and group goals, this matter must be addressed, as well. Individual goals should not sabotage the goals of the group. It is unclear whether or not group goals exist in the first place.

REFERENCES

Association for Counselor Education and Supervision. (1990). Standards for counseling supervisors. *Journal of Counseling & Development, 69,* 30–32.

Association for Counselor Education and Supervision. (1993). Ethical guidelines for counseling supervisors. *ACES Spectrum, 53,* 5–8.

Bernard, J., & Goodyear, R. (1998). *Fundamentals of clinical supervision* (2nd ed.). Boston: Allyn & Bacon.

Borders, L. D. (1991). A systematic approach to peer group supervision. *Journal of Counseling & Development, 69,* 248–252.

Corey, M.S., & Corey, G. (2002). *Groups: Process and practice* (6th ed). Pacific Grove, CA: Brooks/Cole.

Holloway, E.L., & Johnston, R. (1985). Group supervision: Widely practiced but poorly understood. *Counselor Education and Supervision, 24,* 332–340.

Sherry, P. (1991). Ethical issues in the conduct of supervision. *Counseling Psychologist, 19,* 566–584.

Vasques, M.J. (1992). Psychologist as clinical supervisor: Promoting ethical practice. *Professional Psychology: Research and Practice, 23,* 196–202.

PART II

GROUP MEMBER CONCERNS

CHAPTER 20

GROUP RESISTANCE: "OKAY. YOU CAN LEAD THE GROUP NEXT WEEK"

This incident focuses on the dynamics of what may occur when a group member creates resistance in the group.

CRITICAL INCIDENT

Jean Sunde Peterson

Background

Jack, a veteran high school teacher now in charge of a program for gifted students, has taken one counseling course, Theories of Counseling, as a means of exploring a possible career change. Jack has good instincts about counseling, thinks a great deal about what he learned in the course, and has, in fact, been facilitating affectively oriented discussion groups regularly for a year as part of his program's curriculum. Initially he cofacilitated one group with a counselor at the school for one semester and then continued on his own. The group meetings are 55 minutes in length, are semistructured, and focus on a new topic related to adolescent development at each weekly meeting. Groups have been organized according to grade level, with students from grades 9, 10, or 11 specifically comprising each group. There have been no problems with attendance, and the students seem eager to focus on social and emotional issues, which have not been acknowledged or addressed formally in the program in the past.

Incident

The groups have been meeting for approximately 6 weeks. Jack is learning as he goes, of course, but he has noticed that this year he is more relaxed with the groups than during his first year and that the students seem to be willing to talk and find commonalities with each other. He senses that he needs to spend less time on planning and resist functioning as a teacher, even though he is able to use the developmental topics fairly effectively to generate communication. The students generally seem to appreciate having a place to talk together.

Jack is aware, however, that one 10th-grade group has become more and more resistant. He is familiar with this term from the counseling course, but he has not studied how it applies to groups. He does not even label what he is experiencing as *resistance*. He simply feels confused and not in control of the group. When the group disperses each week, he knows he will continue to carry an image of Amy, scowling, home with him. He may even have trouble falling asleep because she is still staring at him sullenly in his mind's eye. He is aware that Amy has great power in the group. Her lack of active participation seems to inhibit the other group members. Group membership is voluntary, and Amy never misses. But she hardly ever participates, even during go-rounds, when each group member has an opportunity to respond or give input on the same question or topic.

After one particular group meeting, Amy approaches him, saying, "Why don't you just let us talk? When I was in the [psychiatric] hospital, we each took turns leading the group. We didn't have a topic." She continues to explain that they talked about all sorts of things—"like drugs and stuff"—in their hospital groups.

Jack tries to explain his goals for the groups to Amy: the focus is social and emotional development of high school students, and the format is meant to ensure that no one dominates and that even shy students have a voice. He further explains that the groups will indeed probably talk about drugs and stuff eventually. However, he senses that his explanation is inadequate. Amy persists with uncomfortable questions. Suddenly he says, with an edge in his voice, "Why don't you lead the group next time then?" Amy seems momentarily stunned. Jack asks her what she would like to do with the group. Amy says, "Maybe drugs and alcohol. We talked a lot about that in the hospital." She mentions that maybe she and Laurie, a friend in the group, can lead the group together. Jack agrees and Amy leaves. He is uneasy and recognizes that he has vague feelings of nonsupport for Amy and her friend's leadership.

Discussion

Amy and Laurie attempt to lead the next group meeting. Jack sits silently at the table, offering no assistance after briefly introducing the two girls as the group leaders for the day. Laurie seems uncomfortable from that moment on. Amy uses closed questions, gets little or no response, and group members are not forthcoming with comments. Jack lets the discussion dwindle into what appears to be extreme discomfort for the girls, amid tense silence in the group, before he takes charge. Jack is feeling somewhat confused as to what happened, wondering what he might have done differently in leading the group.

QUESTIONS

1. When is a counselor ready to facilitate a group?
2. Pertinent to this incident, what does coursework in group process usually teach about resistance that could have helped Jack here?
3. What leader issues are important to consider in this incident?
4. What ethical issues emerge in this incident?
5. What are potential differences between school groups and mental-health-agency/treatment-center groups?

6. What kind of group was Jack leading in his program?
7. What else could Jack have explained to Amy about the groups during the aftergroup conversation?
8. How might Jack have dealt with Amy's outside-the-group challenge at the next group meeting?
9. What should Jack have considered before handing over the reins to Amy (and Laurie)?
10. What responsibility do counselor education programs have for providing all counseling students, including part-time students, even during first courses, with basic ethical guidelines concerning competence?

RESPONSE

Suzanne M. Hobson

This critical incident provides a powerful example of the importance of sufficient counselor training and supervision prior to the facilitation of actual counseling groups. Although Jack was a veteran as a high school teacher, he was also an untrained novice as a group counselor. Despite his good instincts and apparent thoughtfulness about the content presented in the Theories of Counseling class he took, Jack's training was clearly insufficient to render him competent to provide group counseling.

The American Counseling Association *Code of Ethics and Standards of Practice* (1995) clearly indicates that counselors should "practice only within the boundaries of their competence" (section C.2.a). Likewise, the American School Counselor Association's *Ethical Standards for School Counselors* (ASCA, 1998) states that "the professional school counselor functions [only] within the boundaries of individual professional competence" (section E.1.a).

In addition, the Association for Specialists in Group Work *Professional Standards for the Training of Group Workers* (ASGW, 2000) elaborates on the minimum training requirements for group counselors. Specifically, these standards require that group counselors should have developed the "knowledge, skills, and experiences deemed necessary for general competency for all master's degree prepared counselors" and have completed "core training in group work" prior to conducting any group counseling. This core training in group work should address "scope of practice, types of group work, group development, group process and dynamics, group leadership, and standards of training and practice for group workers" (section I.A.). Due to the fact that Jack has neither completed a training program in counseling nor had coursework specific to the facilitation of counseling groups, it certainly appears that Jack is in violation of these codes and standards.

Had Jack completed his master's degree in counseling, including a core course on group counseling that addressed all aspects recommended by ASGW and supervised practicum/internship experiences doing group work, he would have developed considerable knowledge and skills relevant to the challenges he faced while facilitating this group. Specific to this particular incident, he would have learned about the importance of screening potential group members; the value of orienting members to the group; typical stages of group development; the predictability of a storming stage that includes member resistance; skills for addressing resistance and helping a group move through the storming stage to the norming and performing stages; and issues related to outside-the-group conversations.

In preparing for facilitating this group, Jack would then have understood the importance of screening all potential group members. ACA's Code of Ethics section A.9.a, ASCA's Ethical Standards section A.6, and ASGW's Professional Standards section D.1.a all address the importance of screening in the process of forming a counseling group. Had Jack screened group members (with appropriate training), he might have chosen not to include Amy in this group. He seems to have planned for a semistructured psychoeducational group and might have excluded Amy based upon her inpatient treatment history and the unlikelihood that this group could adequately meet her needs. Whereas school groups tend to have a more structured, psychoeducational, and growth focus, inpatient groups and mental health agency/treatment center groups tend to have a less structured, psychotherapeutic, and remedial focus. Given these differences, it is understandable (and perhaps predictable) that Amy became frustrated in a structured psychoeducational group. Had Jack screened Amy, he would have had an opportunity to talk with her about this and to assess the likelihood that Amy would benefit from the group and demonstrate an ability to function effectively within it.

In addition to screening potential members prior to selecting participants for this counseling group, it is important to orient group members to the purpose and nature of the group. Although Jack did provide Amy with information regarding the goals, focus, and format of the group during their later discussion, it is unclear whether this information was also presented to all group members at the onset of the group.

Most importantly, adequate training would have equipped Jack with knowledge about typical stages of group development and the predictability of a storming stage that includes member resistance as well as with skills for addressing resistance and helping a group move through the storming stage to the norming and performing stages. Generally, core coursework in group counseling teaches that groups typically develop in a specific manner and that it is not only common but desirable for groups to go through a storming stage (Tuckman & Jensen, 1977). With this training, Jack would have recognized Amy's complaints as reflective of the resistance that commonly occurs during this stage of group development.

Instead of trying to address Amy's concerns directly during this outside-the-group challenge, Jack would have understood the importance of insisting that Amy bring her concerns back to the group. Doing this is important for two reasons. First, it allows the group to respond and to work through the resistance in order to develop greater cohesiveness and a stronger orientation to action. It helps the group develop as an entity with influence rather than maintain the group leader's power. Second, it embraces the resistance and amplifies it rather than attempts to squelch it. Paradoxically, by encouraging Amy to bring her concerns to the group and using the next group meeting(s) to address her concerns and, fundamentally, the purpose of the group, the resistance will diminish and result in a greater action orientation within the group. By defensively attempting to squelch it quickly, Jack may find that the resistance continues and ultimately results in the ineffectiveness of the group. Because of these insights, Jack could have avoided responding to Amy defensively and could instead have regarded her challenge as predictable and as an opportunity to help the group navigate through the storming stage to the norming and performing stages (Tuckman & Jensen, 1977).

In bringing Amy's concerns to the group, Jack could begin by sharing that Amy had approached him outside of the group and by reiterating the importance of addressing group issues within the group rather than outside of it. He could then invite Amy to share her concerns. After Amy had shared her concerns, Jack should take great care not to appear defensive and to avoid the temptation of providing a quick solution or response. Instead, he should facilitate a conversation among the group members about the purpose of the group and the other group members' perceptions regarding what occurred in the group. He might offer his observation that Amy's silence in past group meetings seemed to inhibit other group members' participation, and ask the group members about this. In addition, Jack could encourage the group members to talk about their personal goals for the group, given the parameters of a semistructured group format.

Ideally, Jack should use the outside-of-group challenge to talk with Amy about the importance of bringing her concerns to the group for discussion. In addition, Jack might talk with Amy about the difference between school groups and mental health agency/treatment center groups. Preferably, this conversation could occur during the screening and orientation process.

Because of his lack of training, it appears that Jack did not screen and orient group members; that he clearly did not recognize and know how to respond to resistance; and that he was not aware of effective ways to address outside-the-group challenges. Therefore, Jack responded defensively to Amy and put her in a position of leading the group. In addition, he allowed her to draw Laurie into this leadership without consulting her. Rather than increasing the group members' sense of safety, feelings of cohesion, and commitment to action, Jack's actions appeared harmful to Amy, Laurie, and the other group members. The lesson seems to be that "If you challenge the group leader and question the effectiveness of the group, you'll be put out on a limb and embarrassed."

In accordance with the ASCA Ethical Standards that state, "the professional school counselor...accepts responsibility for the consequences of his or her actions" (section E.1.a), Jack must accept responsibility for unethically practicing beyond his level of competence and for any harm that results. In addition, the university counselor education program in which Jack is enrolled might need to take some responsibility. The ACA Code of Ethics clearly states that "Prior to admission, counselors orient prospective students to the counselor education or training program's expectations, including…the type and level of skill acquisition required for successful completion of the training" (section F.2.a) and that counselor educators "make students and supervisees aware of the ethical responsibilities and standards of the profession" (section F.2.d).

Because it is unclear whether Jack was aware of the legal and ethical guidelines concerning training and competence as they apply to the practice of counseling, this incident highlights the importance of providing every new student, at the point of admission, with an orientation to ethics. This orientation, in my opinion, should include an overview of the ACA Code of Ethics and relevant state laws that govern the practice of counseling. All new students should learn, at a minimum, the training and supervision requirements prior to being able to provide counseling services. I believe that counselor education programs have a responsibility to protect the public (potential clients) by providing such an orientation to students either during the admission process or immediately following each student's admission. The protection of clients is the joint responsibility of the counselor and the counselor education system alike.

RESPONSE

Kurt L. Kraus

There are two pieces of good news. One is that Jack is considering a great career transition, and with years of experience in schools he will certainly bring an excellent understanding of daily life in a school setting. The other is that in this incident it seems by the students' favorable response to these discussion groups that the opportunity for group counseling in this school setting is great. Adolescent development in general and the complexities many gifted and talented adolescents encounter specifically sound like superb themes for group counseling.

Now consider the bad news. Unfortunately, despite the need for such a relevant group, Jack is in the unenviable position of leading a group without the necessary education and training, neither theoretical nor practical. Perhaps this is Jack's fault, being an overly zealous counselor in training. Perhaps it is a situation in which the existing school counselor is so stretched for time that she or he is unable to continue co-leading this project and gives the group to Jack. Or is it that the counselor is unaware that Jack is unprepared to practice as a school counselor? It is clear from the outset that Jack is willing but unqualified to undertake this type of group work. Such a predicament is scary for Jack (especially so early along his new, professional career path) and risky if not potentially dangerous for Amy and her fellow group members. This incident is certainly in conflict with the ACA *Code of*

Ethics and Standards of Practice (1995) that focuses on protecting clients during group work (section A.9, SP-5). Let us look at several of the many issues this case uncovers.

The school counselor who began these grade-specific affectively oriented discussion groups brought Jack in as a logical co-leader. Jack was interested in becoming a school counselor as a change of career, and Jack is obviously interested and aware of some of the issues unique to gifted and talented youth by his current position as program director. With insufficient training (i.e., coursework and supervised practice) in group counseling, Jack attempts to manage Amy's group by relying on his common sense and his misdirected application of theoretical concepts (e.g., resistance) to this group experience. If the group was to be an educational experience in which the focus was Jack teaching these gifted and talented young people about social and emotional development, Jack might have been the right person for the leader. Instead, as Jack notes, "he needs to spend less time on planning and resist functioning as a teacher." The group has in fact taken on a more group counseling function, one that Jack is ill-equipped to lead.

Theories of Counseling is hardly a group work course. It is wonderful that Jack has "good instincts," but the profession of counseling is not built upon instinct. Adequate preparation for the complexities of leading or co-leading this adolescent development discussion group require both didactic instruction and supervised practice (ASGW, 1998). Although it is unclear whether Jack is formally in a counselor education program, we might imagine that Jack has begun a counselor education graduate degree. If so, it is critical that in his orientation to the program (ACA, 1995, section F.2.a) and the counseling profession, Jack be taught that ethical counselors, as a matter of responsibility to the profession and of adhering to appropriate levels of competence, do not deliver services for which they are inadequately prepared (section C.2.a).

It is clear that as Jack attempts to explain group goals to Amy, she never explicitly understands the purpose of this group. The ACA Code of Ethics (section A.3.a) states that the client is clearly informed as to the purpose of his or her counseling as a matter of client rights in the counseling relationship. In this case it is unclear whether Jack so notified the group members about the purpose of this group. This issue is particularly relevant in the context of school counseling programs. Amy's honest (if not manipulative) misunderstanding of the purpose of the group is likely to be based on her past experience during her psychiatric hospitalization. Although Jack's "focus is social and emotional development of high school students," it seems that Amy is in need of services this group was not intended to provide. It becomes Jack's obligation to refer Amy to a more appropriate intervention rather than change the purpose of the group to try to accommodate or appease her. It is essential and ethical that the theme of social and emotional development remain constant throughout the group experience.

An additional question that emerges is whether Jack (or more critically his predecessor, the school counselor) adequately screened members for this group. The tendency to select members from a rather homogenous group (i.e., the students in the gifted and talented program), without adequate screening, is high. Best practice is clearly met by careful attention to screening potential members to assess their appropriateness and to garner informed consent. The issue of informed consent can be complex in school counseling programs that involve minor clients/students. In some states, the law or school policy requires specific parental permission regarding minors participating in the school counseling program. Although this is not addressed in this incident, school counselors must be vigilant to adhere to and uphold existing laws and policies that may apply to their work environment.

Optimistically, several salient issues that are reported in this incident would be mediated had Jack faced this dilemma as a fully trained, professional school counselor or as a supervised counselor-in-training intern. He would have carefully designed the group and screened members accordingly. When Jack encountered Amy's "uncomfortable questions," it is likely that Jack would have been better able to redirect Amy and her questions back to the group. Jack's offer for Amy to "lead the group next time" would be a decision based upon the purpose of the group, the norms established in its early stages, and the appropriateness of such an intervention for Amy. Further, we would be reasonably assured that had Jack introduced the topic of drugs and alcohol, it would be because it is appropriate to the entire group, not just Amy.

In summary, this incident teaches three important lessons. The first is that effective counselors are well trained and that process cannot be rushed or sidestepped. The second lesson is that group work is a powerful intervention, but it is neither a panacea for overworked counselors nor an appropriate mode of counseling for all students/clients. The third lesson is that resistance in group work has multiple meanings. In this case, it is quite possible that Amy was more unclear and reluctant than resistant. The dynamics in all groups are immensely complex, and it is essential that we examine carefully the many factors that may be involved, such as leader, member, purpose, content, and process, and that influence each group.

REFERENCES

American Counseling Association. (1995). *Code of ethics and standards of practice.* Alexandria, VA: Author.

American School Counselor Association. (1998). *Ethical standards for school counselors.* Alexandria, VA: Author.

Association for Specialists in Group Work. (1998). Best practice guidelines. *Journal for Specialists in Group Work, 23*(3), 237–244.

Association for Specialists in Group Work. (2000). *Professional standards for the training of group workers.* Retrieved from http//www.asgw.org

Tuckman, B.W., & Jensen, M.A. (1977). Stages of small group development revisited. *Group and Organizational Studies, 2,* 419–427.

CHAPTER 21

SUBGROUPING: "WHAT WE DO ON OUR TIME IS OUR BUSINESS!"

This incident describes the development of subgrouping within an outpatient, open-ended group that focuses on early addiction recovery issues. The dilemma deals with one of the requirements for group, which is for each member to attend Alcoholics Anonymous (AA) or Narcotics Anonymous (NA) meetings on a weekly basis.

CRITICAL INCIDENT

Ford Brooks

Background

This recovery group is composed of seven clients ranging in age from 25 to 62. All of the clients, including the facilitator, are male, and two of the members are African American. The group members are making their first attempt in recovery by abstaining from alcohol and drugs, attending this treatment group twice per week, and attending AA or NA twice per week. The group members are randomly tested for alcohol and drugs by the outpatient facility. Two of the group members started the group because they were unable to discontinue drinking without having to go to detoxification services at a local hospital. They were referred from the hospital to the group. Three of the subgroup members are court referred and have various denial mechanisms, which have been strengthened by the subgrouping. The remaining two members have come into the group because of positive urine drug screens at their workplaces, and they are in jeopardy of losing their jobs. They both agree that their cocaine and alcohol use is addictive and that they need help. Overall, four of the group members are invested in the group, and the three who are subgrouping remain in denial and are minimally compliant.

Incident

The group meets two times a week for 10 weeks. This particular group is open-ended, and the newest members are the three who are subgrouping. Prior to group sessions, the facilitator notices the three members together in the parking lot separate from the other four members. This subgroup typically comes in a few minutes after the rest of the group and usually is cracking jokes or making light of the group.

The most recent interaction in group session involved the three members sitting together in the group room and distracting the other four members. One of the members who was referred by his employer was talking honestly and painfully about how he not only nearly lost his job due to his cocaine addiction but also almost lost the relationship with his wife. This group member began to sob and was visibly upset by what he had just shared. It was at this point that one of the three subgrouping members switched the subject, and the other two in that subgroup steered away from the member in pain. The three members began to talk about the weekend and how they went to a racetrack and did not drink.

At this time the facilitator observed very clearly the split in the group and how the subgroup was playing out. The group facilitator said, "I notice that the three of you seem uncomfortable with the feelings that were just shared. ...could you tell us what might be going on for you right now?" Following this question the subgroup remained silent, and then one of them said, "This feelings stuff is for the birds...I went to a racetrack and didn't drink, that was a big deal for me, and I don't think I need to weep and cry over it."

The facilitator then went to the other group member who just shared deep feelings around his potential losses and asked, "How is it for you to share what you shared, and then hear a number of group members say that they don't need to weep and cry?" From the standpoint of the facilitator, the split between those who were invested and those who were still in denial and minimizing was clear.

Discussion

The facilitator is aware of how the group has polarized, and he has made attempts at processing this in the group. The counselor's process comments are consistently met with silence, hostility, and avoidance. It is clear that a number of group members are thinking about discontinuing their participation in the group. The facilitator is unsure how to proceed with the group and how to address the issue of subgrouping, which feeds into a larger issue of denial.

QUESTIONS

1. How might the counselor deal with this situation of subgrouping?
2. What might the counselor do in the preassessment phase of group preparation in order to address this issue?
3. How could the four group members help in addressing the subgrouping and denial issues?
4. What are the ethical issues that need to be addressed with this situation?

RESPONSE

Rebecca A. Schumacher

From the account presented, the facilitator understands that the group dynamics are seriously jeopardizing the effectiveness of this group. Any of the leadership interventions used thus far have not resolved the issue of sub-grouping. There are important elements of group work that the facilitator could consider for this group, as well as future groups, to better assure members that the group experience is productive and beneficial. Elements of content and process are ones that this facilitator will want to reexamine.

The facilitator needs to act on the observations of subgrouping. For the benefit of both the group and new members, observations by the facilitator of the subgrouping outside of group meetings as well as the tardiness to the sessions need to be stated and processed in group. If allowed to continue, these three members may never confront their denial of alcoholism and may simply mark time until they have fulfilled the requirements of the court referral; and the four other members may quit the group. Thus there would be no benefits experienced by any of the members.

An attempt to acknowledge subgrouping seems to have occurred when the facilitator commented, "I notice that the three of you seem uncomfortable with the feelings that were just shared...." Although this comment is an accurate response, it may have been premature to talk about feelings. When working with an all male group, and a group with diversity, the group leader should consider whether a feelings-oriented group is most beneficial. The facilitator needs to identify and then practice sensitivity to the differences in the members of this group. In addition, the facilitator needs to consider whether talk therapy is appropriate for these new members.

Appropriate preparation and orientation to a group experience is essential for a group to become more than simply a collection of individuals. Appropriate preparation and orientation may not guarantee that a group subsequently moves to the working stage in which members accomplish personal goals, but pregroup attention to preparation does set the stage for a greater likelihood that group outcomes will be positive. In addition, ethically, potential members of any group need to be made aware of the purpose, goals, group rules, and confidentiality as well as of the benefits and limitations of groups. Even in open groups, such as this outpatient group, orientation and preparation of members should be addressed. Preparation for group work should include the importance of punctuality to sessions and member meetings outside of group sessions. Yet there is no indication that this group facilitator devoted time to preparing and orienting members to the group experience. Informed consent is missing.

As prevention for future groups, perhaps this group facilitator could meet individually with each new member prior to attending a first group session. If it is not possible to have individual meetings, a portion of the first session with a new member(s) should be devoted to orientation about the group. Current members could assist the facilitator in helping new members understand the content and process of the group. Taking time to orient and prepare a new member(s) will contribute to the development of trust and subsequent cohesion among members. It will be facilitative for the group leader to request input from both the current members and incoming members for suggestions about the group. For example, the facilitator might ask, "How can our group help each of you reach your goal?" or "What other group rules will facilitate our group meetings?" It is important in any group that group members establish shared ownership in the group.

In this incident, the facilitator is confronted with how to address the subgrouping of the three newest members. Even though it might appear as an afterthought, the facilitator may want to devote the next group session to the points of group preparation. This will be the opportune time to discuss the facilitator's observations of subgrouping and tardiness. In addition, having the current four members help describe the purpose, goals, group rules, confidentiality, benefits, and limitations might begin to develop open lines of communication between the four current members and the three new members. The four group members could talk about what it was like to be referred to a group and their thoughts about usage of alcohol and drugs. This may begin to breakdown the barrier that seems to exist between old and new members. In addition, it may provide the facilitator with insight about the new members and their ability to participate in talk therapy and determine the strength of their denial mechanisms.

If every attempt to develop this group into a cohesive, working group should fail, the facilitator ultimately has a responsibility to the group itself. After considerable deliberation and consulting with a supervisor, the facilitator may need to request that the new members, who have formed a subgroup, leave the group. Should this action become the last resort, the facilitator needs to provide alternative resources for these three members.

It is an essential practice that group leaders have ongoing professional development in order to keep abreast of the best group work practices and research. This facilitator may find that ongoing supervision is helpful for continuous development of knowledge and skills for leading groups and dealing with challenging group situations.

RESPONSE

Steven F. Hundley

How might the counselor deal with this situation of subgrouping? Group facilitation becomes optimal when minimal but definite values are created, supported, and practiced by the counselor and the group members. Although cooperation is essential and group cohesiveness a significant goal, it is not unusual for groups to become segmented. The counselor's role may not be to correct group members for subgrouping but to facilitate an understanding of why subgrouping is occurring.

The behavioral norms and values of the group, for example, both spoken and understood, may have contributed to the split. The counselor should be more focused on the process of uniting the group and less intent on addressing individual needs. The three members of the subgroup have perceived the norms within the group as unfair or too demanding and devote much of their time to sabotaging the efforts of the facilitator to whom they attribute their discomfort. The counselor should recognize their resistance as fear and the subgrouping as a mechanism for overcoming their fear. For example, the subgroup was cracking jokes and making light of the group. This incident may be viewed as some form of intentional disruptive behavior, but it is more likely an expression of denial or fear of intimacy with the group. The behaviors need to be addressed as part of the process and not as impedance to the process.

The energy created by the fear of the three group members is powerful but misdirected. The counselor's role is to redirect this fear and to use it for the benefit of the entire group, including the subgroup. Because the actions and attitudes of the three group members are not unusual, the counselor must develop a strategy that uses the subgroup to create a therapeutic process. The counselor must provide an opportunity for the members of the subgroup to invest themselves into the larger group. The counselor should encourage each member of the subgroup to establish personal goals and to consider how the group can influence and support his efforts to meet the goals. The counselor should facilitate a discussion on the limitations of informal grouping and the strengths of the counseling group. The counselor should utilize techniques that enable the subgroup members to recognize common bonds with other group members. One technique may include having the four group members self-disclose circumstances in which they behave in ways similar to the subgroup and why. Another method will be to create dyads with one member of the subgroup paired with a member from the other four. The interactions within the dyads may create a high level of comfort and dissipate fear and anxiety among the subgroup members. Bonds may be formed that will offer more support and cooperation when the collective group resumes.

The counselor needs to recognize that although subgrouping may have a powerful influence on the group, and that the influence may be subversive and disruptive, the members of the subgroup may be actually demonstrating anger with or fear of the counselor. The counselor needs to evaluate his or her style to determine if it is too directive, too rigid, or too threatening. If so, the subgroup members may have sought comfort and intimacy with each other, especially if it appears that a significant bond has been formed between the counselor and the other group members.

What might the counselor do in the preassessment phase of group preparation in order to address this issue? The counselor should ascertain the level of commitment of each of the potential group members. Direct contact with the group members individually is critical for determining whether a prospective member values the group experience. In this case, members of the subgroup would probably have revealed some resistance to participating or at least reluctance to change their behaviors. Their denial would have been evident given an appropriate screening process.

The screening process would have contributed to trust building between the group members and the counselor. If a level of trust had been established, members who later formed the subgroup would have been inclined to devise individual strategies for dealing with their fears and denial, establish personal goals, and be less likely to respond in the way they did. The counselor would have been viewed as an ally in a process rather than as a figure of authority, and the level of comfort that the subgroup members found with each other would have been established with the counselor and then reinforced by the members of the group.

Preassessment gives the counselor the opportunity to discuss group procedures, benefits, and risks, and to talk about ground rules that are established not by the counselor for the purpose of seeking control but for established professional methods to facilitate a positive group experience. The counselor should discuss ways in which risks can be minimized for the group member and how that group member can reduce the harm he or she potentially poses to others and to the process. However, if prospective members are absolute in their determination not to participate or to contribute to the group counseling process, careful consideration should be given to their acceptance into the group and their potential to impede the group process.

In this case, if the counselor had an established method for interviewing prospective members, the similar behaviors and attitudes of the subgroup would have been recognized and possible intervention could have been used to inhibit the subgroup members' activities at the beginning of their experience in the group. More likely, the counselor would have come up with ways of facilitating individual involvement with the group and bonding with members who did not become part of the subgroup.

How could the four group members help in addressing the subgrouping and denial issues? Any responses to the subgroup for their behaviors or denials, although these might be having negative consequences on the group, will probably serve to reinforce the power and control the subgroup is seeking. Self-disclosures that are emotionally painful, like the one described in the incident, may be too unstable and threatening for members of the subgroup. Although self-disclosure is viewed by many as having significant value to the group process and to the individual who self-discloses, there must be a mutually agreed upon attachment range among the members in order for the disclosure to have meaning for the group or the individual.

The members of the group not in the subgroup will have to recognize that their self-disclosures are not compatible with the subgroup members' level of trust and fear and that it will take time and patience for members of the subgroup to work though their reasons for subgrouping and denial. Group members should follow the lead of the counselor in spending more time increasing the subgroup's level of compatibility and creating a balance that encourages all members to feel safe. In this way, the process of self-disclosure is mutually inclusive, resulting in the subgroup empathizing and respecting the self-disclosures of all members and in the four group members recognizing the limitations and appropriateness of self-disclosure.

The members of the group who are threatening to discontinue are themselves forming a subgroup. They are feeling the stress and pressure of having new members join the group, and they are not willing to tolerate particular behaviors. Most likely, members of the group are talking outside the group and forming alliances to counter the effects of the subgroup, including quitting. Again this should become part of the process in demonstrating to all the members of the group why subgroups form and why group members will seek others who will support both appropriate and inappropriate behaviors. Members seek others who sustain their need to change and their need to remain the same. The subgroup members maintain their denial through forming an alliance, whereas the other group members maintain their view of acceptable group behavior through alliances with each other and the counselor.

What are the ethical issues that need to be addressed with this issue? The counselor is not addressing the implications of subgrouping with the group. Furthermore, the actions of the subgroup and the lack of strategies by the counselor appear to be hindering the group process. The competency of the counselor to respond appropriately to the circumstances is in question. According to the Association for Specialists in Group Work *Best Practice Guidelines* (ASGW, 1998), group workers need to modify the techniques that are used to the group's type, stage, and ability to perform core group competencies. Subgrouping is a common dynamic in group counseling, and the counselor should be better prepared to manage the situation.

Open-ended groups often have members who have not been screened to determine their appropriateness to the type of group and are just as important to the practices of the group facilitator or counselor. There is no evidence in the incident presented that the counselor was able to identify that the members of the subgroup might not be appropriate given their denial and inability to form individual goals or goals compatible with the group.

The group included African American members. The counselor should, therefore, be sensitive to diversity effects on groups and individuals within groups. Counselors who lack information of cultural and diversity issues should take immediate steps to develop a working knowledge of diverse populations. The *Best Practice Guidelines* state that "group workers continuously seek information regarding the cultural issues of the diverse populations with whom they are working both by interaction with participants and from outside resources" (section B.8).

REFERENCE

Association for Specialists in Group Work. (1998). Best practice guidelines. *Journal for Specialists in Group Work, 23*(3), 237–244.

CHAPTER 22

MEMBER SELF-DISCLOSURE: "BUT THIS IS HOW I FEEL!"

The following incident explores the impact of member self-disclosure on group dynamics and considers the roles and responsibilities of group facilitators.

CRITICAL INCIDENT

Kelly A. McDonnell

Background

Lisa and Craig are interning at the local high school as part of their formal training toward earning a master's degree in school counseling. Both have nearly completed the degree requirements and are gaining additional clinical experience in small group facilitation.

They are about to begin a new group for students who are experiencing significant stressors at home that are having an impact on their school performance. Some of the prospective group members have experienced confrontations with teachers or peers, some seem to be withdrawing from friends and activities, and all are having difficulty academically. Lisa and Craig have received referrals from teachers and the school counselor. After conducting prescreening meetings with prospective group members, the facilitators organized a group of five members, including two females and three males. Brief descriptions of the members follow:

- Chris is a 15-year-old Caucasian female. Her parents are currently in the process of divorcing after several years of fighting and trial separations. As a result of this change in her family, it appears that Chris and her mother will need to move out of their home, and her mother is considering moving to another city to be closer to her family. Chris is an only child. She has been feeling depressed and has begun to withdraw from friends and her usual activities.

- David is a 15-year-old Asian American male. His mother has been ill for some time and needs much assistance and support. She gets fatigued easily and some days is incapable of getting out of bed. Because his father travels regularly for work, David usually takes care of his younger sister and the household chores while trying to help his mother as well.

- Ed is a 15-year-old Caucasian male. Ed's father just moved out of the family home, and Ed has heard his parents talking about divorce. This is not the first time that his family has experienced this behavior. Just 3 years ago his parents had marital difficulties, during which time his father moved out of the house for a brief time before they eventually reconciled. In response to these recent events, Ed has been spending a lot of time away from home. He often stays out late at night, gets into trouble with the law, and faces being suspended from school for fighting.
- Lauren is a 14-year-old African American female. Recently her elderly grandfather came to live with Lauren and her parents and two younger siblings. Her grandfather has Alzheimer's and has had difficulty caring for himself. This change has been stressful on the family, particularly Lauren's mother who has taken on the primary responsibility for her father's care. This has resulted in Lauren taking on additional responsibility for looking after her younger siblings.
- Marty is a 14-year-old Caucasian male. He lives with his older brother, his mother, and his mother's boyfriend. Marty's father died 3 years ago, and his family has been having a difficult time. Almost a year ago his mother began dating Joe, and about 2 months ago Joe moved in with the family. At first this relationship seemed to be a good one. Joe doted on Marty's mother and spent time with Marty and his brother, but recently Joe has become angry and physically aggressive. Marty, too, has become more belligerent at school and involved in a couple of fights with other students.

Both group facilitators have had an introductory class in group dynamics and theory, which included participating as a member of a personal growth group. Though Lisa and Craig have not previously led a group together, each has experience co-leading with a more experienced facilitator. They co-led groups during their initial practicum as well as during the current internship. In addition, both gained experience working with adolescents in individual counseling. A school counselor who has a Licensed Professional Counselor credential is supervising Lisa and Craig.

Lisa and Craig decided to offer a support group and sought to provide a safe environment in which members could feel comfortable talking about their difficulties. Because the leaders gathered good information during the prescreening sessions, they were aware that the members had some shared experiences. For example, Marty, Chris, and Ed are all experiencing some type of caretaker discord, and Chris and Ed also face the possibility of parental divorce. David and Lauren have taken on additional caretaking roles within their families, and Ed and Marty have been feeling angry and getting into physical altercations.

Although the leaders knew this information about the members, the members did not know about one another. The leaders hoped that by becoming aware of these commonalities, the members would gain support and understanding and not feel so isolated or alone in their circumstances or struggles. In addition, they thought the members might be helpful to one another in identifying ways of coping or dealing with their situations. The leaders were anxious to begin and get the group members talking about themselves so that the similarities could be revealed. Though the members were a little less enthusiastic and initially felt apathetic about being in the group, they agreed to participate. The leaders secured written consent from caregivers so that the adolescents could take part in the group.

The leaders worked together to plan the group format, logistics, and procedures. They decided that the group would meet for 1 hour, twice a week, and made arrangements to hold it after the last period of the day when all of the students could attend. Thus there was no need to secure a note from a teacher, or pull a student out of class. It was organized so that the group members could just go directly to the counseling office after their final class. The group was to meet in a small conference room in the counseling office area, which was quiet and provided an environment for confidentiality.

The leaders decided to meet for 4 weeks (eight sessions), at which point they would assess the progress of the group and individual members and consider whether to continue. This more limited commitment was designed to provide some time for the group members to get to know one another and develop a sense of oneness and cohesion, but not so long as to overwhelm the members with what might feel like a large obligation. In preparation for the first group session, Lisa and Craig drew on aspects of their training and talked about the importance of setting a positive tone from the outset. They wondered how willing these group members would be to talk about themselves during the first group meeting. Craig remembered an instructor talking in class about group member introductions that could help members begin to self-disclose and model group behavior. Lisa recalled seeing a video in which group leaders used different techniques (icebreakers) to help members share about themselves and begin to get to know one another. They decided this would be a good way to structure the first session. Lisa and Craig just knew that when the group members realized what they had in common and could talk about their difficulties they would begin to feel better.

The leaders were excited about this opportunity. Because they wanted to do a good job and provide an experience that would benefit the members, they worked hard to find activities that would help group members talk about themselves and their situations and get to know each other more quickly. Overall, they felt that group cohesion would enhance the accomplishments of the group.

Incident

At the beginning of the first session, the leaders introduced themselves and provided group members with information about their background, experience, and expectations for the group. They gave an overview of the time, duration, and format of group meetings, and they talked about the purpose of the group and how they thought it could be beneficial to the students. In addition, the leaders addressed confidentiality and its limits, and engaged the group in a discussion about group guidelines (norms).

After this initial activity was completed, the leaders led the members through a series of activities designed to get to know one another's names, ages, likes, and dislikes, as well as other information about each other. Although the nature of the information was superficial at first, the group members slowly began to share more personal information. Ed talked about his parents' fighting and their impending divorce. He shared that he has felt as if his life is out of control, and he has been worried about what will happen to his family. He indicated that he has not talked to anyone about what has been going on in his life. Chris had been attentive while Ed was talking, and the leaders thought they saw her eyes fill with tears. Though Chris had not said much during the session, she had remained engaged. Now it seemed that something in what Ed had said struck a chord with Chris, and she began to talk about her family situation. Though it was almost time to end the session, the leaders were hesitant to cut her off as she had said little up to this point and appeared to need to talk. Moreover, they did not want to limit her for fear she would withdraw and not open up again. Chris shared that her home life had been filled with fighting and that her parents were divorcing. Then she revealed that she and her mother might move away and talked about how scared and depressed she was in connection with that possibility. She began to sob openly at this point and seemed overcome with emotion. The other group members were very quiet. Lisa glanced around the room and noticed that some members were looking at the floor or shifting in their chairs, as if they were uncomfortable and did not know what to do. At this point Chris paused, lowered her head and then blurted out that she had even tried to hurt herself so that her mother would not make them move. The leaders made eye contact and looked at each other as if to say, "What do we do?"

Discussion

The leaders are in the position as facilitators of the group to work in the best interest of all the members. Particular concern arises when a group member like Chris discloses information that references possible harm to herself. Consider the questions that follow in terms of how the answers might contribute to Lisa and Craig making a decision about an appropriate course of action when faced with this challenging situation.

QUESTIONS

1. How might the leaders have responded to or addressed the group member's (Chris's) self-disclosure and effectively brought the group session to an end?

2. What factors contributed to Chris's self-disclosure? How did the leaders facilitate/contribute to her subsequent personal disclosure?
3. What suggestions do you have for the group leaders to avoid such a deep disclosure during the first group session?
4. What might be the impact on the other members and the group development as a result of this incident?
5. When selecting activities or exercises for use in a group, what factors should a group leader take into consideration?
6. What multicultural issues might a group leader want to consider in regard to group member self-disclosure?

RESPONSE

S. Lenoir Gillam

Chris's self-disclosure appears to have caught Lisa and Craig off guard. When she first began to speak, well before much disclosure could occur, the leaders could have cut her off by stating something like, "Chris, you seem to be relating to what Ed was saying, and it appears that you might like some time in group. Because we're at the end of this session, I'm wondering if we can bookmark this conversation for now and revisit it next session?" At that point, the leaders could have helped the group summarize and terminate the session. By acknowledging the importance of Chris's issues, her concerns are validated while the leaders model adhering to time limits outlined in the structure of the group.

The danger with this type of intervention is that there is no way to anticipate how serious the issues might be that will be prevented from surfacing. Obviously, if the leaders note that the client's welfare is in danger, they must intervene even if it means meeting with her after group to assess the degree of suicide risk. However, interventions that occur with individuals outside the context of group may lead to troubling dynamics later within the group. The fact that Chris's disclosure happened at the end of the session is not good for the client, for the other group members, or for the liability of the leaders.

Preventing this type of problem is important. Several factors led to this incident, and early leader interventions could have helped to circumvent it. One factor is that Ed was open about his family concerns during this session. Although the complete depth of his disclosure is unclear, it appears from the incident that he was quite open for a first session, especially after it was noted that members expressed some reluctance to participate. The fact that he was allowed to share his story in this manner probably communicated to others that higher risk disclosure was expected, or at least allowed, in these early sessions.

The goal of this session was to introduce an icebreaker to involve members and facilitate connections among them. The leaders should have structured the activity and process to prevent members from going into detail and into depth about their issues this early in the group's development. That is, early on leaders should consider using activities that are low risk, involve the group instead of focusing too much attention on any one member, and avoid deep disclosures from members. As the group progresses through stages of development, members can tolerate higher risk activities that lead to greater depth of exploration.

A second factor, assuming that Ed's disclosure was not too in-depth to be inappropriate for a first group (again, based on what is presented in the incident, it is unclear whether what Ed shared was too deep for the first session), is that Lisa and Craig missed opportunities to draw out Chris early in the session by noting her nonverbal responses to what Ed was sharing. If they had done a better job of scanning the members in an attempt to facilitate everyone's participation and to help members make connections with each other, then the leaders could have prevented Chris from waiting until the end of the session to raise new business.

A third factor is that, even if Chris began to share with the group earlier in the session, the leaders failed to intervene to prevent the depth of her disclosure. They could have diffused her affect by preventing such individual attention on her issues or by redirecting her to focus more on cognitive elements of her issues. In essence, she was allowed the opportunity to make these deep disclosures prematurely.

Attending to the issues just noted could have helped the leaders avoid the problems that ensued from this first-session deep disclosure. Other suggestions for the group leaders to prevent this kind of problem in the future include

- talking with members about the risks associated with group participation during screening;
- being clear with members during the first sessions about structure and ground rules, particularly the time limits of the session;
- preparing members earlier in the session for when each session will end (e.g., reminding them that there are 15 minutes left in the session);
- using low-risk exercises during early groups to model appropriate levels of disclosure;
- cutting off new business at the end of the session by validating the member's concerns and inviting the discussion to continue at the next meeting; and
- considering a different structure for the group format (e.g., weekly sessions for 8 weeks vs. meeting twice each week for 4 weeks, which for this support group might alleviate some of the intensity and allow the process to unfold more slowly).

Chris's disclosure at the end of the session is not an unusual phenomenon. Sometimes members may use raising issues at the end of a session as a defense to exploring those issues in much depth. It is important for leaders to anticipate these occurrences and do their best to prevent them.

As noted previously, this incident is likely to have some impact on group members and group development. Lisa picked up on the discomfort communicated by group members during Chris's disclosure, as evidenced by their nonverbals and lack of participation. Members are probably not prepared to deal with deep disclosure this early in the life of the group. Group cohesion will not have been established, and members cannot be expected to know how to respond appropriately to serious issues and strong affect. Once norms are established, cohesion is formed, people feel safer to take appropriate risks, and members can deal more effectively with their own and others' issues in group. In addition to feeling uncomfortable with others' discomfort, members may fear that they will be expected to disclose at the same level of depth before they are ready. Furthermore, in this case, they observed a lack of response to Chris's disclosure. They may infer that disclosure in this group results in little to no feedback and support from other members. In addition, this experience reinforces that members may not be able to rely on the structure set up by the leaders, given that the time limits were not observed. For all of these reasons, group development may suffer. The leaders, while attempting to facilitate cohesion by structuring sessions twice weekly, are likely to be sabotaging the forming stage of their group as a result of what happened in this session. Given the difficulty in forming this group, and the limited 4-week structure, this group will probably not realize the entire cycle of group development.

It is difficult to make exact comments about cultural issues in this group related to self-disclosure based solely on generalizations about race or ethnicity. However, it is important to remember that cultural differences do exist within this group and that members are likely not to perceive self-disclosure in exactly the same way. In fact, in this group, even intracultural differences in the way that self-disclosure is perceived could exist. Creating a safe environment in which people's differences are appreciated is likely to lead to an understanding of how members, regardless of their race, ethnicity, or gender, think and feel about self-disclosure and other issues. Leaders must be sensitive to peoples' differences and promote this sensitivity in group members as well.

RESPONSE

James J. Bergin

It is obvious that Lisa and Craig's assumption that "when the group members realized what they had in common and could talk about their difficulties they would begin to feel better" was erroneous, particularly as it pertained to Chris as she sobbed and spoke of attempting to hurt herself to gain her mother's attention. Moreover, the other members' silence and withdrawal of visual attention from Chris likely served to exacerbate Chris's negative feelings. Therefore, it was incumbent upon the group leaders to make an immediate intervention on Chris's behalf.

Specifically, Lisa and Craig should have reinforced Chris for her courage and honesty in sharing her story with the group and for having listened attentively to Ed while he described his feelings about his parent's divorce. In addition, because it was time for the group session to end, the leaders should have reiterated to the members the purposes of the group, described how Ed and Chris's courageous self-revelations were significant contributions to the group process, reminded the group of the importance of confidentiality, and then ended the session. Both Ed and Chris should have been kept after the session and debriefed in individual counseling sessions.

Beyond dealing with this immediate crisis, however, Lisa and Craig need to engage in a major overhaul of their group before the group sessions continue (if ever). Three important issues need to be addressed in revising the group, and should have been addressed before the group began: group composition, informed consent, and client safety.

Group composition. Given the information about each client that was obtained during the pregroup screening interviews, there should have been some question in the counselors' minds as to the readiness of each individual for group counseling and as to the compatibility of the group as a whole. Both Ed and Chris revealed that they were confronting divorce/separation issues, which were having an immediate impact on their lives. These issues should have been explored more fully and with greater confidentiality in individual counseling prior to placement in group counseling. Similarly, Marty's sudden physical aggression at school warranted a more private examination to determine readiness for participation in a group. Moreover, both Chris and Marty's situations were cause for further investigation, respectively, regarding possible suicide attempts and child abuse.

David and Lauren did have similar situations in terms of having to cope with family illness and to take on added responsibility in caring for siblings. Therefore, it might have been assumed that these two would benefit from group counseling that focused on caregiving and time-management skills. However, the counselors should have made additional inquiry prior to the group as to David and Lauren's feelings about their family members' illnesses and possible loss of life. Above all, the leaders should have explored the cultural values of each student regarding disclosure of family matters and addressed them individually prior to initiating group counseling.

Informed consent. This issue also needed to be addressed more fully. The counselors did not reveal to the clients the group's plan, purposes, format, and activities until the group met for the first session. According to sections A.3 and A.9 of the American Counseling Association *Code of Ethics and Standards of Practice* (ACA, 1995), counselors have responsibilities to inform clients about what takes place in the group counseling experience in terms of potential risks, benefits, limitations, and other pertinent information. Providing such information should be initiated during the pregroup screening and reiterated throughout the counseling process. Only then can it reasonably be assumed that a client's consent for group counseling is truly informed. Because these clients are minors, Lisa and Craig are well advised to have a written contract with the group specifying that each group member is committed to joining the group, maintaining confidentiality, working on self-improvement, assisting other group members to improve themselves, and following the group rules and procedures. This type of contract would have been particularly valuable to the leaders when the group members became uncomfortable with Chris's self-disclosures and withdrew their attention from her.

Client safety. Lisa and Craig did not exercise sufficient caution in providing for the safety of the group members. They rushed the process of the group, devoting little time to building rapport among the members before moving the group to the transition stage by encouraging Ed and Chris to self-disclose. The result was that both Ed and Chris were exposed to unnecessary risk, especially because the other group members had made no public affirmation of their commitment to help each other and to maintain confidentiality. Indeed, the counselors had only addressed the topic of confidentiality at the beginning of that first session, and had left the issue of members providing support for each other to be determined by whether or not the group members became aware of their commonalities. The counselors had a responsibility to the group members to assist the group in building trust and in teaching members to provide support for each other. By rushing the group process they failed to meet this responsibility.

REFERENCE

American Counseling Association. (1995). *Code of ethics and standards of practice.* Alexandria, VA: Author.

CHAPTER 23

MANIPULATION: "PAY ATTENTION TO ME"

*This incident explores some of the issues associated with manipu-
lation in a group counseling situation.*

CRITICAL INCIDENT

Virginia A. Kelly

Background

Jose and Sandy are counselors at a small private college located in an affluent suburban community. Sandy has grown concerned about the number
of young women who seem to express dissatisfaction with their bodies and
the extreme measures they seem willing to take in order to fit in with the
rest of their peer group. She decided to address this issue through a group
on wellness and healthy choices. She asked Jose to co-lead the group with
her because she senses that having both a male and female leader will
enhance the potential outcomes of the group experience.

Incident

Jose and Sandy begin the process of planning for the group. They seek referrals from cases with which they are familiar as well as from concerned faculty members and administrators. In addition, they advertise the group in
residence halls and in the campus newspaper. They want to limit selection
for the group to individuals who have not displayed characteristics or behaviors associated with full-blown eating disorders and who are not currently in
treatment for such a disorder. They are instead hoping to target students
who they perceive as at risk for an eating disorder diagnosis. They plan for
an 8-week group that they intend to be both psychoeducational and process
oriented. Their goals include the dissemination of pertinent information as
well as the provision of support and a forum for working through some of
the issues associated with the attitudes held by the group members.

When all of the plans had been made, Jose and Sandy began the group.
The group went well, and after the first two sessions, they were pleased with
the group composition and felt positively about the potential for helping
members. However, during the second session some fairly subtle but disturb-
ing dynamics began to emerge. One of the group members, Yvonne,
appeared to be extremely needy. Within virtually every conversation, she
expressed her association with the specific issue under discussion. For exam-

ple, Sarah, one of the group members, began to disclose regarding the nature of her difficult relationship with her mother. She described how demanding and critical she perceived her mother to be and stated, "It does not seem to matter how good I am. My mother always seems to find the negative; always points out what I did not do well." At this point, Yvonne broke in: "You think that's bad? My mother just doesn't even care. I can come home with straight A's and she won't even notice." This pattern with Yvonne repeated itself three more times within the session. It became clear that she was intent on redirecting the focus of attention to herself whenever she felt that another member might become the center of attention.

When Sandy and Jose discussed these dynamics at the close of the second session, they discussed the possibility of intervening and discussed their role and function in the group. However, they agreed that this was a tough situation and decided that they would remain conscious of these dynamics, but essentially observe the next session to see if the issue might be one that could be worked through by the group without intervention on the part of the leaders.

The third session proved even more of a challenge. Although Yvonne seemed to minimize her attempts at directly controlling the focus of the group, the manipulation of members seemed to increase. Throughout the course of this session, Jose and Sandy observed Yvonne cry, refuse to disclose the nature or cause of her upset, and threaten to simply stop eating. When one group member began to disclose that her older sister had suffered with anorexia, and was describing the impact that this had on her own attitudes toward these issues, Yvonne began to cry softly. When another member asked her what was wrong she replied, "Oh, nothing. Don't pay any attention to me." When at another point, Yvonne was asked to disclose what she was experiencing, she said, "It doesn't really matter anyway. Don't worry about me. I will be fine." And finally, at the very end of the session, while the group was closing for the evening, she made the statement, "I am thinking that I will just stop eating altogether. What's the point anyway? Nobody really cares about me."

Discussion

After this session, Jose and Sandy both expressed their discomfort with Yvonne's behavior. Although they experienced Yvonne's behavior as manipulative, they felt strongly that she was vulnerable and at risk. In addition, they were convinced that her behavior was not good for the rest of the group. However, they agreed that they did not know where to go with this and ultimately decided to see what direction the group might take.

QUESTIONS

1. What are the responsibilities of the group leaders regarding Yvonne's manipulative behavior?
2. How do you describe the suitability of these two counselors for leading such a group?

3. What are the leader issues exhibited in this incident that may interfere with the success of this group?
4. How might the leaders proceed with the group?
5. What other ethical issues are important regarding the planning, implementing, and postreview of this group session?

RESPONSE

Craig S. Cashwell

The case of Yvonne is complex and requires an intentional response from Jose and Sandy. Yvonne's behavior in the second and third sessions seems quite different, but the common thread is that all of these behaviors appear to be manipulative and attempt to force responses from other group members. For the purpose of my response to this incident, I am assuming that Yvonne's behavior is primarily occurring outside of her conscious awareness. Although there are several important issues, such as theoretical orientation, experience at facilitating process groups, and expertise related to eating-disordered behavior, that may affect the responses of group leaders to clients who are attempting to manipulate the group, there remain some general guidelines as to how to respond to Yvonne.

One issue involves preliminary screening. Though Jose and Sandy were highly intentional in determining the focus of the group and the characteristics of a desirable group member (e.g., at risk rather than having a full-blown eating disorder), little information is provided about how they screened group members for acceptability into a group based on other factors, such as personality dynamics. It is important to note, though, that these preliminary screens often are not helpful. Clients who become manipulative in group may know how to make a good first impression, or may only become manipulative in the context of the group and may, in fact, be the clients most in need of the group process (Kottler, 1994).

Other issues relate to the climate of the group that has been established by the leaders and the stage of group development. Because Jose and Sandy have chosen to facilitate a group that combines psychoeducation and group process, the group is likely to be still in an early stage of developing its norms. Though it would be ideal for members of the group to confront Yvonne's manipulative behavior, this may or may not happen contingent on the personalities and previous experiences of other members of the group. If this does not occur spontaneously, Jose and Sandy have a clear responsibility to address this issue in the next group session.

There are a number of reasons why Yvonne's attention-seeking behavior needs to be addressed. One is that if Jose and Sandy continue to adopt a wait-and-see approach to Yvonne's behavior, waiting to see what the group does, things are likely to get worse. In behavioral language, attempts to extinguish this attention-seeking behavior only by providing no reinforcement are likely to fail for several reasons. Among these are that it is likely that other group members will inadvertently reinforce the attention-seeking behavior. It is common for group members to respond to "nobody likes me" statements with reassurances that they do indeed care for the individual. This is the nature of this game, and if it plays out this way, group members will be reinforcing Yvonne's undesirable and manipulative behavior. Even if group members refrain from providing this reinforcement (on their own or at the direction of Jose and Sandy), this intervention is likely to be incomplete. When reinforcement is withdrawn, manipulative clients often engage in an extinction burst, in which the manipulative behavior initially increases in frequency, intensity, or duration in an effort to receive the reinforcement, in this case attention and reassurance from others. Yvonne might increase the frequency of her attention-seeking behaviors or move to a different attention-seeking behavior, such as suicidal ideation, to gain the attention. Such an extinction burst may be particularly difficult for this group with only five sessions remaining and given that portions of these sessions will be dedicated to psychoeducation.

It seems, then, that Jose and Sandy have some clear responsibilities in the fourth session. It will be important to assess the seriousness of Yvonne's threat to quit eating. My response focuses on dealing with the manipulative behavior and is predicated on the assumption that Yvonne does not have a full-blown eating disorder and is not in clear and imminent danger. Although the exact method chosen to challenge this behavior depends on the theoretical approach of the group leaders, an approach that I recommend is that Jose and Sandy work together to create relationships between members of the group and Yvonne that are characterized by mutuality, openness, and directness—a true dialogue. Though some group leaders may choose to start the next session by revisiting Yvonne's disclosure from the end of the previous session ("…What's the point anyway? Nobody really cares about me"), I recommend waiting until this type of behavior/disclosure occurs again (and I believe it will) so that the approach can be phenomenological and work in the present rather than the past. Responses from Jose and Sandy may include process observations ("I notice that when Yvonne says 'nobody cares about me,' many of you begin to reassure her that you do care about her") or facilitative questions ("What are your reactions to what Yvonne has said?"). The intention of either type of facilitative response is to engage Yvonne in a genuine and conscious interaction with group members to raise her awareness about her manipulative behavior and how this keeps her from having honest and healthy relationships with others. In this way, Jose and Sandy are facilitating a group process rather than waiting to see if it will occur without facilitation.

If these efforts are unsuccessful, the group leaders may choose to use skills of immediacy to confront the manipulative behavior themselves. If so, the two primary considerations are which of the two group leaders should challenge the behavior and whether this should occur within the group session or outside. The dynamics of co-leaders who are male and female may set up a family reenactment (Gladding, 2003). Based on information that

Jose and Sandy have about Yvonne at that point, an intentional decision should be made as to who will confront this behavior. The decision to challenge within or outside of the group session is a difficult one. Although challenging this behavior within the group is ideal, as it will allow other group members to provide feedback and enter into a dialogue with Yvonne, the ultimate goal is for this behavior to stop. Jose and Sandy must make a clinical decision about whether Yvonne can enter into this type of genuine dialogue in front of the group and intervene accordingly.

Another possibility is to consider individual counseling sessions for Yvonne concurrent with the group. This is a common approach to working with manipulative clients (Kottler, 1994). Though removing Yvonne from the group and providing only individual counseling remains an option should her manipulative behavior have an adverse effect on other group members, concurrent individual and group sessions are preferable. This approach may help Yvonne become more aware of her manipulative behavior and engage in behavior rehearsal within the group.

RESPONSE

Robert K. Conyne

Labeling group members usually leads to practice-oriented problems. The group co-leaders, Sandy and Jose, are justifiably concerned about Yvonne's functioning in the group and need to generate a variety of intervention choices from which they may choose. Yet if I were their supervisor, I might encourage them first to develop some alternative explanations and understandings of Yvonne. Avoiding being locked into any one descriptor for behavior, especially a negative one such as manipulation, can serve to provide a more comprehensive and expansive view and, therefore, a broader range of intervention possibilities.

Protecting and promoting member welfare, that is, Yvonne's and that of each of the other members, is the sine qua non of the Association for Specialists in Group Work *Best Practice Guidelines* (ASGW, 1998; Rapin & Conyne, 1999). The effects of Yvonne's behavior, then, both in terms of what it reveals about herself and in relation to other group members, need to be accorded highest priority by the co-leaders. Yvonne's expression of potential self-harming behavior at the close of session three is, at the least, troubling. The co-leaders certainly hold a responsibility for appropriately addressing Yvonne, but within the context of the group and its members. It is important for co-leaders to frame their work ecologically (Bemak & Conyne, 2004). How consistent is Yvonne's behavior in group with her behavior out of group? Certainly, Yvonne seems to behave within this group in ways that are drawing undue attention and concern, ways that are becoming more dysfunctional to group progress. What are these ways? What are the contextual circumstances within and outside the group? What contextual circumstances surround other forms of behavior she exhibits? Are there positive interpersonal behaviors that Yvonne has displayed? Again, what are the circumstances? Can these positive behaviors form a basis for launching co-leader interventions? These kinds of questions would have been appropriate for co-leader processing following session two and might have led to a more guided session three, in which an escalation of Yvonne's attention-seeking behavior might have been better anticipated, along with a range of intervention possibilities from which to select.

The *Best Practice Guidelines* (ASGW, 1998) call for leaders to devote considerable time and care with planning and processing, as well as in performing group leader functions within group sessions. These co-leaders are stumbling across performance challenges that might well have been eliminated or at least reduced through conducting more effective planning and between-session processing.

Improved screening during planning could have withdrawn this more preventively oriented psychoeducation group from being offered to Yvonne, whose tendencies toward high neediness might have been discovered. Including her within this type of group (psychoeducation group type for prevention purposes) was from the beginning a poor fit for someone who might benefit more from a counseling or a psychotherapy group (ASGW, 2000).

Engaging in a higher quality of between-session processing, as opposed to what appears to be a fairly cursory effort in this important activity, can provide the opportunity for better in-group performance. Inadequate co-leader between-session processing has contributed to a higher risk situation in the group and to a greater opportunity for both individual and group failure. Group members and groups themselves are not like fine crystal, easily broken. They tend to be resilient (Kell & Mueller, 1966), allowing mistakes to be turned into successes if proper leader processing occurs (Conyne, 1999).

What about Jose and Sandy's preparation for leading this group? Is their training and experience compatible with this type of group, concern area, and population (ASGW, 1998, sections A.3.a; B.2)? Being a counselor in itself is no particular signal that the answers to these questions will be affirmative. In addition, even the most thoroughly prepared group counselors must develop a good working relationship to be able to function well as co-leaders. There is no evidence presented attesting to the quality of the working relationship between Jose and Sandy.

Sandy and Jose's only partial adherence to the *Best Practice Guidelines* (ASGW, 1998) in group work weakened their capacity to function as effectively and as appropriately as is needed. If the case of Yvonne had not emerged, some other challenging issue would surely have exposed this deficit.

What should the leaders do in this situation? They need to do a lot between session three and session four in terms of processing what has happened, what the contexts were, what the effects seem to be, what intervention choices may be possible, and what strategies are most likely to be successful going into session four. I want to place the emphasis here on between-session processing (ASGW, 1998, section C). Performance options can then be created and selected much more responsibly and with better outcomes. Certainly, the leaders need to be open with their supervisor. If no supervisor is available (which is too often the case), they should seek the consultation of a trusted and respected group work colleague (section A.8.d) and refer to valuable group work texts and guidelines for assistance.

I anticipate that from this improved between-session processing, the co-leaders will develop a more comprehensive and nuanced understanding of the situation and of the possibilities for their own action, which may enable them to see what the group did.

REFERENCES

Association for Specialists in Group Work. (1998). Best practice guidelines. *Journal for Specialists in Group Work, 23*(3), 237–244.

Association for Specialists in Group Work. (2000). *Professional standards for the training of group workers.* Retrieved from http//www.asgw.org

Bemak, F., & Conyne, R. K. (2004). Ecological Group work. In R. K. Conyne & E. P. Cook (Eds.), *Ecological counseling: An innovative approach to conceptualizing person-environment interaction* (pp. 195–218). Alexandria, VA: American Counseling Association.

Conyne, R. (1999). *Failures in group work: How we can learn from our mistakes.* Thousand Oaks, CA: Sage.

Gladding, S. T. (2003). *Group work: A counseling specialty* (4th ed.). Upper Saddle River, NJ: Merrill Prentice Hall.

Kell, B., & Mueller, W. (1966). *Impact and change: A study of counseling relationships.* New York: Appleton-Century-Crofts.

Kottler, J. A. (1994). Working with difficult group members. *Journal for Specialists in Group Work, 19,* 3–10.

Rapin, L., & Conyne, R. (1999). Best practices in group counseling. In J. Trotzer (Ed.), *The counselor and the group: Integrating theory, training, and practice* (3rd ed.). Philadelphia: Accelerated Development.

CHAPTER 24

ASKING A MEMBER TO LEAVE THE GROUP: "THE LAST STRAW"

This incident illustrates some of the issues involved when a group leader finds it necessary to ask a member to leave the group.

CRITICAL INCIDENT

Carolyn Henshaw

Background

Sarah is a certified addictions counselor with 3 years of experience at the outpatient recovery program of a nonprofit hospital. She is a recovering addict with 5 years of sobriety. Clients are self-referred, employer referred, or court ordered into the 12-Step-based program, and most undergo detoxification in the hospital's inpatient unit before beginning their recovery. Daily group therapy is a major component of the treatment. The group is open, with clients rotating in and out of the program at various times to complete the required 6 weeks of treatment. Clients participate in other types of group experiences as well, including psychoeducation. Clients must maintain abstinence and negative urine drug screens during treatment. The current group that Sarah leads has eight members, including two women and six men, until the two women dropped out, each after attending only two sessions. Four of the members have been in the group for approximately 2 weeks. Harry has just arrived.

Incident

Harry has come into the treatment program (his third time in 2 years) and announced that he has no intention of giving up his addiction but is only attending to meet the requirements of a court order and to "avoid going back to prison." He is somewhat charismatic and seductive in his behavior and is often the center of attention during breaks in which group members appear to talk freely and generally have a good time. He is quiet during group time, volunteering little and speaking only when asked. After his third week in the program he continues to test positive on his urine drug screens and now must attend daily 12-Step meetings (versus the usual two per week) as a requirement for remaining in the program. Harry reports that he attends his 12-Step meetings as often as possible and is doing his best to complete the additional assignments as required by Sarah.

Sarah's style of counseling is intrapersonal. Most of the group time is spent attempting to work on individual issues. There is little interaction, and Sarah has been reluctant to push the members because several have become angry when confronted. The discussion often becomes storytelling, and the members remain avoidant of feelings. When negative feelings arise, the members glance at one another and then remain silent. From time to time during a session Sarah will ask members to respond to what another has shared, but after a sentence or two they are quiet again. She has told them on several occasions that it is their group and they are responsible for giving feedback to one another, but often it seems that most of the talking is provided by Sarah, and the sessions are more characteristic of a psychoeducation group.

On this day, 1 1/2 hours before the group is to begin, Harry storms into Sarah's office, argues loudly with his wife, who has come for the weekly family education session, and requests a brief consultation with Sarah beforehand. Sarah asks Harry to leave and he does, but when he comes back for the group session later, he is inebriated. Sarah tells Harry to report to the office for a urine drug screen and says she will see him there shortly. Sarah continues to lead the group in the usual opener of checking in physically, emotionally, and spiritually. There is no discussion of the incident during the next half hour, and then Sarah tells the group members to take a 10-minute smoke break. She meets with Harry and tells him that this incident is the last straw, that he has continued in noncompliance and has exhausted all possibilities of being allowed to remain in the program. She tells him that she does not want to deny him services and therefore will refer him to a related treatment program, if he so chooses, where he will receive the same treatment but in a different group setting. Harry calls a friend to take him home. When the group reassembles, Harry is not present. Several of the group members ask about him and express concern, to which Sarah replies, "He left!"

Discussion

On the next day Harry was absent. When the other members asked where he was, Sarah said, "He didn't come in today." A week later the group members heard through the grape vine that Harry had transferred to another program. Sarah did not discuss the incident with the group members, and they eventually stopped asking about him. Sarah continued to lead her therapy group, with the current members completing their 6 weeks and new members arriving periodically.

QUESTIONS

1. What group leadership strategies or styles might have prevented the escalation of the events surrounding the necessity of removing Harry from the group?

2. What issues on Sarah's part may have interfered with a successful group experience for Harry and the other group members, and what recommended actions could help resolve these issues?

3. What was the impact of Harry's behavior and removal from the group on the other members?
4. What are other issues or ethical considerations involved in processing the event (asking Harry to leave the group) with the remaining group members?
5. How would you describe the group dynamics that may have played a part in Harry's behavior and subsequent removal from the group?

RESPONSE

Jean Sunde Peterson

Regardless of leadership style and group type, whatever happens in a group can be processed. Such processing, of a member's or group's disruptive behavior or of a surprising disclosure, gives group members an opportunity to reflect on their experience, articulate feelings and thoughts, and hear what other participants are thinking and feeling. Sarah missed many opportunities to process group events, thereby inhibiting individual and group growth in response to those moments.

Much might have been gained had she facilitated group members' exploration of feelings and thoughts related to Harry's coming to the group inebriated, of Harry's absence when the group reassembled, and of Harry's absence at the next meeting. Those were events in the life of the group that undoubtedly had an effect on group members, perhaps provoking anxiety connected to earlier abandonment, discomfort related to the inebriation, relief at Harry's absence, or resentment over the fact that Harry was causing commotion.

Besides demonstrating that feelings can be shared and validated, group processing might have moved members toward empathy with Harry as they explored their own anxieties related to recovery and control, their skepticism and hope regarding group participation, and, potentially, their concerns about the charismatic Harry. Processing various occurrences during Harry's first group sessions might have helped him to feel connected with other members, even though his controlling behaviors might have persisted.

Processing group experiences could have occurred in connection with group phenomena, not necessarily related to Harry's actions, and might have helped Sarah move the group beyond stories. The fact that this was an open group probably meant that group dynamics varied greatly from meeting to meeting. Sarah could have helped members process that reality, especially in terms of their response to change, such as changes in group membership. In fact, Sarah may have discovered that this open group, in this outpatient hospital setting, could benefit from a more flexible and different leadership style, especially because her intrapersonal style did not seem to be effective in addressing individual needs and intrapersonal conflicts, including Harry's, not to mention the apparent interpersonal issues within the group.

When the two women dropped out, especially if there was no warning, Sarah might have explored group members' reactions to the fact that the only two women in the group elected not to continue. She could have helped the group to process the glances surrounding expressed negative feelings. Sarah could have used regular end-of-session processing to explore members' anxieties about actively participating in a group, get feedback about her leadership style, and learn about members' wishes, needs, and discomforts, especially because her leadership apparently did not generate comfortable and sustained dialogue. In addition, a small amount of self-disclosure by Sarah, not about her own recovery but related to the group's effect on her, might have modeled an important behavior and promoted similar risk taking by group members.

It is easy to speculate that Sarah's lack of skills, or her own issues, inhibited her from asserting herself as a group leader, from encouraging or modeling appropriate risk taking, from moving to a more effective leadership style, or from engaging Harry or the others in processing. Sarah missed opportunities to explore and attend to Harry's and other members' concerns. She was not skilled enough to use group time equitably, to move members beyond storytelling, for example. No matter how frustrating Harry's behaviors were, Sarah's responsibilities to him and to the group included inviting participation, protecting group members, respecting individual differences, and processing what occurred in the group. Appropriate processing could have given all members an opportunity to gain skills and important insights and might even have resulted in Harry's becoming more compliant in treatment and becoming more comfortable with group participation.

Harry's noncompliance in several areas of treatment, including his inebriation, appears to have warranted dismissal from the group. Sarah appropriately and ethically offered to refer him to another program. However, according to the information presented, her poor leadership prevented group members, including Harry, from maximizing their gains from the group experience. Group leaders should not expect members to know how to behave when they enter a group, particularly when experiencing stressful transitions. It is the leader's responsibility to lead, to facilitate interaction, and to model and encourage effective group behaviors.

RESPONSE

James V. Wigtil

Sarah could have employed other group leadership strategies or interventions to prevent the escalation of events related to removing Harry from the group. Her repertoire of group leader interventions should build on her intrapersonal style and be broadened to include both feedback and process interventions to take advantage of the power and curativeness of group member interaction. At a more basic level, though, it is not clear what ground rules Sarah introduces to group members. A no-storytelling guideline can help members eliminate their antitherapeutic behaviors and increase the therapeutic behaviors they are offering in the group. Cross talk, or giving feedback, is another ground rule that can help Sarah's group members benefit from the therapy group experience. These and other basic group rules can help her direct the group members toward behaviors that create positive group norms, and the rules should be reintroduced each time new members join this open group.

Sarah should model the giving and receiving of feedback. A dynamic that may need to be addressed in this group is that the members could be confused and only offer corrective feedback at the expense of positive feedback or think confrontation has to be negative and accompanied by anger. Sarah could have helped the members understand that confrontation should be done with an act of caring and support, which is especially important for group members dealing with substance use and abuse issues. This could be the reason why the two women members dropped out after two sessions. Member unwillingness or inability to give or receive feedback, coupled with storytelling, could be indicative that this group is in the transition stage and lacks qualities such as trust and cohesiveness. Leader process interventions that focus on Harry, other members (interpersonal), or the group itself, and on what seems to be occurring in the here and now, can help move the group beyond the plateau Sarah is experiencing.

In addition, Sarah should consider providing some cognitive frameworks for change or other meaning attribution functions to the group, such as interpreting, explaining, and clarifying. For example, Sarah could respond to Harry within a whole person framework (that is broader than the spiritual, emotional, and physical check-in she typically uses) or costs in one's life framework related to substance use and abuse. This approach could help Harry with a holistic inventory of past and present costs, such as the relationship with his wife, costs around participating in this treatment program for the third time in 2 years, and costs around his current use of alcohol and other drugs.

Issues on Sarah's part that may have interfered with a successful group experience for Harry and other group members include the issue that Sarah is a recovering addict with 5 years of sobriety. Does she have a recovery program, and importantly, how is she working it? This is an important topic to explore in peer or more formal supervision. For example, a parallel process could be operating in that Sarah may be stuck or plateaued in her life, and this is also occurring in the group. Sarah may need to add counseling or therapy to her own recovery program so that she can more appropriately deal with her personal recovery issues. Although Harry has responsibility for what he did both within and outside the group, Sarah should examine her role in Harry's unsuccessful treatment/group therapy experience. Further, the level of Sarah's leadership knowledge and skill is not clear, so an appropriate focus in supervision is on her group leadership strengths, her growth areas, and her plans to address the growth areas. For example, does Sarah have trouble dealing with feelings and therefore cannot encourage the group to deal with feelings?

Asking Harry to leave the group is significant to both Harry and the other group members. This should be addressed graciously by making the experience as therapeutically constructive as possible (Yalom, 1995). Sarah might have anticipated that the members would experience anxiety related to abandonment, rejection, and dislike, and that she would get little support from the group, even though the members might have agreed that Harry should have been asked to leave. If this indeed occurred, Sarah should have helped the group move from this interpretation to one in which it was clear that in her actions she had had the best interests of Harry and the remaining group members in mind, and that Harry had been responsibly referred to another treatment program.

The impact of Harry's behavior and removal from the group is not fully clear. However, one possible impact is member ambiguity and a possible message that "In this group we will not discuss when a member misses or departs from the group." Sarah was succinct and brief in her comments on Harry's leaving the group, and she provided one-line responses when asked by group members. Sarah may have taken Harry's failure in treatment personally, or she unintentionally glossed over the impact of Harry's leaving on the rest of the group members. Importantly, three members had 1 week left of the 6-week therapy group. An additional leader concern may be the group history (legacy) that will confront new members as they are integrated into the group.

Sarah should consult the American Counseling Association *Code of Ethics and Standards of Practice* (ACA, 1995) regarding group work (section A.9) and termination and referral (section A.11) for further direction on these issues related to her work with this group. In addition, the Association for Specialists in Group Work *Best Practices Guidelines* (ASGW, 1998) sections regarding self-assessment (A.3.a), professional development (A.8.c, A.8.d), self-knowledge (B.1), and therapeutic conditions and dynamics (B.4) will provide effective direction to her. An important ethical and legal consideration for Sarah is abandonment. It is not clear if Harry's referral to another treatment program was mutually agreed upon, as is typical in traditional group therapy. It is also typical to mutually agree on a member's departure from the group, although in this case Sarah had a responsibility to terminate Harry based on the treatment program's philosophy. Because his termination occurred quite abruptly, she further needed to suggest an appropriate referral rather than abandon him.

It is not evident, though, what procedures staff were to follow in terminating someone from the treatment program. Because the therapy group is the main part of a larger treatment program, perhaps Sarah should have processed the possible termination of Harry with her supervisor or staff colleagues, even if this was not a program requirement.

Group dynamics that played a part in this critical incident and that merit increased emphasis include the here and now: establishing and maintaining positive therapeutic norms, an interactional approach to group therapy, parallel processes with the group leader, and the availability of curative factors.

Paying attention to denial, minimization, and resistance; taking advantage of natural group synergy and energy; and working through problem member behaviors are other group dynamics that merit increased emphasis in this critical incident.

REFERENCES

American Counseling Association. (1995). *Code of ethics and standards of practice.* Alexandria, VA: Author.

Association for Specialists in Group Work. (1998). Best practice guidelines. *Journal for Specialists in Group Work, 23*(3), 237–244.

Yalom, I. D. (1995). *The theory and practice of group psychotherapy.* New York: Basic Books.

CHAPTER 25

CONFIDENTIALITY: "DON'T TELL"

This incident explores the issue of confidentiality in the group work setting and how it might be different than in an individual counseling setting.

CRITICAL INCIDENT

Mary A. Hermann

Background

Susan is finishing her first year as a school counselor in a suburban high school. She is eager to provide developmental guidance activities related to current student issues, and she has a strong desire to incorporate her training in group counseling in her work with students. The number of students at her school who have been struggling with eating disorders has appalled Susan. Accordingly, she implemented a counseling group for sophomore girls that counselors, teachers, and coaches identified as at risk for developing an eating disorder.

Incident

During the first session, Susan remembered that her group counseling professor stressed the importance of establishing a safe, trusting environment in the initial group session. Sensing that the group members were a bit anxious and tentative about disclosing information, Susan told them, "I assure you that everything you say in this group will remain confidential." Susan noticed that after she made that statement the group members began to relax and speak more freely.

When Susan asked the group members if they felt pressured to be very thin, one of the members, Selena, began to cry. Selena explained that she is passionate about dancing. She takes lessons, dances with a local dance company, and is a member of the high school dance team. She told the group that she has been under a lot of stress because her English term paper is due next week. She added that when she is under stress, she eats more than usual. Three days ago her father told her that he thought she was putting on some weight. He told her that if she gained any more weight he was going to quit paying for her dance lessons. Selena confessed that she has not eaten anything since then, and she feels weak and depressed. But the dance team weigh-in is the next day, and she needs to "make the weight." If she does not make the weight, Selena said, she has "no reason to live."

Immediately after the session, Susan called Selena's mother to express her concern over Selena's suicidal ideation. At dance team practice that afternoon, a group member told her friends on the dance team to be nice to Selena because she is suicidal. Another member of the group told Selena's English teacher that she is worried Selena is so stressed out over the term paper that she might "do something stupid."

Discussion

Selena is upset because she feels that her privacy has been violated. She only spoke about her dilemma because Susan had promised that everything said in the group session would remain confidential. Now Selena thinks she hears members of the dance team gossiping about her, and she is sure she is the topic of conversation in the teachers' lounge. Selena thinks soon everyone at school will know her personal business and will think that she is a nut case. Furthermore, according to Selena, her mother is freaking out because she thinks Selena is suicidal.

QUESTIONS

1. What are your thoughts on whether it is ethical for a group leader to assure group members of complete confidentiality?
2. What are the exceptions to the general requirement that counselors keep group member disclosures confidential?
3. What are a counselor's ethical obligations when a group member makes a reference to suicidal behavior?
4. How might the issue of confidentiality become more challenging in certain settings such as school settings?
5. What can group leaders do to promote confidentiality?

RESPONSE

David M. Kaplan

The editors of this book asked me to respond to two group counseling critical incidents. In my response to the other one, Dual Relationships: "I Think I Know You," I stated my conviction that the vast majority of ethical dilemmas in counseling revolve around the single issue of informed consent. So it is not surprising that Susan's mistakes center on problems with informed consent. What is informed consent? It simply means that clients have the right to know the rules and to withdraw at any time if they feel that the rules are not in their best interest.

Susan needed to tell Selena (and all group members) the rules, including the rules about confidentiality. This should have been done both in writing (as an informed consent brochure) and verbally before any counseling took place. Why in writing? Because, contrary to our opinion as counselors, clients and students do not hang on to our every word and so need a document that they can refer to in order to review the rules. In addition, a printed informed consent brochure with a sign-off sheet for your files provides documentation in case any questions are raised later by parents, supervisors, courts, or insurance companies. Susan may feel that as a school counselor, informed consent brochures only apply to other types of counselors. Let me assure all readers that school counselors have the same responsibility to construct informed consent brochures as any other type of counselor. Students have the same right to informed consent as clients in a mental health, substance abuse, private practice, or any other setting. For an excellent discussion about the construction of an informed consent brochure, I refer you to the book, *The Paper Office* (Zuckerman, 2003).

The informed consent rules that Susan neglected to tell to Selena and the other group members revolve around confidentiality. Confidentiality in group counseling cannot be guaranteed. The lack of ability to assure confidentiality is acknowledged in the American Counseling Association *Code of Ethics and Standards of Practice* (ACA, 1995), which states in section B.2.a that "The fact that confidentiality cannot be guaranteed is clearly communicated to group members." Why is this so? For the obvious reason that a leader cannot control the disclosures of group members outside the group. The counselor can certainly set privacy norms, and group participants can agree to keep statements within the group. However, there are no guarantees that members will not tell their friends, family, teachers, and others what occurred during group sessions. That is why Susan was wrong to state to the eating disorder group, "I assure you that everything you say in this group will remain confidential."

Susan was also wrong in making the statement because it fails to let the students know about the exceptions to confidentiality. The Association for Specialists in Group Work *Best Practice Guidelines* (ASGW, 1998) mandates in section A.7.d that "Group workers define confidentiality and its limits (for example, legal and ethical exceptions and expectations; waivers implicit with treatment plans, documentation and insurance usage...and that legal privilege does not apply in group discussions (unless provided by state laws)."

The ACA Code of Ethics states in section B.1.g that "When counseling is initiated and throughout the counseling process as necessary, counselors inform clients of the limitations of confidentiality and identify foreseeable situations in which confidentiality must be breached." Therefore, Susan needed to inform every student before the group began about the specific situations in which confidentiality would be broken. One of those would be when clear and imminent danger is present (section B.1.c). If Susan had done that, she would have been able to let Selena know that her lack of eating for 3 days and suicidal ideation constituted the clear danger that had been discussed with group members. She then could brainstorm with Selena the best way to inform her mother. Why should Susan involve Selena in the decision about how mom is informed? She should involve her because it allows Selena to be involved in her counseling. It allows Selena to ask her mom not to tell her friends and therefore avoid the embarrassing aftereffects cited in this incident. It is the only way that Susan has a fighting chance to keep Selena from feeling betrayed and therefore to keep a relationship. All of these reasons support the importance of informing clients about the disclosure of confidential information when it is required (SP-9).

RESPONSE

Mike Hubert

Confidentiality is essential to building a foundation of trust upon which individuals can engage in the risky business of self-disclosure. Groups, in which respect for the privacy of information is the norm, reduce the risk of harm and encourage self-disclosure by members. This results in increased trust and willingness to reveal and address thoughts and feelings that place the individual in a more vulnerable yet changeable state. However, promises of complete confidentiality in a school group counseling setting is an unethical practice that demonstrates disregard for the principles outlined in the American Counseling Association *Code of Ethics and Standards of Practice* (ACA, 1995, section B.2.a) and the American School Counselor Association *Ethical Standards for School Counselors* (ASCA, 1998, section A.2.f). Counselors are taught to recognize the importance of these principles, but who taught the members of Selena's group? We have no way to guarantee the privacy of information shared in a group. Selena's fellow group members do not have to adhere to our professional standards and may choose to inform friends and teachers.

Protecting a client's privacy is foundational to providing effective counseling, but it is not the only underlying principle in counseling that an ethical practitioner must consider related to confidentiality. There are times when revealing information obtained in counseling is appropriate and necessary to protect the client or another individual from harm. Some counselors sign contracts with schools whose policies or governing statutes require releasing confidential information to building administrators. Counselors must consider the balance between the student's rights and best interests, as well as those of parents (ASCA, 1998, sections B.2.a, B.2.b, B.2.c). In addition, a student may request a release of private information to a third party, such as a parent or therapist. These exceptions are based on the ideal that parents, the school, and the state must share responsibility in protecting minors from harm.

Selena's expression of suicidal thoughts has triggered a process of decision making that the counselor in this group must begin. Ultimately, it will be the counselor Susan, not Selena or the other group members, who will make the assessment and determination of what is necessary to protect Selena from harm and what information must be shared with whom. In a situation such as this, Susan and other group members may continue to explore and clarify with Selena what is behind the words "no reason to live." However, when an individual reveals intent to do harm, the counselor must ensure that she engages the group member directly on what has been revealed. For Susan to do less might communicate either fear or disinterest resulting in Selena increasing her disconnect from life. This point in the group process would be a good time to reaffirm both the need for and limits of privacy within the group.

Susan retains a responsibility to meet with Selena individually to make a complete assessment as to the degree of risk to her life. As part of that assessment, Susan should consider consultation with someone expert in the diagnosis and treatment of eating disorders. Our training as school counselors does not automatically provide us with the skills necessary to handling the complex issues related to a health condition such as an eating disorder. Both of the ethical codes (ACA, 1995, section C.2.a; ASCA, 1998, section E.1.a) speak directly to working within the boundaries of the practitioners' professional competence. A complete understanding of the impact of such a health condition, combined with the suicide ideation, would be helpful to Susan in making a decision to share confidential information.

Should Susan make the determination to reveal what Selena has shared in the group to protect Selena from harm, Susan must first discuss her decision with Selena. Susan is responsible for reviewing how she has reached her decision to the degree that Selena can understand and to attempt to empower Selena to take the appropriate next steps in helping identify and contact others, such as Selena's mom, who may have a responsibility and capacity to protect her from harm. The responsibility for the counselor to ensure that needed steps are taken is not conditional upon the student's agreement with the counselor's decision, but Selena's acknowledgement of her personal risk would create a degree of ownership that may help motivate her to receive any needed assistance.

In most cases, those individuals needing to act on behalf of a student in imminent danger will include parents (not necessarily in cases of suspected abuse within the family) and a designated mental health specialist or agency that can provide a safe and secure environment. The school counselor may have an institutional requirement to share information with the building principal. It is imperative that disclosure include only as much information as necessary to obtain needed interventions consistent with section B.1.f of the ACA Code of Ethics. We must continue to value confidentiality even when it is necessary to limit it.

A school setting is a challenging environment in which to ensure confidentiality. Students may be in the same counseling group, share the same classes, and serve on the same dance team. Compartmentalizing confidential information shared in a group from other contexts can be challenging for teens.

Working within her ethical responsibilities as a school counselor, Susan must adhere to district and school policies as well as the lawful requirements of building supervisors. However, if Susan finds that her ability to provide ethical services is at odds with a building or district policy/directive, counselors are under an obligation to support and protect against any infringement not in the best interests of students (ACA, 1995, section D.1.l; ASCA, 1998, section D.1.a).

Likewise, parents often expect that protecting information shared in a school counselor's office should not apply to their real and perceived rights to know what the counselor has learned from their child. So the school counselor is tasked with helping parents, administrators, and teachers to respect the need for confidentiality as a counseling tool, and not as a means to either undermine the interests of parents or reduce counselor accountability in a school. This author has found enthusiastic support for providing the conditions of counseling, including confidentiality, as the result of implementing a comprehensive, developmental counseling and guidance model within the school and district. Designing and implementing a counseling program that openly addresses the needs of all key stakeholders will result in respect for the norm of confidentiality.

Susan should implement both a verbal and written disclosure process prior to the initiation of any counseling group. As part of the prescreening process, she should outline conditions and limitations of a counseling group. This kind of discussion is consistent with ethical standards (ACA, 1995, section A.3.a; ASCA, 1998, section A.2.a) and offers a platform for stressing the importance of confidentiality within a group as well as its limitations, which include the "harm to self or others" that led to Selena's sense of betrayal by her counselor Susan. The counselor should ask whether an individual believes he or she will be able to keep information revealed in a group as confidential. Some students may have difficulty keeping such secrets, and may be better suited for individual counseling services. Informing a prospective group member that confidentiality cannot be fully enforced is critical.

Finally, Susan has a responsibility to reinforce the importance of confidentiality at appropriate times within a group, such as the beginning and ending of each session. If individual members identify some anxiety about whether they can comply with the expectation of confidentiality, this creates a great opportunity to discuss who they might want to tell, what they would tell, and their purpose in telling. Ultimately, however, if an individual group member feels he or she may not be able to fully comply, a proper termination and referral from Susan to an individual form of counseling is in order. This protects the group as well as the exiting member.

REFERENCES

American Counseling Association. (1995). *Code of ethics and standards of practice.* Alexandria, VA: Author.

American School Counselor Association. (1998). *Ethical standards for school counselors.* Alexandria, VA: Author.

Association for Specialists in Group Work. (1998). Best practice guidelines. *Journal for Specialists in Group Work, 23*(3), 237–244.

Zuckerman, E. L. (2003). *The paper office* (3rd ed.). New York: Guilford.

CHAPTER 26

DOMINATING MEMBER: "YOU DON'T UNDERSTAND HOW DIFFICULT THIS IS FOR ME!"

This incident outlines a situation within a longstanding, open-ended group composed of eight addicted impaired professionals with narcissistic traits, one of whom has significantly dominated the group.

CRITICAL INCIDENT

Ford Brooks

Background

This relapse prevention group is composed of impaired professionals (two physicians, one nurse, three lawyers, one teacher, and one police detective) who have been mandated by their licensing/certification boards for ongoing counseling in lieu of losing their license/certification. Most of the members have been in this outpatient group for approximately 2 1/2 years, meeting once per week for 90 minutes. The group is composed of six Caucasian men and two Caucasian women, and it is cofacilitated by a Caucasian male and female. Prior to becoming a member of this group, each group member has participated in at least three inpatient treatment experiences and at least two outpatient alcohol and drug treatment programs in their lifetimes. Each of the group members is required to be urine tested by their respective certification/licensing boards on a random basis. At least half of the group members have relapsed once since beginning the group experience. All are attending at least three Alcoholics Anonymous (AA) or Narcotics Anonymous (NA) meetings per week in addition to the group, along with receiving individual counseling. Group members are admitting their addiction and, for the most part, have moved through the denial that they can control their use of chemicals.

Incident

One of the group members consistently dominates the group, taking a great deal of time and energy from the group each week. Many of the group members, however, appear to find comfort in his behavior as they do not feel the need to bring up current personal issues, and use the dominating member as a way to avoid exploring those issues in the group sessions. The dominating group member as well as other group members have met attempts by the cofacilitators to intervene with the dominating member with resistance.

The cofacilitators know that many of the group members are struggling with their recovery, yet the dominating member pulls the focus away from the group. The dominating member recently returned from long-term treatment after having relapsed and losing his job at a local law firm. He had been back from treatment approximately 1 month when he reentered the group. Prior to his relapse he had been a member of the group for almost 3 months and had exhibited similar dominating behavior.

The most recent interaction in the group went as follows: Check-in of group members was made; however, the dominating member started with the check-in and then continued to talk about his week in detail. "You know, this has been a long and difficult week for me. I learned that I've lost my job for sure and that the relationship with my wife is probably going to end in divorce. I don't know what I will do without her and my children." Group facilitator response: "I hear a great deal of pain and uncertainty in your voice and would like to explore this after we finish check-ins with the rest of the group. Is there one particular issue you would like to focus on?" Dominating member: "I have so many issues to talk about...ever since I was released from the hospital, I feel so alone and struggling. I continue to attend AA and meet with other AA members:..." (he continues to keep the focus on himself). Cofacilitator: "It sounds as though you have a great deal on your plate; what would you like to focus on in this group tonight?"

After two focus questions, the dominating member continues for the next 20 minutes and describes how difficult his transition from treatment has been. This leaves half of the group members to check in with and minimal time to interact. The cofacilitators, although trained as group counselors and knowledgeable about addiction recovery, are perplexed by this situation. They continue to struggle with the dominating member and realize that the group members are sitting back and not addressing their recovery issues.

Discussion
The group facilitators are poignantly aware after this particular group that the dominating member is wrestling with issues of control and emotional vulnerability. Although he is talking about the situation, the feelings associated with them are not readily shared. In addition, it is beginning to be apparent that a few of the group members are tiring of the dominating member's behavior, yet are unable to confront it. The facilitators are concerned about the welfare of the other group members and question whether it is ethical to allow the dominating member to continue in the group unless his behavior improves.

QUESTIONS

1. Is the dominating member appropriate for this group? How might you address the facilitator's ethical concern?
2. What could the cofacilitators do differently in their pregroup assessment to prevent or address this behavior of the dominating member?

3. When the dominating member was returning to the group, what could the cofacilitators have done differently to address his behavior?
4. What process comments could be made by the facilitators to bring the group into the discussion?
5. What would you as a cofacilitator do to let the dominating member back into this group after he had just returned from treatment?

RESPONSE

Ann Vernon

Although the dominating group member clearly needs this group experience to work on his issues, it is apparent that his behavior is inappropriate because he is taking up too much time at the expense of other group members. Although some of the other members appear to be comfortable or even support his behavior to some extent because it takes the focus off them, it nevertheless does prevent them from addressing their own issues and working toward their individual recovery.

There are several ways to address the facilitators' ethical concerns about this member. First, they could approach him individually prior to the next session and indicate that they realize he has an exceptionally high amount of stress at this time and can benefit from talking in the group, but that it is important that other group members have an opportunity to have equal time. The facilitators could try a casual approach, telling him that they understand that he may not even be aware of how dominant he has been while asking him if he could please be mindful of it and work hard on giving others a fair share of time. This is a low-key confrontation that may not work because he has narcissistic traits; however, it can be a first attempt to change his behavior and therefore allow him to remain in the group.

A second approach is for the cofacilitators to do more to confront the dominating member. For instance, because the empathic response might not slow him down, they might try holding up a hand and cutting him off, saying something like, "We realize you have things to share, but we need to move on now; we will come back to your issues at a later point as time permits." And then if he keeps on talking, they will have to repeat this procedure and encourage the next person to begin sharing.

A third approach is to empower the group members to confront his behavior because it is beginning to wear on a few of them. One way to do this is to use more process questions when the dominant member begins to talk on and on. For example, a facilitator could say something like, "I'm sorry to interrupt you, but I'm wondering how the rest of you are feeling about what is happening right now?" In the event that no one speaks up, the leader might model a confrontation by saying, "If I were a member of this group and were attending it in order to help me deal with my own substance abuse and relapse issues, I might feel cheated if I wasn't able to address them in this group because so much time is being taken up by one member." If these approaches do not work, and if the member continues to dominate at the expense of other group members, it may be necessary to remove him from the group.

In the pregroup assessment, the cofacilitators should clearly state the purpose of the group and indicate that the advantage of a group format is that everyone has an opportunity to share issues of concern and receive feedback and assistance from other group members. They should be explicit that it is not appropriate for one or two persons to dominate the group. It is possible that they will pick up on this individual's behavior during the assessment, and they could point out to him that even in this meeting he seemed to do most of the talking but that in the group setting this will clearly not be appropriate.

Because this individual had been dominating prior to relapsing and being in long-term treatment, it seems imperative that before letting him rejoin the group the cofacilitators meet with him and give him clear feedback on what they had observed about his behavior prior to leaving the group for treatment. They should indicate that this is a difficult time for him, and that he may need more individual counseling for a period of time because the group experience is intended to involve everyone in dealing with issues. They should never ask him to begin first with the check-in; they should reiterate the rules at the beginning of each session, and they should be more assertive if his behavior does not change.

Process comments that the facilitators could use include the following:

- "I notice that several of you seem a bit impatient with what is happening within the group today."
- "I sense that it may be more comfortable to let one person talk so that you don't have to deal with your issues, but I'm wondering how that is helping you?"
- "I'm wondering how you are feeling about what has happened so far in our group today...."
- "I'm aware that so far today nobody has said anything except_____."

Comments such as these will hopefully put ownership back on the group members and redirect the process.

If the dominating group member's behavior is as bad as it seems, the cofacilitators could consider having this individual sign a behavioral contract in which he agrees to talk less and listen more. It might be helpful for him to have some sort of nonverbal signal from one or both of the facilitators, something to help him realize that he was being too dominant and serve as the signal to stop. They might consider using a timer, giving everyone a few minutes of check-in time, and then negotiating with the group on how to give more equal time to all group members throughout the session. If this procedure seems too rigid, the facilitators could even use a technique such as tossing a ball to a member to start the discussion, and the member in turn toss it to another member, and so on. Another idea is for the cofacilitators to introduce more structure into the group by assigning each member to be in charge of a group session. Or they could introduce a topic for discussion or some type of experiential activity that would help other group members identify and deal with their own issues relative to this topic. Although the danger of this is that they "stay in their heads," it might encourage more participation by all members.

In the event that none of these suggestions works, the facilitators will need to discuss other options with the licensing board because the group treatment is mandated.

RESPONSE

Diana Hulse-Killacky

This incident presents a number of implications for leaders to consider both for the present group situation and for the preparation and facilitation of future groups. The presence of a dominating member is not unusual in therapeutic, task, and educational group settings. There are many reasons why people take up air time in a group. Some individuals use talk to clarify their thoughts; others talk because they are focused only on their own concerns and have a need for uninterrupted attention from other members. Some individuals talk to reveal information that may or may not be appropriate for a particular group setting.

In this case the dominating member may not be suitable for the current group experience. Although groups can be and are powerful mediums for therapeutic work, the question arises, "What is the best fit for this person at this time?" This group member appears self-absorbed and so overwhelmed with his own concerns and issues that his ability to be concerned with the needs of others or simply to listen to others is obscured. He may be best suited for individual counseling, which can address his pressing concerns. He may need some guidance and clarification about the purpose and function of group work. It is difficult to know if he has ever had any pregroup preparation and participated in any group screening interviews. From the description in the incident, it seems that the group experience is not working for him, for the other members, or for the facilitators.

The group facilitators have options to consider with regard to this current situation. The American Counseling Association *Code of Ethics and Standards of Practice* (ACA, 1995) addresses the match between group member needs and goals and the group's goals (in section A.9.a). Here the leaders should carefully assess whether the dominating member's goals and needs are truly compatible with the goals of the current group. If they decide they are compatible, then the leaders need to review the norms for the group and guidelines for participation in the group. If norms and guidelines were not developed and agreed upon, the leaders need to address these points immediately. For example, what are the guidelines concerning attendance and participation? Have the leaders promoted conversations about each member's expectations for the group experience? Have the leaders discussed such issues as taking turns, providing all group members the opportunity to speak, and agreeing that one person talks at a time? The facilitators may need to define (or redefine) what a check-in involves. Check-in rounds are usually brief methods that give each member an opportunity to share an idea, need, or concern. Such rounds provide leaders with information about how to structure the conversation for that particular group session.

The fact that this dominating member is taking up lots of time in the group and that others may or may not be concerned about this situation is not unusual. If I am in a group and someone else does all the talking, then I do not have to participate and thus reveal anything that might lead to a focus on me. However, the potential contribution of the group process is thwarted by factors described in this incident. Have the facilitators communicated to the group members that they want to hear from everyone and that group members benefit through the interaction of all members?

It is clear that the facilitators need some review of basic skills for keeping conversation going in the group. Knowing how to cut off unproductive communication in the group is an important skill to master. In addition, leaders need to develop skills for drawing out less vocal members and to demonstrate other skills such as linking, holding the focus, and shifting the focus. It is clear from reading this incident that these skills need to be quickly implemented.

In terms of future planning, this incident points to the importance of screening. As noted earlier, group work is not indicated for everyone, and this dominating member client may need other counseling interventions before he is ready to be a productive and useful group member. If individual screening procedures are not feasible or practical, then leaders need to think strategically and use the first and perhaps second meetings to conduct in-group screening sessions to prepare members for the purpose and function of this particular group. Such preparation gives the facilitators an opportunity to explain their expectations for the group and to enlist the members' expectations. Leaders can explain how the sessions will proceed from the check-in through the working phase and can educate the members to the various behaviors the leaders will exhibit to keep the group on task. Through this type of preparation the leaders can introduce the need to hear from everyone. Leaders can conduct a quick assessment by finding out who likes to talk, who talks easily in front of others, who prefers to listen and reflect, and who does not like to talk. Leaders can explain that their use of certain skills such as drawing out, cutting off, and shifting the focus will help the group stay on task and ensure the participation of all members. Through these various discussions, the leaders are clarifying the purpose of the group and the reasons behind their own behaviors. As a result, the members know in advance what to expect in this particular group setting. The leaders need to develop a conceptual map for the effective practice of group work. They need to identify what they think is conceptually possible. Having a clear conceptual map will help guide their behavior in the group. Ultimately the leaders want to work with the members to create an environment that is likely to maximize the probability that all group and member goals and needs will be met.

REFERENCE

American Counseling Association. (1995). *Code of ethics and standards of practice.* Alexandria, VA: Author.

CHAPTER 27

HOSTILE MEMBER: "HOW DARE YOU!"

This group situation addresses the potential challenges involved for beginning counselors when a group member becomes hostile during a session.

CRITICAL INCIDENT

Louisa L. Foss

Background
Juan and Elise are counseling practicum students who co-lead a group for court-ordered domestic violence offenders. Both students have successfully completed two practica in individual counseling and are pursuing this third practicum for the purpose of acquiring group leadership skills. Both students have had limited experience with groups, including group counseling coursework and a variety of task groups. Juan, in particular, tends to be fairly shy and slow to become involved in the group process. Juan and Elise have been leading this open group for offenders for approximately 3 months. Most group members complete the group between 16 and 23 sessions. All group members are male.

Incident
The group is composed of nine men, all court ordered for domestic violence charges. Eight of the nine men are present for this session. One individual, Jeff, just learned during the last session that because of his lack of progress, he will need to complete an extra 10 sessions beyond the typical 16-session requirement.

The men enter the room, and Juan asks the members to do their typical check-in: "You know the routine, go ahead and share with the group what your name is, your partner's name, and how it is you ended up here." Some group members openly admit their violence against their partners, but others need to be questioned further by the group leaders. Elise jumps in a great deal of the time to facilitate this mild confrontation. From the beginning of the group session, Juan notices that Jeff is visibly agitated and more negative toward the group leaders than is typical. Elise asks Jeff to take his turn at check-in, and he replies, "This group is really just a bunch of bullshit, and everyone's just saying what they need to say to get out of here. Okay, what is it you want me to say?" Jeff is staring at the floor, bouncing his knees and wringing his hands. Elise repeats the question adding that if Jeff has been court ordered, then the group must assume that he has done something wrong, "Well, Jeff, you know, you're here, so that leads me to believe that you can get something out of the group. It's part of your contract to keep working on goals, so what do you want to do?" Jeff replies, "Well, you just keep extending the contract, lack of progress, what does that mean?"

Elise waits for Juan to begin to defend the co-leader decision, and Juan replies in a shaky and quiet voice, "Jeff, you know that you weren't admitting that you hit Judy, and that's one of our requirements, so we really need to have you do that." Jeff gets up out of his chair, raising his voice, "It's like I said, I didn't do anything wrong. She fell into my elbow. It's not my fault!" At this point, both leaders are visibly shaken and become silent. Members of the group begin to appear uncomfortable. Elise states in a low, quiet voice, "Jeff, I need you to sit down now. If you don't sit down and calm down, we'll have to have you removed from the group." Jeff does not de-escalate, but instead accuses Elise of being just like his partner, Judy, and mutters something profane about Elise under his breath. Juan remains silent.

Discussion

When a group member's hostility is acted out in the group, it can result in an uncomfortable situation for the group leaders as well as the members. Feelings of confusion, worry, surprise, lack of confidence, and perhaps fear serve to challenge the group leaders as they work toward facilitating an appropriate course of action. Answers to the following questions may help the group leaders in finding the most appropriate way to deal with this incident while at the same time serving the best interests of all the group members.

QUESTIONS

1. How can hostile group behavior be defined?
2. At what point in the incident do safety issues become more pronounced?
3. What strategies should be developed to address the hostile group member at this time?
4. How can the group members effectively process the hostile member's behavior, given their own presenting concerns?

RESPONSE

Edward Neukrug

Hostility in a group is usually manifested by some kind of blame game. For instance, hostility can be directed at another group member, the group leader(s), a real person in the individual's life, or an imaginary person or event ("It's all my dad's fault! If he was present when I was a kid my life would have turned out so much better"). Hostility can sometimes result in a group member becoming a scapegoat, particularly if more than one group member is focusing anger toward one particular person in the group. Regardless of the type of hostility being expressed, it is most likely masking some deeper feelings. Further, it is an indication that a group member is coming close to some important issues that are in some way threatening, and it is a convenient defense against uncovering this sensitive material. In fact, within the group setting members will often become hostile rather than leave themselves vulnerable by opening up. This is particularly the case if trust has not yet been built in the group.

Safety issues in a group such as the one presented in this incident are, of course, a concern from day one. In this group the members have a track record of harming others and of not being able to control their anger. Thus the group leaders should be particularly careful concerning anger getting out of control. As might be expected, such vigilance is supported by the American Counseling Association *Code of Ethics and Standards of Practice* (ACA, 1995) in reference to protecting clients: "In a group setting, counselors take reasonable precautions to protect clients from physical or psychological trauma" (section A.9.b). It is critical that group members learn that they can express their feelings without their feelings being associated with violence. The leaders should be wary of Jeff's anger and vigilant about keeping tabs on it. At the same time, it gives the leaders an opportunity to have Jeff express his feelings in meaningful ways. For me, the key is to keep a precarious balance between letting Jeff express his feelings and assuring that he is not going to get to the point at which he could act out. I am particularly keyed in on how angry Jeff is toward Elise because the anger toward her is likely to be mimicking his anger toward his partner and women in general.

Jeff is asserting that he did not hit Judy. The rules of the group state that the members must admit they have been abusive to their partners. Jeff and the group leaders are in a double bind. To assert the rules and try to confront Jeff into admitting he hit Judy is not respecting Jeff, could lead Jeff to withdraw from the group physically or emotionally, or could lead him into becoming so enraged that he could potentially act out in the group. Jeff has stated he did not hit Judy, and for him to suddenly change his statement would be particularly difficult. Typically, abusive men are burdened by large egos, and it would be demeaning for Jeff to suddenly admit he had been lying all along. It is unlikely that an intervention would lead Jeff, at this point, to admitting this behavior. Thus Jeff and the leaders are at a stalemate.

Although I am likely to believe that all the group members have been abusive, I am left with a gnawing feeling that perhaps Jeff is telling the truth. As unlikely as this is, if this were the case, I am asking Jeff to admit to something he did not do, and the rules of the group give me no other way to respond. Thus if I were the leader of this group I might respond in a somewhat unusual manner in this case. Modeling genuineness, I might say to Jeff and the group, "You know, my experience has been that men who have been in this group have been abusive toward their partners, and I suspect that you have been, too. However, you are telling me otherwise, and I want to believe that you are being honest with me. As the rules stand, I have no choice but to ask you to admit to this behavior. However, perhaps we need to revisit the rules. Let's open this possibility up to all of the group members and see what they think and where we might take this."

This response does a number of things. First, it allows Jeff to be left with his ego intact. I am saying to Jeff that even though it is quite unlikely, perhaps he is telling me the truth. It gives Jeff an out. Second, it allows the power of the group to take over. I am asking the group members to help me with this dilemma, and I am saying that I will respect where they go with this. Showing that I trust them, I believe, is critical to my ability to build solid, respectful relationships. Third, I am modeling openness and genuineness. For these men, such behaviors, especially exhibited by a man, are probably few and far between. I am showing them a new way of living in the world and dealing with conflict and suggesting that it is possible to come to a resolution by talking a problem through. Fourth, I am modeling uncertainty, a behavior that most of these men probably have a difficult time expressing. Men are taught to be definite and self-assured, even when they know they are wrong. Thus I am showing all of the men, especially Jeff, that it is all right to act in another way. In fact, in a rather indirect but powerful manner, I am saying to Jeff, "I admit that my rules may be flawed, that I am flawed, and it's okay if you admit that you are flawed too."

The issue of ground rules, and being able to change them, is key to this incident. Usually, as a natural part of the group process, members will challenge the rules of a group. An effective leader must learn how and when to stand firmly by the group's rules, and when it might be more effective to be flexible. This is not always an easy decision, and it is critical that the group leader recognize the issues involved when making a decision of this kind.

RESPONSE

Suzanne M. Hobson

Hostile behavior within a group may be defined as a form of resistance that involves the intimidation or ridicule of another group member/leader. As in Jeff's case, hostile behavior may take the form of raising one's voice, using profanity to describe the group process, name-calling, or standing above group leaders (or members) as a form of intimidation. Hostile behavior does not always take such an overt form. At other times hostile behavior may take less direct forms. Anger-based changes in attendance, sarcastic comments, uninvolved body language, and passive-aggressive behavior may also signal hostility in a group member (Corey & Corey, 2002).

It is essential that counselors recognize hostile behavior as a form of resistance and respond to it in a therapeutic, rather than defensive, manner. Indeed, the effective handling of resistance is essential to a positive outcome of the group counseling process. Recognizing and helping the group member understand the source of hostility is key to the effective handling of this situation. Resistance, including hostile behavior, most often reflects an attempt by a group member to increase feelings of safety and decrease feelings of vulnerability. In doing so, the group leaders need to consider ways in which they might increase the feelings of safety for the hostile group member and the other members of the group.

In this group, Juan and Elise must respond to Jeff in a caring and inquisitive manner while simultaneously enforcing some clear boundaries. To err on the side of only communicating caring and interest in Jeff's concerns is to miss an important opportunity to address anger management in the here and now and to condone the escalation of anger into physical intimidation and verbal aggression. Clearly, the purpose of this group is to help these offenders learn more effective ways in which to manage feelings of anger and to internalize the importance of not violating the boundaries of others. To err on the side of only enforcing boundaries is unlikely to help increase Jeff's feelings of safety and is instead likely to maintain or intensify his resistance. Similarly, although the enforcement of boundaries may temporarily assist other members in feeling safer and more protected, it is likely to result in decreased feelings of safety by all members of the group. Indeed, Jeff may not be the only person in the group who believes it is "just a bunch of bullshit." If this is the case, other group members now have an opportunity to vicariously learn how the group leaders will handle any future objections or concerns they may raise. By allowing such complaints to be aired and explored, the possibility of accomplishing true change rather than using group time to go through the motions unproductively is increased dramatically.

It is my belief that Juan and Elise did not adequately balance their response to include both caring and limit-setting qualities, and that the lack of balance contributed to Jeff's escalation. In analyzing the interactions, I notice that Jeff expressed hostility as he expressed criticisms of the group and questioned his need to be there. In response, Juan hesitantly confronted Jeff with the reality of the court order but did not acknowledge Jeff's anger and resentment. This response did not effectively address Jeff's safety issues, and predictably, he escalated his hostile behavior in an attempt to be heard.

After being confronted by both Elise and Juan, Jeff escalated to the point that he got out of his seat and raised his voice. It is at this point that safety issues may emerge. Jeff seems to be struggling with self-control and management of anger. Although this clearly made Juan and Elise uncomfortable and is likely to do the same for many counselors, it is important to recognize that this is a moment of therapeutic opportunity. Elise and Juan now have the opportunity to help Jeff regain control over himself, to process what happened for him internally, determine how he manifested this behaviorally, and begin to take steps to learn new ways of being. Despite the discomfort inherent in such a moment, this is the moment counselors might hope for! Here Jeff brings his outside behavior into the group. The group has now become a social microcosm within which Jeff and other members can work toward new ways of managing their behavior, thoughts, and emotions.

One way to help shift this session toward greater productivity is for Elise to now respond to Jeff with a better balance between offering caring and support and enforcing clear boundaries. Using Landreth's (1991) steps for therapeutic limit setting, Elise might respond with the statements in the Table 27.1.

In addition to directly responding to Jeff's confrontation, it is important that Elise and Juan utilize the power of the group. Knowing that each group member was court mandated because of domestic violence, these leaders should understand that everyone in the group now has an opportunity to learn and to model new skills or attitudes. Once Jeff has de-escalated, it will be helpful to invite group members to share their observations. Questions to facilitate a discussion about anger management and hostile behavior might include

- "What did you see happen with Jeff just now?"
- "When did you first notice that he was angry?"
- "What signs do you notice in yourself that first signal anger?"
- "How did Jeff's feelings escalate to the point that he got up, yelled, and called me names?"
- "What would you do if you got that angry here?"
- "What's the difference between being entitled to your own feelings and violating the rights of others?"

Table 27.1. Steps for Therapeutic Limit Setting

Steps for Therapeutic Limit Setting	Statement
1. Acknowledge the feeling or desire.	"Wow, Jeff! I can see you're really upset by this and I'm sorry if it seemed as if I wasn't taking your concerns seriously. I'd really like to hear more about it. I want this group to be a safe place for you to share your concerns."
2. Communicate the limit.	"But I also want this group to feel safe for the rest of us. And right now, I'm not feeling safe. It's not okay for you to stand over me, call me names, or yell at me."
3. Target acceptable alternatives.	"If you'd like to express your doubts about this group and about your need to be here, you're welcome to do so. But I need you to stay seated and to treat us well as we talk about it. Or, if you prefer, we could wait until next week's meeting to talk about it."

It is important that the group leaders use this encounter as an opportunity to explore member feelings of ambivalence. If, as Jeff suggested, "everyone's just saying what they need to say to get out of here," the group is unlikely to be productive without direct attention to issues of resistance, ambivalence, and denial. Some questions that might be useful in discussing member resistance and ambivalence about change include

- "If you have ever questioned the value of being here, what was that about?"
- "What keeps you coming?"
- "Is there any reason besides the court mandate that you want to be here?"
- "What would you like to get out of the group?"
- "How do you want your relationship with your partner to change?"
- "What part of you feels defensive and judged for being here?"

To react in such a way requires a fair amount of confidence on the part of the group leaders. This confidence may be developed as a result of experience, supportive supervision, or an understanding that the confrontation represented an opportunity and not a problem. As new counselors, Juan and Elise were understandably shaken by this encounter. My hope is that they will seek supervision and explore ways in which they could respond in the future. In addition, Juan and Elise will do well to regularly meet to plan and rehearse for group meetings. In both supervision and the planning meetings, Elise and Juan could benefit from debriefing, from anticipating problems, from practicing new skills, and from coordinating their roles in each session.

In anticipating problems, supervision and planning meetings could address typical problems often encountered when counseling mandated clients. For example, mandated clients are often upset and angry about being mandated and tend to express anger toward both the counselors and the system that mandated their attendance in counseling. Additionally, mandated clients often fail to agree with the system about what the problem is and whose responsibility it is. This supports denial and creates more challenge for counselors during the engagement process. Similarly, clients who have a history of domestic violence often have anger management difficulties and tend not to respond well to challenges to their power. Male perpetrators of violence against women frequently have difficulty respecting women, including female counselors. Before beginning the group counseling process as cofacilitators, Elise and Juan should have already used supervision and planning meetings to anticipate these issues and plan for these predictable problems.

Even with such planning, Juan and Elise are novice counselors and may encounter some difficulties in managing this group. It will be important for them to use these meetings to practice and rehearse new skills and to coordinate their roles within the group sessions. In practicing new skills,

Elise and Juan may want to role-play ways in which to verbally respond to group member anger, challenges from group members, and expressions of denial. As group leaders, they will want to have frank discussions about their own individual strengths and weaknesses and to discuss skills that they each want to develop while facilitating this group. Finally, in coordinating their roles, Juan and Elise will benefit from discussing situations in which each person should step in to assist the other counselor and situations in which each person should step back and allow the other counselor to proceed. Knowing when to step in is especially important in groups that may present safety risks so that the co-leader can serve appropriately as backup in order to maintain safety. Knowing when to step back is important in any group in order to have the leaders avoid being split by group dynamics. Stepping back and allowing one's co-leader to proceed is essential in these splitting moments and communicates trust and cohesion between the co-leaders.

By using group supervision and planning meetings for these purposes, Juan and Elise will increase their ability to anticipate problems, develop skills, and coordinate their efforts. The result will be increased effectiveness in their counseling efforts and improvement in their skills as group counselors.

REFERENCES

American Counseling Association. (1995). *Code of ethics and standards of practice.* Alexandria, VA: Author.

Corey, M.S., & Corey, G. (2002). *Groups: Process and practice* (6th ed.). Pacific Grove, CA: Brooks/Cole.

Landreth, G. L. (1991). *Play therapy: The art of the relationship.* Muncie, IN: Accelerated Development.

CHAPTER 28

RESCUING:
"EVERYTHING WILL BE OKAY"

This incident explores some of the issues group leaders may encounter when members do not allow each other the opportunity to experience and explore certain emotions.

CRITICAL INCIDENT

P. Clay Rowell

Background
Joe has been a counselor for 2 years working with students at a small, liberal arts college. He recently joined a group in private practice that specializes in relationship counseling. The counseling firm has decided to start a 10-week closed group for male clients who are experiencing divorce. Each group session will last for 50 minutes. At his former job, Joe led a support group for freshmen dealing with college transition issues. His coworkers have asked him to facilitate the group under supervision of one of the Licensed Professional Counselors at the firm. Joe will also work with this counselor for his supervision requirements for licensure.

Incident
The group had been assembled prior to Joe's employment. The counselors had screened male clients they had engaged in individual counseling and comprised a group of six who were in the process of divorce and wanted to join the group. Joe gathered the screening notes and discovered that each of the six men were in their 30s, had been married for more than 7 years, and had college degrees.

The first night of group entailed the getting-to-know-you details. The group discussed norms, and the members decided they would have an open format, with no topics brought in by the group leader. This was a little unnerving for Joe, as he had always presented topics with his college group. However, he felt it would be a wonderful learning process, and he could obtain help from his supervisor.

During the second session, each of the members described his personal reasons for being in the group. The men mostly discussed the facts of their relationships. Joe felt the group was somewhat resistant but appeared to be connecting with each other as the session progressed. He knew the group was still in its initial stage and hoped to deepen the focus as the weeks went on.

That focus became quite deep the night of the 3rd week. The members began to explore feelings about their relationships. They were sharing coping strategies with each other, and there were no apparent conflicts between any members. Joe was feeling good about the group process and progress of the members. He was feeling good about himself, too. After all, he had never led a group like this before, and everything was going so well.

During this third session, one of the group members, David, mentioned that he was having a hard time being alone. He said that he did not feel as if anyone was on his side and that he was having difficulty communicating with his family about the divorce. Joe recognized he had an opportunity to do some linking. He asked, "Is there anyone else here who can identify with the feelings of isolation that David just shared?" Joe thought to himself, "This should inspire good discussion." "I do," replied another member, Calvin. "Would you share those feelings with the group?" Joe asked.

Calvin began to speak emotionally in a way that Joe did not expect. Calvin quietly said, "Everyone in my life has cut ties with me. My ex-wife has gained full custody of our child, and I am only allowed to see my son 1 weekend a month. My ex-wife refuses to allow my son to talk with me at any other time." Joe observed the somber faces in the group. Calvin, looking at the floor, continued, "My parents want nothing to do with me. They are religiously against divorce and view me as a failure. Calvin was visibly shaken. As tears began to roll down Calvin's face he finished, "I don't know what to do." Steven, a group member sitting next to Calvin, patted him on the shoulder. "It'll be alright," he said. "You'll get through this fine." "Yeah," replied David, "I'm sure your wife will calm down and let you talk to your son more. She's just angry right now." He added, "And your parents are your parents. They'll love you no matter what. Just give it some time, Calvin." "I agree," said another member, Damien. "Don't cry. I know it will work out."

Feeling good the group members were showing compassion for each other, Joe asked other members to share their personal struggles with isolation until the session was over.

Discussion

After the session ended, Joe thought about the powerful moment that had occurred in the group. He felt great that a member was willing to open his feelings to others. He also thought how wonderful it was to see the other guys help Calvin the way they did. "Now that is deepening the focus," he thought. He decided this was the breakthrough he had been waiting for, although admittedly he was not prepared for it during the third session.

Reviewing the session with his supervisor, Joe commented on how the members were progressing. He told his supervisor the men were beginning to discuss feelings and seemed to be relating well to each other. He mentioned how easy it seemed to lead this group because of the members' willingness to share and explore.

QUESTIONS

1. How can rescuing be a negative force in the group dynamics?
2. How does rescuing affect the progress of individual members?
3. How does rescuing affect the group as a whole?
4. How could Joe have handled the situation differently when the other group members rescued Calvin?
5. How can Joe use the willingness to rescue others as a positive in the development of the group?
6. Is rescuing ever okay? Why or why not?

RESPONSE

Gerard Lawson

Using the term *rescuing* for the incident just described is something of a misnomer. In a group, rescuing more often has to do with the rescuer's discomfort than with actually assisting the group member in question. Whenever a group member rescues another there is the implicit message that some sort of behavior or expression is uncomfortable or unacceptable. Although there may be momentary relief for the group member, a rescue of this sort is something like a Band-Aid on an open wound. The rescue does not do anything to help in healing; it merely covers up that which is difficult to face.

When rescuing is allowed to happen in a group setting, the material that is actually able to be processed in the group becomes significantly curtailed and often limited to only those issues that are comfortable for the group members. Yet issues that are uncomfortable are often fertile ground for progress and growth in a group setting. In addition, rescuing behaviors are often initiated by a group member who is a strong presence in the group, who is then joined by other group members. A result is that rather than just limiting the range of discussions to what is comfortable for group members generally, the range becomes limited to that which is comfortable for one member in particular.

There are implications for all of the group members and the group as a whole if rescuing behavior is allowed to go unchecked. For the group member who is rescued a clear message is again delivered that what he or she was expressing is both uncomfortable and (worse) unacceptable in the group. The group member is left with an unresolved issue, which most likely took a great deal of courage to bring up in group in the first place.

Further, this group member has to wonder what issues will be acceptable in the future and may choose the safer route of simply not sharing anything of substance, thus avoiding the risk of another rescue. The group setting had the potential of being a place to express the member's genuine thoughts and emotions, but it has become a place of uncertainty in which any genuine expression seems unsafe. The same message of uncertainty and insecurity is as clear to the group members who witness the rescue as it is to the member who is rescued.

What are the implications for the rescuer? To understand, we must first make some assumptions about why that group member made the choice to make the rescue. The most likely explanation is that something in the other group member's expression of emotion hit too close to home for the rescuer's comfort. But not only is the rescuer denying other members opportunities to express themselves openly and honestly, the rescuer is also most likely denying him- or herself opportunities to address his or her own issues.

In our incident Joe allowed Calvin to be rescued by Steven, and other group members joined in to pacify Calvin's expression of emotion. By allowing the rescue to go forward, Joe gave his tacit approval of the message the other group members were sending. Joe could have done a number of things differently in order to allow the group members to help Calvin rather than rescue him. First, Joe could verbalize aloud to the group how difficult it is, for men in particular, to express or witness the expression of strong emotion. Joe could use this opportunity to normalize the expression of emotion and to explore the urge to problem solve and how it can have the effect of stifling the expression of emotion that often needs to happen. Then Joe could help the group understand that the best way to help one another in the group is to allow and encourage the expression of emotion, and to explore the emotions that each member is feeling. By taking this approach, Joe could communicate that the expression of emotion in the group is welcome; and he could name as a specific goal of the group an issue, which if addressed, will apparently benefit the group members. The result from this different tack could have been a challenge for the group members to assist one another by struggling with their own issues.

It is possible there are times when rescuing is appropriate in a group setting, but safeguarding clients is the responsibility of the group facilitator, not group members. A rescue may be appropriate, for example, when a group member is struggling to put words to his or her experiences and the group facilitator helps the member to name those experiences through clarifying and reflection. Even in such situations we will hope that the group facilitator is aware of both the content and the process of the group member's struggle. For the facilitator to rescue a group member who is struggling with the process sends the same message as if a group member rescued them, but much more powerfully.

RESPONSE

Nancy Bodenhorn

Rescuing can occur in many variations. Group leaders or members may attempt to rescue one another from challenging situations both within the group and in the outside world by shielding them or offering to intervene.

I see this example of rescuing as a self-rescuing form of resistance. In other words, the group members rescued themselves from entering into the deep level of emotions that Calvin was entering. By reacting in the way they did, they not only rescued Calvin from those depths but also avoided those depths for themselves. Although the members were not overtly negative in their reaction to the sharing, the platitudes offered were clearly inviting Calvin to leave the emotional level where he was at the time. In essence, the group was indirectly saying "we do not want to go there" in reference to that level of emotion. We know the session continued with sharing of struggles with isolation but are not sure what the level of conversation was. Because Joe singled out this moment as the powerful one, I am assuming the continued sharing was not at the same level. If this indeed was the case, then the result of rescuing had the negative effect of setting an unstated group norm of acceptable levels of emotions. By not processing this, the leader implicitly approved this norm.

Although we know that during the first session the group discussed some of the norms and expectations of the group, we do not know what the purpose of the group was, and we do not know how it was presented or agreed upon with the group members. The responsibility of the leader partially depended on the purpose. If the group was strictly a support group to focus on the immediate feelings and experiences of the members, then the leader's primary responsibility was establishing and ensuring a safe environment for the depth of emotional sharing that Calvin exhibited while also respecting the comfort level of the entire group. Talking directly about the incident when it unfolded would have been an appropriate role for the leader. Through this immediate processing, the group would have been supporting each other while talking directly about the norms and comfort levels instead of leaving them unstated.

If the group was established as an avenue to explore the communication style of each member in order to understand some of the personal reasons behind a divorce, then the leader had an additional responsibility of interpreting the communication as it unfolded and reflecting on that communication in a larger context. In this situation, for example, if the members regularly responded to their spouses' emotionality in the same way as they responded to Calvin, this may have had an impact on the marital relationship. Although addressing this issue would be helpful in a group designed for understanding relationships, it might be inappropriate in a group designed for support.

In either case, the leader had the responsibility to recognize and process the group dynamics. He could return to this the following week, but it certainly would be more effective if processed immediately. The group members were apparently feeling positive, compassionate, loyal, and connected to each other, which is probably why they demonstrated their own resistance in a benevolent way. If group members did not have these positive feelings toward the other members and toward the group, the resistance could have shown itself in a variety of other, more destructive, ways. The leader should recognize these positive aspects to the dynamics.

CHAPTER 29

RESISTANCE:
"I'M TIRED OF WALLOWING"

This incident looks at resistance and how it may affect the group process.

CRITICAL INCIDENT

Cathy Woodyard

Background
Melissa was leading an ongoing personal growth group for women that lasted for 12 sessions. A psychiatrist referred a new member named Elizabeth to the group. Elizabeth had attempted suicide with a serious drug overdose after being told by her husband of 18 years that he had moved out and wanted a divorce. She had been hospitalized and released the day before the group began. Elizabeth was from England but had lived in the United States for many years and was a very successful businesswoman. She had supported her husband, who was 10 years younger than she and who was disabled with arthritis. When she first began group, she was in intense emotional pain and talked of her despair and hopelessness. She shared with the group her feelings of shame over two failed marriages and her lifelong belief that she was ugly and would never find another partner. She admitted to having focused on taking care of her husband and her job to such a degree that she knew little about herself or her interests.

Incident
On the night of the fourth group session, Elizabeth came into group laughing and smiling. As the session began, Melissa mentioned to Elizabeth the difference in her affect. She replied, "Yes. I've decided I wallowed in my slop long enough. I'm getting on with it." Surprised, Cathy asked, "So, how are you going about getting on with it?"

"Well," Elizabeth explained cheerfully, "I'm putting my house up for sale. I'm selling all the furniture and everything in it. Anyone want to come to a great garage sale this weekend? Or better yet, anyone looking for a Victorian home?"

Startled, one of the group members asked, "But Elizabeth, didn't you tell us you and your husband worked years renovating that house? And you've got all the handmade furniture he made? What brought all this on?" "Yeah, he did," she replied. "But it's just a house. He can take what furniture he wants, but I want to be done with all the rest of it."

When group members asked how this dramatic change had come about, she told a long yet delightful story of her past week. With great animation, gestures, and humor, she related an incident during the week in which she was home alone going through closets and drawers selecting items for the garage sale. Like a professional storyteller, she entertained group members with images of herself sitting amidst piles of clothes, photos, and books deciding what to discard, what to sell, and what few items to hold onto. She ended her story, saying, "So, I've moved on. I'm tired of feeling sad. I never should have gotten so upset about it all to begin with. This summer when the divorce is final, I'm going to celebrate with a trip back to England. Enough about me! Let's move on to someone else! Next!" Melissa, skeptical of Elizabeth's sudden recovery, asked group members for their reactions to what Elizabeth had shared. One said, "I think it's great! I wish I could have gotten over my ex that quickly."

Another said to Elizabeth, "I'm worried you're going to be sad later if you sell all your stuff. Aren't you scared you'll regret it later?" "Oh, pooh! It's time to downsize! I'm tired of regrets. I've spent a whole month dealing with regrets; now I want to put it out of my mind and focus on the future. I've already started looking for a new house. There are some great ones in the same neighborhood, and some even have gardens!" One member said, "I'm really glad for you. You've been so down, and I've really worried you'd try to hurt yourself again. I'm glad you're past all the darkness." "I am, too," she replied. "I never should have let it get me down like that anyway. Okay. Move on to someone else."

Melissa was uncertain what to do. She did not believe Elizabeth was through experiencing the grief of her marriage ending, and she was concerned that Elizabeth was making such large decisions at this time. She knew that deciding to sell her home and her belongings could be an indicator of suicidal thinking, but nothing else that Elizabeth said indicated that she was considering suicide. Instead, she was making plans for the future and had mentioned looking for a new home and planning for a summer trip. Melissa believed Elizabeth was running from her grief, but she was uncertain whether to confront this or allow her to experience the temporary joy. Before she could decide, another group member spoke up and said, "I need some time to talk about something that happened to me this week." Melissa chose to let the group member continue, believing that life and time would bring Elizabeth back to her grief. At that time she and the group would help her through it.

Discussion

As Melissa was writing her case notes after the session ended, she wondered about her decision not to try harder to break through Elizabeth's resistance to dealing with the pain of her divorce. She decided that this was a phase in Elizabeth's grief process and that it was not her place or responsibility to move her from the temporary happiness back into the sadness. She felt satisfied with her decision.

QUESTIONS

1. Should Melissa have addressed the question of suicidal thoughts directly to Elizabeth?
2. How might Melissa have better assisted the group members in confronting Elizabeth?
3. Did Melissa respect Elizabeth's resistance or ignore it?

RESPONSE

Charlotte Daughhetee

The first thing that strikes me about this incident is the way the counselor, Melissa, rationalized away her own intuition about the actual state of the client, Elizabeth. My experiences as a counselor have taught me to listen to those little red flags that arise within us during the counseling process. Melissa needed to listen to her skepticism and uncertainty about Elizabeth's sudden turnaround. Instead, she made a tentative and ineffective effort at eliciting the group in an exploration of Elizabeth's true affective state. Later, she engaged in the type of wishful thinking that can have dire consequences when a client is considering suicide.

Intuition should lead a counselor to check things out and explore further, verifying his or her hunch with specific data. The facts in this case bear out the counselor's gut feelings and concerns. There are marked suicide risk factors evident in Elizabeth. She has a recent history of a lethal suicide attempt including hospitalization. She has suffered a loss not only of her marriage but also, in a sense, a potential loss of purpose, given that for the last 18 years she has been the support system for her disabled husband who has now moved out and has initiated the divorce. Elizabeth has expressed a sense of hopelessness concerning her chances for future relationships. She has spent her life focusing on others and acknowledges that she barely knows herself; she seems adrift and afraid.

Her "great garage sale" sounds like a method of giving away prized possessions, another sign of suicidal intention. Her flippant attitude about the Victorian home that she has so lovingly renovated is highly suspicious as well. In addition, the cultural issues should be considered as well. Though Elizabeth has lived in the United States for at least 18 years, her stated desire to return to England implies a longing to reconnect with her culture of origin and could be significant information. On a more serious note, this stated wish may be a way of signaling a desire to go home as a euphemism for wanting to die and escape her pain.

Elizabeth's energetic demeanor is a major red flag because severely depressed individuals will often experience a lifting of mood once they have come to a decision to kill themselves. It takes energy to commit suicide, and individuals who are serious about an attempt will often appear upbeat and lively just prior to an attempt. Melissa's uneasiness with the sudden turnaround and the myriad suicide risk factors present in Elizabeth justify further investigation into Elizabeth's state of mind and the level of her suicidal ideation and intention.

The group members are also initially startled by Elizabeth's turnaround and express surprise. They are quickly cajoled out of their own intuitive hunches and become unwitting participants in Elizabeth's façade. Melissa rightfully picks up on the group's doubts and uses this as an opportunity to challenge Elizabeth. However, Elizabeth deftly minimizes and evades further exploration, and the group drops the confrontation when Elizabeth steers the attention of the group to another member.

Melissa could have tapped into the here-and-now impressions expressed by the startled group members. Using confusion as a confrontation tool, she could have explored the reactions of group members as a way to gently confront Elizabeth. The manner in which Elizabeth presents herself is greatly at odds with her past feelings of shame, grief, and hopelessness. Several group members seem to be aware of this contrast, and Melissa could have used their awareness and confusion and explored these reactions ("There seems to be some confusion about how Elizabeth's statements today contrast with her feelings last week"). Melissa's timidity in confronting sets the tone for the group process and a theme of avoidance prevails. Confronting Elizabeth about her 180-degree turnaround by using the confusion of the group is an effective way to initiate exploration into Elizabeth's true internal experience and potential lethal plans. This would also provide the group with a learning experience about ways in which they minimize and evade painful feelings and experiences.

Melissa must clearly address Elizabeth's intentions. If using group members' confusion as a springboard to confrontation proves ineffective, Melissa must directly ask Elizabeth about her plans and any suicidal ideation. Melissa ignored Elizabeth's resistance and minimized the serious signals sent during the session, thereby reinforcing and paralleling the avoidance exhibited by Elizabeth. The discussion section states that Melissa "decided this was a phase in Elizabeth's grief process and that it was not her place or responsibility to move her from the temporary happiness back into sadness." This sentence alarms me because it is Melissa's responsibility to help Elizabeth deal with her situation in a genuine and therapeutic manner. At the very least she is reinforcing denial and minimizing; at the worst she may be turning a blind eye to a serious suicide threat. Melissa is unsure and avoidant when she needs to be courageous and direct. Confrontation, ideally as part of the group work, is necessary in this incident.

RESPONSE

Marcheta Evans

The focus of this incident is the counseling issue of resistance. When a counselor attempts to make a determination of whether or not the client, in this case Elizabeth, is being resistant, a definition of resistance must be assigned. Corey (2002) has given a basic definition of resistance as being anything that impedes the movement of therapy. In its simplest form, resistance refers to any idea, attitude, feeling, or action (conscious or unconscious) that promotes the status quo and gets in the way of change. As Corey has noted, Freud viewed resistance as an unconscious dynamic that clients will utilize to withstand the unbearable anxiety and pain that would surface if they were to become aware of their repressed impulses and feelings.

In this particular case, Melissa did a quick risk assessment in the group regarding Elizabeth's mental state. She made a decision to not address whether Elizabeth was contemplating suicidal thoughts at the moment. Melissa did attempt to engage the group in the process of Elizabeth's decision; however, Melissa did relatively little to confront Elizabeth's "new attitude."

As the therapist in this situation, Melissa should have taken some additional time to explore with Elizabeth her sudden decision. Based on an understanding of how resistance manifests itself and the stages of grief, Melissa should have allowed additional work and time to focus on Elizabeth during this session. Melissa should have attempted to ascertain Elizabeth's state of mind and her planning toward the future. In addition, Melissa should have taken into consideration Elizabeth's culture in regard to her traditions, beliefs, and values, and to the impact these could have on her decision making and choices.

According to the background information, Elizabeth, who had been a successful businesswomen, was in intense emotional pain and talked of her despair and hopelessness when she initially entered the group 4 weeks ago. As the group leader, Melissa should have explored how her new affect is in sharp contrast to her affect upon entry into the group. Of course, through all of the discussion, the therapist should have been constantly monitoring Elizabeth's reaction to the inquiries.

As a therapist, Melissa must realize that resistance can be positive when utilized appropriately. It may be seen as a defense or coping mechanism for the client to manage intolerable or intense emotions until a time when the client is able to cope with them consciously. That being the case, the therapist must not push too hard, but enough to be assured, as much as possible, of the client's intent or level of suicidal ideations.

This could have been a very valuable and rich teaching moment for the group. It could have been a time for the group to realize that there are moments when you must look beyond or below the surface to truly ascertain what is really going on inside the individual. It could have been a time for the group to realize that just because someone is saying or looking as if they are in great shape, this may not be the reality.

The initial reaction of the group participants was one of excitement because of this major change in Elizabeth. Initially, the group was excited about her new, positive attitude and decisions. As noted, one of the group member's expressed how she wished she could have "gotten over my ex that quickly." Some of the members did express concern about her decisions, but Melissa did not engage the group in helping Elizabeth deal with the issues or explore them to the depth or extent that could have been helpful to all the members. Particularly, getting the group to express the repercussions of making impetuous decisions with lifelong consequences could have proved to be quite beneficial to the whole group.

Most beginning therapists view confrontation as a negative process, but in reality, it is a process of attempting to get the clients or group members to look at their choices and decisions in a mirror before making them. Confrontation should have been employed in much more detail than Melissa allowed for the group to process and grow. Melissa really had no idea of what to do with Elizabeth's resistance. As a therapist, she let the group move on through her indecision on how to proceed. Melissa attempted to engage the group in this decision made by Elizabeth, but she allowed her feelings to cloud her professional responsibility by wanting to see Elizabeth happy. While completing her case notes, she attempted to rationalize the process and her decision to leave Elizabeth's decision alone, but she allowed a prime teaching opportunity to slip through her hands.

Of course, all of my comments are based on hindsight. I do recognize that when you are in the moment, it is harder to follow the ideal, especially when you want to see someone work through their problems; however, as therapists, we must constantly be conscious of the fact that counseling is work and requires our full competency and commitment to the well-being of our clients. It was Melissa's responsibility to assist her client in making the best decision, not just to give her temporary pleasure with the risk of life-long regrets.

REFERENCE

Corey, G. (2002). *Theory and practice of counseling and psychotherapy* (6th ed). Pacific Grove, CA: Brooks-Cole/Wadsworth.

CHAPTER 30

SEXUAL FEELINGS: "THIS GROUP IS NOT A DATING SERVICE"

This incident explores some of the issues of sexual feelings among group members.

CRITICAL INCIDENT

Jodi Ann Mullen

Background

Sarah has recently begun a new position at an outpatient chemical dependency clinic. Her responsibilities include both individual and group counseling. Sarah is enthusiastic about her role at the agency. She has 6 years of expertise in both facilitating groups at an inpatient chemical dependency clinic and working with individuals. Also, she has volunteered at a local high school for a number of years as a mentor to adolescent women. She currently is facilitating two groups at the clinic. Both of the groups are relapse prevention groups. Each group is a closed group that meets weekly. The difference between the two groups is that one is designed only for women and the other has both men and women members. The groups were designed to follow a similar format. Another difference is that in the women's relapse prevention group, special attention is given to issues that are particular to women in recovery.

The agency has recently experienced an increase in the number of female clients, which led to the agency's director to contact Sarah about facilitating a group designed especially for women. Sarah has been interested in women's issues since her undergraduate years and considers herself a feminist.

The women-only group has been meeting for three sessions, and all has been going quite well except for one problem. Sarah has noticed that two of the group members, Andrea and Gail, are regularly whispering to each other while other group members are talking. It is distracting to Sarah and the other group members. She has also noticed these two women nonverbally communicating during the sessions, appearing to flirt with each other. Although she hates to admit it, she is totally annoyed with Andrea and Gail's behavior. She is also annoyed with her own inability to manage the group. She is beginning to question her adequacy as a counselor.

Incident

During the fourth session of this group, Sarah begins her session as always by posting an agenda. As usual, she asks if any group members want to add anything to the agenda. Leann replies, "I want to say that it is not appropriate for people to use this group as a dating service." Sarah, wide eyed, turns around to face the group from her position at the flip chart. Embarrassed, caught off guard and confused, Sarah says, "What do you mean, a dating service?" Other members express their shock that Sarah has not realized that Gail and Andrea are together, and that this group has been part of the courting process.

Andrea, a sensitive woman, looks scared and puts her head down. Gail, a survivor, gets up and leaves. On her way out Sarah pleads, "We are a group, let's work this through as a group. If you leave you don't come back." Gail says she has enjoyed coming to the group, but she will not have her private life put on display. "I have learned a lot about myself and the life I want to lead. It does not include alcohol, and it does not include being made to feel there is something wrong with me. I wasn't aware I did anything wrong. Don't blame Andrea, I initiated things," she says. She turns to the group, face reddened and eyes teary, "And I cannot even leave you losers because I'm mandated" she says. Sarah and the other group members are shocked. Andrea stays in her seat, face buried and crying.

Discussion

After listening to Gail, Sarah realizes she may have acted before thinking. She has a vague recollection of her clinical supervisor saying, "Counseling is about thoughtful spontaneity." Sarah realizes what her supervisor meant as she realizes that she was clearly spontaneous yet lacked thoughtfulness. She tries to get the group back to the agenda of the day's tasks, but is flustered. The group members are also flustered. Andrea remains in her seat sobbing; no one attempts to comfort her. Sarah suggests the group should call it a night. "We will get back to business next week, same time," she says. The group members do not linger and leave the agency quickly. In her office Sarah feels remorseful about what happened in the group and attempts to figure how this all happened. She decides to call her clinical supervisor to schedule a session for tomorrow morning. She hopes to debrief and figure out how to salvage the group.

QUESTIONS

1. Are there any ethical issues raised in terms of Sarah's handling of this situation?
2. What steps could Sarah have taken to ensure that all participants were aware of the expectations of the group?
3. Is it possible for group members to be intimate but still benefit and contribute to a group?
4. What within Sarah might have contributed to her actions during this group session?

5. How should Sarah proceed from here in handling this situation?
6. What are the mandated members' issues that interfere with the success of this group?
7. How can the intimate relationship between group members be addressed within the group? Should it be addressed at all?

RESPONSE

Walter B. Roberts, Jr.

One of the most important aspects of the counselor's ability to be helpful to others is a thorough understanding of his or her own personal attributes and how they impact the helping relationship. Having a firm understanding of how psychosexual psychology impacts counselor-client interactions is critical in both individual and group settings, particularly if such subject matter may become a component of the counseling venue. We must assume that psychosexual energies will be a part of the transference-countertransference matrix.

The psychosexual aspects of the helping relationship cannot be ignored. Unfortunately, great pains are often undertaken by both parties to do just that. Both the client and the counselor come complete with their personal histories and perspectives on a wide variety of issues. Sexuality is just one of those many issues. The expectations that the client and the counselor bring into the relationship about gender impacts communication, that is, what is said, the way it is said, and how it is perceived. These personal histories and expectations do not always lend themselves to the most effective of counselor-client interactions, particularly in the sexually dishonest culture in which we live.

Americans do not deal honestly with the issue of sexuality. Although our culture is saturated with sexual images and sexual stereotypes, we have shied away from discussions about true sexuality—about what it means to be biologically female or male, how we relate to and treat those whose sexual identity does not follow traditional or stereotypical expectations, how the sexes relate to each other, what each gender needs from one other to form healthy and meaningful relationships. Indeed, furious debate rages in public K-12 education over these very topics. Subsequently, the failure of American culture, including schools of the helping professions, to realistically discuss the sexual aspects of humankind helps create the Sarahs of our profession.

Sarah is not a newcomer to the profession. Although she may have just started a new position, she has 6 years of prior counseling experience in different capacities. She has apparently facilitated groups for the same period. Six years of group facilitation is quite enough time to have more-than-adequate knowledge of the permutations of group dynamics and processes and to be well versed in the expect-the-unexpected world of group member interactions, especially in a treatment setting.

Sarah in this instance appears to be naive, oblivious/blind (willfully?) to the interactions of members within the group, or not well versed in how to manage confrontation when it emerges in the group setting, a situation that was apparent to everyone in the group—including her! Sometimes confrontational incidents do, indeed, just happen. This situation was heralded for weeks by Andrea and Gail's distractive behaviors. Sarah had every opportunity to be ready to turn a confrontational incident into a facilitative enlightening moment for group enrichment. She chose not to do so. One questions the basis for her being "wide eyed...embarrassed, caught off guard, and confused." The group is now in turmoil; the group leader has allowed her power to be taken by a dominant group member (who is taking that power out the door with her—how symbolic!); a fragile group member has been injured by the fracas; and the group leader has chosen to abandon the group in its critical state by concluding the session early immediately following the incident and taking shelter in her office (under her desk, too?) to feel remorseful and attempt to figure out how all this came to be.

This is what 6 years of group facilitation has taught Sarah? What must that first year have been like? For whatever reason, Sarah has chosen not to take responsibility for her leadership position and to be prepared to facilitate a pending confrontation, which everyone knew was coming. What could those reasons be? Did Sarah not learn basic group theory and skills in her graduate program? Has she practiced with benignly neglectful supervision for all these years in clinical settings? Or is Sarah afraid of the same-sex relationship intimacies that emerged between Andrea and Gail during the course of the sessions and was too confused or afraid to confront her own uneasiness about how to deal with the situation? The right to privacy dictates that group members choose what and how much they share. Members often develop relationships external to the group, including romantic alliances among members of the same sex. Such external-to-group relationships, regardless of gender or nature of the relationship, often pose potential problems during full-group sessions. The external-to-group relationships almost always become in-group alliances that create dynamics different from those of single-cell member interactions. It is not the nature of any type of romantic relationship between the members of Sarah's group that is the issue. The Andrea-Gail relationship has created a power imbalance that was strong enough to disrupt the entire group's forward motion. Any issue or topic on the table for group discussion has now been delayed or permanently trashed. The group's energies and focus will now become the fallout from the confrontation initiated by Leann in expressing her concerns and resentment about the Andrea-Gail relationship.

Sarah's self-assumed status as a feminist may also have contributed to her blunders and refusal to address the pending conflict within the group. Self-attributions and assumptions of knowledge in the absence of reality are accidents waiting to happen. Sarah may well have operated under the delusion that she relates well to all members of the same sex because she is a woman and views herself as an advocate for all women. Therefore, she believed that she knew everything necessary to handle any situation that might arise among and between the women in her group. Leann, Andrea, and Gail might have other opinions on this matter.

Sarah has a lot of work ahead of her for the sake of the group. Hopefully, Sarah's supervisor will be able to provide her with ideas that will assist her in the weeks to come. Additionally, Sarah's supervisor might well benefit everyone by monitoring Sarah's group work more closely and providing in-service educational opportunities for her.

The group will need to discuss the critical incident. Everyone will need to feel free to openly express their viewpoints. This is likely to be difficult for Andrea. She has not only been embarrassed in the group, specifically by Leann, but she may well have lost her relationship with Gail. Sarah may need to have individual sessions with those group members determined to be most vulnerable in order to encourage them to continue as valued members of the group. The focus of the group sessions, however, needs to get back on track toward the initial relapse prevention initiative. Deal with the confrontation, then move forward to the goal. This may be easier said than done, of course, in view of the intensity of emotions aroused in the incident. However, failure to acknowledge critical incidents such as this and the emotional energy they create can leave members feeling powerless to address conflict. Effective group leadership demands effective and knowledgeable group leaders.

RESPONSE

John V. Farrar

It appears that the source of many of this group's problems can be attributed to the leader's lack of assertiveness. A legitimate definition of assertiveness, and one often used by clinicians in their work with individual clients, involves respect for self and others. Passivity, or nonassertiveness, occurs when an individual fails to respect him- or herself while unduly deferring to the feelings and behaviors of others. In this incident, Sarah fails to behave assertively in the execution of her role as the group facilitator. As is often the case with passive individuals, Sarah is aware of, and frustrated by, her own lack of assertiveness. This is evidenced when she expresses annoyance with "her own inability to manage the group" and subsequently begins to question her own professional skills.

It is axiomatic in leadership theory that effective leaders must address two key functions: task activities and relationship-building activities. In her role as a group facilitator, Sarah's task activities include establishing structure and boundaries by leading the group in setting its rules. Relationship-building activities typically involve establishing rapport, modeling respectful communication with group members, and reflecting empathy in both comments and responses.

Unfortunately, it is apparent that Sarah's concern about her relationship with the group, and specifically with Andrea and Gail, has allowed her to either neglect or ignore her task responsibility. It is not clear from the incident whether or not Sarah established the proper ground rules for the group or is allowing the rules that had been established to be violated. Either way, the group has deteriorated as a result of the absence of structure. Sarah's lack of assertiveness and appropriate group facilitation skills are evidenced by her unwillingness to address the disrespectful conduct of Andrea and Gail while others were speaking. She observed this conduct, was annoyed by it, but failed to act. This represents classic nonassertive behavior. Her failure to address this violation of group rules fueled the escalating volatility and resentment of the group.

Because this is a chemical dependency recovery group, it is worth noting that a common clinical expectation for recovering individuals is the avoidance of new emotional relationships during the first year of recovery. The clinical rationale for this guideline is that recovering people need to focus on their recovery. New and potentially emotionally demanding relationships are seen as creating possible relapse conditions. Because this is apparently a mandated group, it may be more difficult to have participants adhere to that expectation, however. A more generic rule that should apply to both recovery groups and other groups is that cliques or alliances not be formed. All groups expect that both confidentiality and the avoidance of secondary agendas be maintained.

Nonassertiveness can lead to episodic manifestations of hostility. This is within the classic passive-aggressive tradition. Sarah's admonition, "If you leave you don't come back," certainly reflects her frustration with her own failure to function as an assertive leader. Clearly, her response after the initial outburst within the group was inappropriate. Attempting to "get the group back to the agenda of the day" was another passive ignoring of the proverbial elephant in the living room. It is not surprising that her group members were both upset and nonresponsive. Sarah clearly should have attended to the here-and-now principle rather than hiding behind her agenda. She failed to address Gail's abrupt departure and Andrea's sobbing. Additionally, Sarah did not speak to the failure of other group members to provide any emotional support or response to Andrea's upset.

Of course, the bedrock of group counseling dynamics is that members be honest with each other. When Leann expresses her objection to people using "this group as a dating service," Sarah, possibly trying to appear either accepting or nonjudgmental, responds, "What do you mean, a dating service?" This is obviously a disingenuous comment because of the concerns that Sarah expressed prior to this outburst. Other group members express incredulity that Sarah was not aware of Gail and Andrea being "together." Sarah failed to model honesty and revealed a lack of willingness to address this behavior with the group immediately. Perhaps inviting the entire group to discuss their feelings on this topic could have provided a detour from the course the group eventually ran.

It should be noted at this point that the sexual orientation of Gail and Andrea is not germane to the issues of this incident, unless Sarah's personal need to appear nonjudgmental about sexual orientation fostered her nonassertive conduct. A budding heterosexual relationship would have been inappropriate to the same degree as the one described in this incident.

Given the fact that Sarah has allowed the group to deteriorate due to her lack of assertiveness, what should she do now? Probably the most appropriate behavior attributed to Sarah was her stated plan to contact her supervisor. Obviously, this is very late in coming. Sarah needs to contact the group members individually, urging them to return to the group while avoiding any triangular communication with them in making this request. Her initial plea to "work this through as a group" was an appropriate one at the time and needs to be raised at the next session with those willing to return. This invitation to return should be extended to both Andrea and Gail as well. Assertiveness requires that Sarah accept responsibility for her prior failure to either establish or enforce the group's rules. She then must clearly express her expectation that they follow those rules in the future.

In conclusion, it is important that Sarah examine (preferably with her supervisor or her own therapist) the factors that led an experienced therapist into such an inept execution of her role. Clearly, her lack of assertiveness ultimately harmed the group's operation.

CHAPTER 31

SILENT MEMBER: "SILENCE IS NOT ALWAYS GOLDEN"

This incident explores the issue of a group member whose continued silence rattles both the group facilitator and the group's members.

CRITICAL INCIDENT

Jody J. Fiorini

Background

Angela, an Italian American counselor, has volunteered to facilitate a support group for individuals with cognitive impairments at a local rehabilitation agency. This group is an open-ended group that has been meeting casually on and off for years. Until recently, attendance had been fairly low with two or three people showing up to the group. The group was more of a social gathering than a counseling group. The agency has recently experienced an increase in the number of clients with traumatic brain injuries and other cognitive impairments. This has led the agency's director to contact Angela about facilitating a more structured group for these individuals. Angela has been consulting for the agency on a volunteer basis for a number of years and has a great deal of expertise in both facilitating groups and working with individuals with disabilities, but she has had no direct experience working with individuals with traumatic brain injuries.

Since Angela began facilitating the group, five new members have joined the original three who have been attending the Wednesday night group, as they have called it, for years. The group has been meeting for six sessions, and all has been going quite well except for one problem. Try as she might, Angela has not been able to engage one of the original members, Vesa, in the group's activities. Vesa is a 35-year-old male of Finnish descent who has some residual memory difficulties left from a car accident suffered during his college years. This member remains silent throughout all sessions unless directly addressed, and even then he responds only with one-word responses. Angela has wracked her brain for ideas for bringing this gentleman out of his shell. She has posed open-ended questions to him. She has structured activities that require interaction of group members. Each attempt has resulted with virtual silence.

Despite Vesa's seeming disinterest, he attends faithfully and has never missed an appointment.   Angela's patience with Vesa is wearing thin. Although she denies it, she has become angered by his continued silence and views her inability to engage him in the group process as her personal failing as a counselor.

Incident

During the seventh session of this support group, Angela begins her session as always by conducting a round check-in with each member to discuss how his or her week has gone.   As has been typically the case, when it is Vesa's turn, he replies with "Everything went fine" and turns to the person next to him. Angela suddenly turns to one of the more outspoken group members, Dawn, and asks her "Dawn, how does it make you feel when Vesa continually remains silent during each of our group meetings?" Dawn immediately responds with, "Yeah, I've been wondering about that? Vesa, why do you even bother to show up here when you obviously don't contribute anything to the group?"   Other members likewise chime in with similar sentiments. One suggests that Vesa is purposely trying to be disruptive to the group, and another calls for his expulsion from the group.

Vesa looks stunned and pushes his chair even further away from the rest of the group members. He says that he has enjoyed coming to the group for years. He learns a lot by listening to each of the members' stories and considers the other members of the group to be his good friends. He says he has been unsure of what to do with this new group format. "I keep wondering when this part will be over, and we can bring in cookies and play cards like we always used to do," he replies. "I don't know what I did wrong, but if you all want me to leave I'll go," he says. He picks up his hat and coat and proceeds to leave the room. Angela and the other group members look at one another in dismay.

Discussion

After watching Vesa leave, Angela realizes she may have mishandled the situation. She tries to bring the group back to a working state, but the members seem flustered and Angela herself feels too confused to continue. She quickly summarizes the session and dismisses the members a bit early. On the way home, Angela feels guilt over the group's events and tries to piece together what may have happened. She determines that she will contact a colleague in the morning for supervision and to try to make sense of what transpired in her group.

QUESTIONS

1. What ethical issues are raised in terms of Angela's handling of this situation?
2. What impact might the cultures of Vesa and Angela have had on their interactions and expectations during the group process?

3. What steps could Angela have taken to ensure that all participants were aware of the expectations of the group?
4. Might Angela's unfamiliarity with the common characteristics of individuals with traumatic brain injuries have impacted her ability to understand Vesa's behavior?
5. Is it possible for group members to be silent but still benefit and contribute to a group?
6. What within Angela might have contributed to her actions during this group session?
7. How should Angela proceed from here in handling this situation?

RESPONSE

Suzanne M. Hedstrom and Deborah E. Renard

Angela began her work with the support group at the rehabilitation agency as though it was a continuation of the ongoing group. In fact, the group she began is quite different from the one the three members of the original group, including Vesa, participated in for years. The original group was one that was or had evolved into a social gathering, replete with card playing and cookies. It bears little resemblance to a counseling group.

Because the focus, goals, and format of the group that Angela is now leading are so very different from the ongoing group, she should consider this to be a new group and engage in appropriate leader activities. The beginning of any new group requires significant preplanning and pregroup interviewing of prospective members prior to the initial session. Angela cannot assume that Vesa and his colleagues from the original group will be interested in and willing to participate in a group with goals and expectations that differ dramatically from their previous group experience.

It would have been appropriate for Angela to have provided specifics for the new and more structured group: group goals and objectives, format for the group, expectations for member and leader behavior, group process, confidentiality issues, risks and benefits to membership, and member rights and responsibilities. This information is best provided in a written format, including details regarding group meeting days and times, location, and leader qualifications. Providing written material for later reference and clarification is especially appropriate when working with a population that has memory and/or cognitive processing difficulties. The leader should also consider placing the information on audiotape for the benefit of those members whose reading comprehension may be compromised. The leader may wish to format this into a contract or provide it in the form of a professional disclosure statement. A prospective member can give informed consent only after this information is provided and a discussion is held between a leader and a prospective member. After this discussion the leader, too, is in a better position to decide whether or not this particular prospective member will be a good fit with this particular group. Additionally, pregroup interviews provide important information for counselors about potential group members, including who they are, how they communicate, how they function interpersonally, and what they want and need.

Because this pregroup discussion does not seem to have occurred, both Angela and Vesa have misunderstandings concerning the group. Vesa seems to be puzzled by what is happening in the group, though he has patiently waited for "his" group to resurface, complete with card playing and cookies. Angela seems in the dark about who Vesa is and why he is in the group.

In addition to Angela's shortcomings in not providing screening to prospective group members (American Counseling Association, *Code of Ethics and Standards of Practice*, 1995, section A.9.a) and not disclosing to her clients information pertinent to the group (section A.3.a.), she also is conducting the group so that she is meeting her own needs at the expense of her clients (section A.5.a), thus compromising the primacy of client welfare (section A.1.).

Angela seems unaware that some of her own issues and needs are interfering with her ability to be an effective leader in this group. Her need to see herself as a competent counselor has clouded her perceptions of Vesa. She interprets his behavior self-referentially, as though his silence is due to her personal failings as a counselor. She does not consider other possibilities or interpretations for his apparent lack of involvement in the group. She seems to not be aware of the contradiction between his faithful attendance and his virtual silence. Unfortunately, Angela's lack of self-awareness surrounding her competence issues results in impatience and internal anger toward Vesa as well as inappropriate leader behavior in the seventh group session.

Angela misuses the check-in, meant to be a brief go-around to touch base with all group members, to serve her purposes. She orchestrates a confrontation by an outspoken group member, the negative tone of which is picked up by other members. In fact, the statements lead to requests for Vesa's expulsion from the group. Sure enough, upon hearing these statements from his "good friends," and explaining his confusion with the new group format (and the benefits he has accrued by listening), Vesa exits the group. Although Vesa leaves believing he has done something "wrong," it is Angela's behaviors that are most questionable. Clearly, confrontation is acceptable in the life of a group and can be a wonderful stimulus for learning and growth. In this instance, however, there is no evidence there was previous modeling of appropriate confrontation by the leader, and the confrontations from the group members were not appropriate. Sadly, because of the anger generated by her own issues and needs, Angela does not block what became an attack on Vesa. The leader does not protect her client from a situation that may result in psychological trauma, contrary to the responsibilities of an ethically competent counselor (ACA Code of Ethics, section A.9.b).

Angela needs to become more aware of her own needs and how they impact her work as a counselor. Her awareness of guilt over the events of the seventh session and her seeking supervision are steps in the right direction. Participating in a supervisory relationship (peer or otherwise) can be helpful to all counselors, no matter how experienced. In Angela's situation, she is aware of her need to feel/be competent. Through supervision she may realize that her need to be competent may actually work to decrease her competent functioning as a counselor. It may be that countertransference-like processes are interfering with her capacity for empathy and effective counseling interventions. These same processes, if present, may be stirring up her own personal fears of disability (especially cognitive/affective disabilities) and/or not-quite-conscious memories of past experiences involving significant others who were either cognitively compromised or nonresponsive in the ways she expected. Angela may decide to seek personal counseling to work on these issues.

Why was Vesa silent? Angela did not know, but believed she could do something to make him participate more fully. She looked at Vesa through her eyes and worldview, not recognizing that there might be many reasons for his silence. She interpreted his behavior self-referentially rather than attempting to explore the meaning behind his silence from Vesa's own perspective. To what extent is Vesa's silence reflective of his lack of understanding of what this new group is all about? Might a lack of trust in the leader have influenced his contributions to the group? To what extent might Vesa's cultural background and/or his residual memory difficulties have influenced his behavior? Angela overlooked many factors that could have influenced Vesa's minimal verbal participation in the group.

How might Vesa's cultural background have affected his behavior in the group? Some cultures do not value qualities that are central to group counseling: verbal expressiveness, emotional openness, self-disclosure, unstructured interactions and the role of the counselor in the group. Indeed, if we assume that both Angela and Vesa have been socialized to behave and interpret social interactions in keeping with their respective cultural backgrounds, we would find them at opposite ends of the continuum. Angela's Italian-American heritage carries norms of a great deal of emotional expressiveness, high-verbal/low-context communication styles, and active (even interruptive) interaction styles; the norms of Vesa's Finnish heritage include restraint of overt emotional expression, a communication style that does not rely heavily on verbal exchanges, and a reserved presentation of self in public that is consistent with his quiet participation. Although Angela's cultural heritage and her professional training may have been more in sync with the values that are central to mainstream group counseling practice, the cultures represented by Vesa and perhaps other group members may value behaviors that are contradictory to those deemed central to group counseling. Greater awareness, sensitivity, and adaptation to cultural differences and their potential impact on Vesa's participation in the group would be appropriate expressions of multicultural counseling competencies.

Angela's lack of familiarity and experience in working with clients with traumatic brain injuries contributed to this critical incident. Many times the residual deficits of traumatic brain injuries are subtle and not immediately perceptible, even to trained professionals. These hidden difficulties are typically identified by clients' self-report and/or observations over time, or they may emerge under conditions of stress and change. Angela did not consider the possibilities that Vesa may have had such problems as word finding, diminished verbal comprehension and expression, slowed processing speed, and/or difficulty interpreting social cues and complex social situations accurately in addition to the residual memory impairments that were noted. Furthermore, individuals who have cognitive impairments are often encouraged to use situational cues as memory and behavioral guides as part of their repertoire of coping skills; it may have been beneficial to Vesa and to other members to change the time, date, or place for the group meeting in order to clearly mark the new group as distinct from the old group. Along the same lines, some type of opening/closing ritual and/or a consistent and overt pattern to the group session may help to promote participation and positive outcomes in this type of group. In a group where high-level cognitive functioning cannot be assumed, the leader should provide, at least initially, a greater amount of structure (e.g., turn taking, as in games) and modeling, perhaps introducing concepts and activities in smaller steps with more practice, repetition, and built-in memory cues than in groups for which at least average cognitive functioning can be assumed. A smaller group size may be warranted.

The events of the critical incident were likely to have been countertherapeutic for other members of the group as well. Although individual differences among individuals with traumatic brain injuries are great, Angela would have fared better had she considered the status and needs of all group members. For instance, irritability, disinhibition, and impaired ability to consider cause-and-effect relationships are common problems for those with traumatic brain injuries. If Dawn's treatment goals included working on these issues by practicing social and cognitive/affective skills (such as "think before you pop off," "monitor/adjust your phrasing and tone," and "consider the other person's feelings before you act"), Angela's mishandling of the confrontation inadvertently exploited Dawn's weaknesses in a way that was countertherapeutic for her as well as for Vesa. For the other members of this traumatic brain injury group, issues such as accurate interpretation and appropriate responses in social situations, management of confusing situations, the ability to perceive events from more than one perspective simultaneously, and problem solving should generally be appropriate to focus on. Using the group as a microcosm or practice venue in which such skills are modeled, coached, refined, and reinforced could be therapeutically beneficial for all members. Angela may be able to address these matters to the group 's advantage as she attempts to regroup after the critical incident.

Can silent members still benefit from and contribute to a group? Not all group members need to be equally verbally active in order for clients to benefit from the group and for the counseling group to be effective. However, if one or more members remain virtually silent, the group is affected. Although the case might be rightly made that the silent member is learning vicariously by listening, the other participants may not be aware of this. It is not uncommon for silent members to attract negative reactions from their peers because their silence allows opportunity for multiple projections (e.g., "you're judging us," "you think you're better that we are," "you're playing it safe while we take all the risks," "you're just an observer, not one of us"). Ultimately, both the silent individual and the other group members benefit by having the meaning of the silence explored.

When looking at the future of this group, three specific aspects/fronts need to be addressed: Angela, Vesa, and the group. Angela has sought supervision; she should continue in a supervisory relationship throughout the duration of the group. She may consider personal counseling to deal with some of the issues raised by this incident. It will also be wise for Angela to set a personal development goal of enhancing her multicultural counseling competencies, perhaps through further formal training, independent study, and/or supervision. Further, Angela's willingness and enthusiasm for leading this group cannot substitute for her knowledge and skill deficits regarding traumatic brain injuries and their associated counseling issues; she needs to increase her competencies in these areas as quickly as possible. Community resources, rehabilitation specialists, supervisors, formal training, and self-study may be ways to accomplish this needed task and address this front.

Vesa's well-being needs attending. He left the group feeling hurt and confused, believing that he had done something wrong. Angela should call Vesa and admit she made some mistakes. She should apologize for allowing the situation to progress as it did and for not clarifying for him the change in the group's focus and goals. She should also invite him to an individual session to debrief the incident and to talk about his needs and goals (i.e., how they might be met inside and/or outside the new group format). She should take responsibility for the mishandled incident and invite him to return with her assurance that that type of incident will not recur. If he chooses to reenter the new group, they should go through the informed consent process and plan together how his return to the group might occur most therapeutically for all concerned. If Vesa is still interested in attending a group like the previous group, Angela could take the initiative within the organization to request the former group be reconstituted.

To the remaining group members, Angela needs to recognize her responsibility regardless of whether or not Vesa chooses to return to the group. She needs to acknowledge to them the mistakes she made in handling the situation in the previous session and to process their reaction to the situation and to her disclosure. Angela has the opportunity to use this experience as a growth and learning opportunity for the group.

RESPONSE

Joyce A. DeVoss

A number of ethical issues are raised in this incident. According to the ACA *Code of Ethics and Standards of Practice* (ACA, 1995, section A.3.a), "When counseling is initiated, and throughout the counseling process as necessary, counselors inform clients of the purposes, goals, techniques, procedures, limitations, potential risks and benefits of services to be performed, and other pertinent information." Angela did not inform her group members of the purposes, goals, and techniques to be used and give them important information so that they could make an informed decision about whether to participate in the group.

In addition, the ACA Code of Ethics states that "Counselors screen prospective group counseling/therapy participants" (section A.9.a). Angela did not screen her prospective group participants to get to know them and learn about their needs, goals, and capacity to benefit from the group. The ACA Code of Ethics also states that "In a group setting, counselors take reasonable precautions to protect clients from physical or psychological trauma" (section A.9.b). Angela did not take reasonable precautions to protect her group members from psychological trauma and even contributed to the psychological traumatization of one member by others, ultimately affecting the entire group.

The ACA Code of Ethics further states that "Counselors practice only within the boundaries of their competence" (section C.2.a) and that "Counselors practice in specialty areas new to them only after appropriate education, training, and supervised experience" (section C.2.b). Angela practiced outside the boundaries of her competence by accepting this assignment with a population of traumatic brain injury clients without appropriate education, training, and supervised experience. She did not understand the disabilities of the clients she was working with, and she did not seek proper training to prepare herself for this work.

The cultural background of Vesa and Angela may have had a major impact on their interactions and their expectations during the group. Angela did not appear to make an attempt to understand Vesa's cultural background and did not seem especially aware of how her own cultural background affected her approach to counseling others. It was her responsibility as a counselor to actively seek to gain such an understanding of her clients and to develop personal awareness of her impact on her clients.

Angela could have interviewed each of the group members individually and gotten to know their needs and expectations as well as shared her own goals and expectations. She could have met with the group for an orientation session, explaining verbally and in writing the format and expectations of the group. She then could have invited questions and/or concerns from group members verbally and in writing.

Angela's unfamiliarity with traumatic brain injuries may have been a major factor in her limited understanding of Vesa's behavior. Vesa's silence and limited verbal expression might have been primarily or partially a result of his brain injury. Angela must receive adequate training to work with the traumatic brain injury population before she can provide ethical treatment for Vesa and her other group clients.

Group members can gain a great deal even when they are silent. Some members are quiet and reflective, but nevertheless, they listen attentively and can provide stability and consistency in a group. They do need to be acknowledged, however, and respectfully invited and encouraged (not coerced) to participate to best of their ability.

Possible contributions to Angela's actions during this session are that she may not have received adequate training in cultural sensitivity in working with diverse clients; she may have lacked awareness of the impact of traumatic brain injury on functioning; and she may not have dealt with some personal issues that arose as countertransference with Vesa that need to be addressed. Furthermore, Angela's expectations for herself and the group may have been unclear and/or unrealistic.

Angela should seek training in working with traumatic brain injury clients. In addition, she needs supervision with this group, ideally through cofacilitation with a supervisor who has expertise in working with the traumatic brain injury population. She should contact all group members and, with the help of a supervisor who has expertise in working with the traumatic brain injury population, obtain an assessment of each group member's current status. She needs additional training in cultural awareness and sensitivity. Angela may consider individual counseling to increase her self-awareness as to the impact and influence of her own cultural background on her interactions with others.

REFERENCE

American Counseling Association. (1995). *Code of ethics and standards of practice.* Alexandria, VA: Author.

CHAPTER 32

RESPECTING DIVERSITY: "WE'RE REALLY ALL THE SAME"

This incident examines the multicultural competence of a school counselor who fails to recognize the effects of cultural differences on group participation.

CRITICAL INCIDENT

Randall L. Astramovich

Background

Mark is a Caucasian high school counselor in an affluent suburban school district. After several requests from teachers, Mark decides to conduct a small group for students coping with divorcing parents. The group contains three senior Caucasian females, one junior Caucasian male, and a sophomore second-generation Japanese female, Anna. All of the group members have recently discovered their parents are in the process of divorce. Because he feels pressured to get the group underway, Mark decides to forego any individual meetings with the group members prior to beginning the group. He also plans to keep the group unstructured and allow the group members to take the lead.

Incident

At the beginning of the first session, Mark gives group members a few minutes to tell about themselves and how they came to find out about their parents' decision to divorce. Mark notices that Anna, unlike the other students, seems very uncomfortable and timid when it is her turn to introduce herself. The male group member interrupts Anna almost immediately after she begins speaking, asking her, "Can you crank it up a notch, please?" Mark gently tells Anna that it would be helpful if she spoke louder and gives a frustrated stare at the male group member. Anna complies with the request and speaks louder, but Mark notices she is very brief and says nothing about her parents' divorce. Because he wants to get Anna off the hot seat and to model self-disclosure, Mark decides to tell the group about his own parents' divorce. Mark ends the first group by reminding group members that opening up and discussing their feelings and experiences surrounding their parents' divorce will help them stay on track in school.

After the initial session, Mark reflects that Anna seems like an outsider in the group. He attributes this to her being the youngest group member and being from one of the poorest families in the community. He decides to make a concerted effort in the next group session to include Anna in the group process more actively.

During the second group session, one of the Caucasian female students discusses feeling pressured to take sides with either her mother or father. Mark notices that Anna looks very sad and thinks she seems moved by what the other student was saying. Anna looks down and nods her head. Mark decides to continue reflecting Anna's feelings in an attempt to get her to open up and share her experience with the group. However, Anna says nothing. After a moment of silence, other group members jump in and start sharing their own frustrations at feeling pressured to take sides during the divorce. Mark facilitates the discussion and decides he has given Anna enough opportunity and will let her be responsible for her own participation. As the group ends, Mark notices that Anna seems relieved and ready to get back to class.

Discussion

After the second session, Mark decides he may have made a mistake in inviting Anna to participate in the group. He thinks Anna is too quiet and not verbal enough to be an effective group member. He makes plans to meet individually with Anna and tell her the group experience seems too overwhelming for her at this time. Because he has no time to do individual counseling, Mark also plans to refer Anna to a local community agency if she wants to continue to work on the divorce issues.

QUESTIONS

1. How do you assess Mark's awareness level of his own biases and of the potential cultural differences that might impact Anna's group participation?
2. What knowledge would have been helpful for Mark to obtain prior to initiating the group?
3. How could Mark have responded more skillfully to Anna's participation?
4. What are some of the dominant discourse assumptions about ideal group counseling members? How do these assumptions impact group leaders?
5. What are some ways Mark can improve his multicultural counseling skills?

RESPONSE

Cheryl W. Forkner

Mark can be assessed as operating from a color-blind perspective regarding his own biases and cultural diversity. This limited perspective prevents him from seeing or even imagining the distinctiveness of Anna's culture and its impact on her within the group environment. In fact, Mark's behaviors reflect a Caucasian individual who is in the contact status of White Racial Identity (Helms, 1995). The contact status characterizes an individual as being oblivious and unaware of racism and color-blind to racial and ethnic differences. Additionally, Mark's counseling skills reflect Westernized counseling values that are associated with traditional counseling intervention, such as valuing self-disclosure, verbal communication, nondirective and unstructured processes, and emotional expressiveness. These counseling values are culturally encapsulating and are limited in their effectiveness with individuals from non-Western cultures, ethnic minority populations, and those who possess a collectivist worldview. Skilled counselors with good intentions who ascribe to Western counseling values isolate clients who are culturally different from themselves because of the incompatibility of counselor and client values and counselor inflexibility or incompetence in working with individuals different from themselves. Awareness of one's own cultural identity, values, and beliefs in addition to awareness of clients' cultural identity, values, and beliefs is an ethical responsibility for all counselors (American Counseling Association [ACA], 1995; Association for Specialists in Group Work [ASGW], 1998b, 2000).

If we broaden the definition of diversity to include nonracial and ethnic dimensions, there are several differences among the group members that can solely or interactively impact the group dynamics. Mark's group represents diversity across race and ethnicity, age or developmental stage, gender, and socioeconomic status. Mark, however, is not completely blind to all cultural differences. By the second session, he began to consider how Anna might differ from her fellow group members and identified age and socioeconomic status as possible contributors to Anna's assigned status as an outsider.

The ASGW *Professional Standards for the Training of Group Workers* (2000) makes it clear that noticing and acknowledging diversity and considering how the group's diversity may impact group dynamics is an ethical start in planning for the success of any group (section II.C). Unfortunately, due to Mark's color blindness, he was unable to expand his question ("How is Anna different from other group members?") to include other variables of diversity, especially a variable as salient as race and ethnicity.

Mark's level of awareness and knowledge of cultural dynamics in groups also renders him blind to the interplay of power that coexists in the group sessions. Mark, a Caucasian adult male and an agent of the educational system, represents a higher status of power and authority than Anna's position as the youngest, non-Caucasian, and less affluent female group member. Even the other group members (older, Caucasian, and affluent) represent a higher status in the power hierarchy than Anna. Anna is the group's only minority member. Therefore, Mark's oblivion to Anna's cultural heritage prevents him from acknowledging and hypothesizing that Anna's presentation in the sessions (observed by Mark as discomfort, timidity, quietness, low level of self-disclosure) could be a function of Anna's ethnic socialization as a second-generation Japanese female adolescent versus Mark's pending conclusion of her being an outsider or inappropriate for the group. Because of

Mark's position as an authority figure (group facilitator, adult, Caucasian male), Mark's behavior in the first group session modeled more than his intended lesson on self-disclosure. Mark modeled his value system and an intolerance of cultural differences among the group members. In essence, regardless of Mark's good intentions and efforts to encourage Anna's overt participation, his cultural identity status (limited awareness of his biases and cultural differences) virtually positioned Anna as an invisible group member against the culturally homogeneous backdrop of the group's Whiteness.

Mark offered the divorce group in response to a need expressed by several teachers in his high school. He responded immediately to the request and initiated the group without adequate planning and preparation prior to the first group meeting. As part of the planning process, Mark would have benefited from acquiring knowledge about the familial and cultural background, the level of distress, and coping strategies of each group member; theories of multicultural counseling and working with culturally diverse populations; theories of group development and group process; and issues affecting adolescents of divorce.

Screening prospective group members provides group leaders with an opportunity to learn more about each group member and potentially how the individual will respond to or interact with fellow group members. If Mark had met with each member prior to the first group, he could have inquired about the student's family of origin history, how the student learned of the parents' pending divorce, how the divorce was affecting the student emotionally and academically, the student's interpersonal style and coping strategies, and the student's expectations and goals from participating in the divorce group. The pregroup meetings would have revealed both similarities (other than the issues of divorce) and differences (e.g., cultural background, interpersonal style, maturity level, circumstances surrounding the divorce, student's coping strategies) among the group members. Mark would have been more prepared to meet the needs and challenges of individual members and of the group as an entity. The pregroup meetings would have revealed the immediate concerns facing the students, and Mark could have put more forethought into the group structure and interventions. (In fact, it is unclear what type of group Mark was offering the students; therefore, the actual goals for the group and for the individual members are unknown.) It is my hope that Anna's cultural heritage could have become more salient for Mark.

Subsequently, he could have taken the ethical steps to learn more about Anna's Japanese culture and level of acculturation, confronted his own biases concerning and skills for working with culturally diverse populations, and considered how culture would affect the group dynamics. According to the ACA Code of Ethics (1995), and the ASGW *Best Practice Guidelines* (1998a) and *Principles for Diversity-Competent Group Workers* (1998b), counselors are ethically obligated to be aware of their biases and cultural issues when working with diverse populations. The *Principles for Diversity-Competent Group Workers* outline multicultural counseling competencies as beginning with counselors' awareness of their own biases and values and continuing with counselors acquiring knowledge of clients' culture and worldview and of culturally sensitive skills and invention strategies. If Mark had knowledge of Anna's cultural heritage, he would be aware of the profile of worldview, values, and beliefs associated with Asian American culture (Sue & Sue, 2003).

With this information, Mark could have interpreted Anna's behavior in the group not through his original concerns and hypotheses but by associating her behavior to ethnic socialization. For instance, Mark could have considered

- Anna's level of acculturation as a second-generation Japanese adolescent and the degree to which Anna and her family embrace Western and Japanese customs, values, and beliefs;
- how Anna was referred to the group. Anna's participation may have resulted from the cultural value of deferring to the recommendation of authority figures (e.g., her teacher) versus Anna's desire to join the group. Anna also may not have understood or been familiar with the process of group counseling;
- Anna's omission of how she learned of her parents' divorce as a reflection of her respect for her parents and family. Anna may have been torn between complying with Mark's instructions to the group members on how to introduce themselves and revealing information about her family. Discussing her family publicly may produce feelings of shame and embarrassment;
- the unstructured format of the group and the link between emotional expressiveness and academic performance, which may have been too ambiguous and contradictory to Anna's expectations for a counseling intervention; and
- Anna's possible experience of incidents of discrimination or prejudice (due to her race/ethnicity and socioeconomic status) from her classmates. She may be mistrusting and uncomfortable with her fellow group members.

Information from the counseling literature on the effectiveness of groups with high school students and stages of group work could have been helpful. Mark's decision "to keep the group unstructured and allow the group members to take the lead" may not be appropriate or the most effective means for this setting, age, and developmental stage of group members. Additionally, if Mark had a full understanding of the initial stages of group work, he would have conducted individual pregroup meetings and facilitated the first session differently. As mentioned previously, pregroup meetings allow the group facilitator to gather in-depth information on each prospective group member. The meetings also function as an orientation to group process and provide group members with pertinent information on the group experience, such as goals, structure, meeting schedule, confidentiality, and group norms. Even if a group is unstructured, group leaders have an ethical obligation to reveal all details regarding the group experience to prospective members so they can give their informed consent for participation (ASGW, 1998a). It is customary for group leaders to review the group rules (e.g., confidentiality), expectations, and norms in the first group meeting (and throughout the process as needed) as a means to create an environment of safety and security for group members. Having the knowledge of what to expect from the group, the experience is demystified and group members are better able to meet the challenges of participation. Mark had an obligation to review the goals, expectations, and norms of the group before having members disclose sensitive information such as how they learned of their parents' divorce. Mark had an ethical obligation to explain the importance and practicalities of group confidentiality before members revealed themselves in the group.

Many concerns affect a family facing a divorce, and the effects of the divorce on children vary according to the age and developmental stages of the children and the level of marital conflict in the household. There are many misconceptions and fears about the effects of divorce, and having concrete information on the topic is be helpful. It would have been helpful for Mark to consult the research literature and other mental health and legal professionals to determine what issues are unique to adolescents (i.e., their rights in custodial issues, grief) and what counseling strategies are most effective for this age group. Mark would then be better able to assist his group members in understanding how their parents' divorce may change their lives and potentially affect their level of functioning. Mark would have been able to incorporate cultural factors by exploring with group members how their cultural backgrounds affect their perceptions of family and divorce and either provide a blanket of support or exacerbate their stress levels.

Although Mark believed he was being helpful to the group by modeling self-disclosure in the first session, the group probably would have benefited more from Mark providing information that normalized the challenges of divorce on children, noting the commonalities among the group members (information he should have gathered from the pregroup meetings), and instilling hope that the group experience could provide group members with a sense of security and support and help members meet their goals during the familial transition of a divorce.

It was obvious to Mark that Anna's presentation in the first group differed from those of her fellow group members, and he attempted to be supportive. It would have been beneficial for him to review the group norms of being civil, respectful, and accepting of each other's style of engaging in the group and to begin modeling and reinforcing these good group behaviors. By normalizing the anxiety or discomfort typically experienced by group members in the early group sessions, especially in the first group meeting, Mark could have educated the members on group process. Mark could have made a process comment reflecting his observation of Anna's discomfort in speaking in the group and then provided Anna with positive reinforcement for attempting to be a good group member by complying with his request for introductions. Mark could have stated his appreciation for her (and other members') willingness to take great risks in the first meeting (when the first meeting can be uncomfortable for many group members). He also could have acknowledged Anna's omission of the information surrounding her parents' divorce, inquired if discussing the situation is difficult for her, and reassured everyone's difficulty in talking about a difficult situation. If Anna did not verbally respond to Mark's process comments, Mark could have reiterated the difficulties of a first session, reviewed how the group could become a safe place for members, and expressed hope that everyone would grow more comfortable as time progressed. Mark could also explain to members that each individual can control how much information he or she reveals in group. Throughout this time, Mark could continue to observe Anna's nonverbal behaviors to assess her level of engagement and connection to the group. Unfortunately, because Mark valued self-disclosure in group and expected members to jump into disclosing information (and modeled this value by revealing his experiences with his parents' divorce), Mark's process comments may have been considered as insincere by Anna.

Mark's contemplation of Anna's status and participation in group is part of the continual planning and reflective process for group leaders. Group leaders should reflect on prior sessions, explore how each group member participated in the sessions (verbally and nonverbally) and affected group dynamics, and plan the next steps for the group. Mark's concern about Anna becoming an outsider is understandable, although possibly premature. His decision to put forth more effort in inviting her into the group process for the second session was a good plan. Anna appeared to be responsive to Mark's reflection of her reaction to her fellow member's reporting. However, Mark's value that verbalization is a measure of group participation sabotaged his connection with Anna and left him feeling discouraged and frustrated. It is unfortunate that Mark did not recognize Anna's nonverbal behaviors as an indication of active participation and engagement, as a reflection that Anna had connected with either the group member who was speaking or with the situation of being pressured to take sides. Mark might have encouraged overt participation from Anna by posing a direct question, such as, "It seems like you can relate to the member's story. What part of her story sounds familiar to you?" If Mark's inquiry met with silence, he could reflect the anxiety of talking about the divorce in a group format and directly say to Anna, "I am glad you were able to connect to the member's story. My hope is you will become more comfortable with us over time." I agree with Mark's thoughts on letting her "be responsible for her own participation." However, I believe that Mark, as the group facilitator, should continue to make conscious efforts to invite Anna into the group process. Unfortunately, Mark dismissed Anna's engagement in the second session. Mark's discouragement and frustration resulted in his reversion to his original position of seeing Anna as an outsider and led to his belief that she may be inappropriate for the group for the sole reason that she does not self-disclose or verbalize to the same degree as the other group members. Because Mark did not conduct pregroup meetings, I think meeting with Anna after the second session is a good idea. However, I do not agree with his assessment that she is inappropriate for group. The individual meeting would be an opportunity for Mark to learn more about Anna and for him to provide more information about the group process. The individual meeting may help Mark connect and have more empathy for Anna and, subsequently, assist him in helping her with the group experience. Without any of this information and this individual intervention, Mark cannot determine whether Anna (or any other group member) is inappropriate for his group. Mark has not established a working alliance with Anna. His unilateral decision to terminate her from group and refer her to an outside provider is unethical (ACA, 1995, section A.11) and reflects the paternalistic dynamics between the majority and minority cultures. Without discussing his concerns with Anna, Mark decided on an intervention for her. As previously mentioned, Mark's lack of awareness about his cultural biases reflects the abuse of power in an imbalanced power relationship.

The incident reflects the most dominant discourse assumptions that the ideal group counseling members are homogeneous in their personal characteristics and experience of a specific concern or situation. In regard to personal characteristics, there is the assumption that an ideal group counseling member is verbal, open to full self-disclosure, emotionally expressive, and psychologically healthy. Without preparation and modeling, group members are expected by group leaders to enter the group experience ready and skilled to interact with other group members, fully disclose their personal situation, publicly discuss their feelings, and possess a level of insight and sophistication that can connect the group experience with improvements in their lives. These expectations are seen in this incident via Mark jumping into the first session without providing an orientation to the group experience and expecting members to follow his lead and vision for the session. The group leader's emphasis on these characteristics often results in a group member being deemed as inappropriate for group (as Mark concluded about Anna) or in a failure of the group leader's facilitation skills if group members do not exhibit these characteristics in group.

I believe group leaders know in theory there is variation in individuals' response to the group process; however, there is a visceral expectation, especially in inexperienced group leaders, that a good group session has all members actively participating (talking) and connecting with each other; is filled with fluid, insightful discussions; and is on task with the structure and goals of the group. In addition, there is the assumption of homogeneity, especially surrounding theme groups like the divorce group offered by Mark. Groups potentially provide a less contrived environment of safety and support to group members because there is the knowledge upon entering the group that there is a shared commonality (surrounding the theme or topic) among group members. I believe group leaders believe homogeneous groups are easier to organize and manage, provide more security for group members, experience less conflict, and achieve cohesion sooner than heterogeneous groups. However, diversity is prominent in theme groups and should be acknowledged and addressed throughout the group process. Operating from an assumption of homogeneity may deter group leaders from addressing the differences observed among group members, keeping the group process focused on the specificity of the topic or problem, and minimizing the interpersonal dynamics among group members. Group leaders may overlook the opportunity to explore other factors (e.g., cultural variables) that affect an individual's coping style and overall group dynamics. Another dominant discourse is the assumption that all counselors are effective group leaders. Group leadership is a skill that builds on general counselor training but is specific in its theory and application of treatment strategies and interventions. The incident description did not indicate whether Mark was an experienced group leader. However, we can assume that Mark felt comfortable in offering the experience for the students as opposed to offering them individual sessions. Assuming group counseling is similar to individual counseling, a group leader can sidestep the planning process for group work, not realizing that behind-the-scene planning and preparation before the first group session are essential and ethical ingredients for a successful group. The incident discussion indicated Mark was too busy to offer Anna individual counseling. So whether Mark believed offering the group would be more efficient, more effective, or both is unclear. What is clear is that Mark succumbed to feelings of being pressured and skipped the vital steps of meeting the students individually and explaining informed consent. The assumption that any counselor can jump into a group and facilitate a good group experience is an erroneous assumption.

Counselors are ethically responsible for acquiring and maintaining a level of multicultural competence. Mark can improve his multicultural skills through a variety of activities. First, Mark can review the ACA and ASGW documents already referenced and listed in the references section. Mark can attend continuing education workshops and seminars on ethics, multicultural counseling, and working with culturally diverse populations. Mark can become more knowledgeable through readings and independent studies. To improve his counseling skills, Mark can seek supervision or peer consultation from a colleague who is multiculturally competent. Mark can also step outside his comfort zone and expand his personal experience with diversity by mindfully attending and participating in activities with people who are culturally different from himself. Multicultural counseling training will challenge Mark's worldview, biases, and values, and provide him with a foundation of sensitivity, awareness, and skills that would have benefited Anna and the entire group.

RESPONSE

Nancy Bodenhorn

There are a number of situations in the incident description in which it is evident that Mark is oblivious to his own biases. His decision to forego any individual meetings with students before starting the group indicates that he believes all of the students have the same understanding of the group process and of the expectation of belonging to a group. By unwittingly making this assumption based on his own biases, Mark has set up a situation in which Anna (or any other student who might have different ideas and expectations about sharing personal experiences in a group setting) is not recognized in terms of her cultural differences. To couple this decision with allowing the group members to take the lead is very problematic. This combination of decisions is dangerous and backfires in this situation. When biases are not recognized, and performance is judged only through one cultural lens (Mark's), the group does not have the possibility of coalescing. Genuineness within the group is in jeopardy because the implication is that difference is unacceptable.

In the first session, Mark attributes Anna's behavior to discomfort and timidity without considering the possibility that her behavior might be culturally appropriate. This, again, is an indication of a lack of cultural awareness. Many Asian and Asian American students are more reluctant to disclose their personal and family situations; but this is not an indication of discomfort. The fact that Anna returned to the group (assuming there was an option) is an indication she was not uncomfortable. Rather, it seems that Mark's discomfort is directing his actions. He also assumes that opening up about one's feelings is a healthy approach to life. This, too, is a cultural pattern and may not be the same assumption that Anna makes based on her cultural background.

Mark gives no indication of recognizing that others may have a different worldview or that any of his behavior is culture bound. In his further reflection about the first session, he indicates his belief that Anna seems "like an outsider," but attributes this to her age and socioeconomic status. Not considering a cultural factor is further evidence that Mark is oblivious to his own biases. He cannot envision that culture could be playing a role. Making a decision to take her out of the group and "tell her that the experience seems too overwhelming for her" is again a result of Mark's own biases. Talking with Anna individually will probably be appropriate, and hopefully there can be an exchange of ideas and information rather than a unilateral decision, especially one based on personal biases.

Primarily, it would have been helpful for Mark to obtain knowledge directly from each individual group member, including cultural information. Ideally, he would understand the values of many Asian cultures and the implications of the acculturation process. Furthermore, by recognizing the importance of individual differences within a cultural context, Mark could first talk with Anna in an attempt to understand her situation within the complexity of her life. Learning cultural values (i.e., not talking about family issues outside of the family, which is more typical of Asian cultures than the mainstream American culture) can be helpful, but the danger is attributing that cultural value to all people with a relationship to that culture. Background knowledge is helpful, but it should be seen as a starting point rather than an ending point.

I also think it will be helpful to find out about other group members who might have difficulty working with someone from another culture. In this situation, the male group member interrupted Anna and asked her to "crank it up a notch," indicating his own impatience with and intolerance of others different from himself. This, too, is a hindrance to the group process. By gathering information about the other students' experiences with and attitudes about students from other cultures, the group initiation could be much more productive.

Mark should have conducted individual meetings with each student prior to initiating the group. In this session, while describing the process and expectations of group membership, Mark could have mentioned to Anna an understanding that cultural values are diverse and ask her whether any of the expectations seemed uncomfortable.

Mark needs to acknowledge my assumption that Anna might be reticent about sharing her family experiences because of cultural values and recognize that her apparent reticence to express her own experiences is culturally appropriate. With this understanding, he could monitor his own expectations and judgments about her behavior in the group. He might allow more time for the students to get to know each other and build trust rather than start the first session with asking how each student learned of their parents' divorce. He could help the others in the group understand that all of us have various levels of what is considered appropriate to share with others. One of the goals of a support group is to help students understand they are not unique in their personal reactions to common experiences, and Anna might be gaining more in that direction than the other students. Mark could also have been more direct in establishing acceptable communication within the group. There is no indication that ground rules were established or discussed, but doing this would help the process. When the other student interrupted Anna, Mark could have expressed his displeasure more directly. This would have encouraged an acceptance of personal and cultural differences.

We tend to talk about ideal group members as being verbal, self-aware, and respectful of others. When group members do not fulfill those expectations, the group leader can feel a sense of failure, try to make all the group members fit that ideal, or decide to remove nonideal members. After the first session, Mark decided to "make a concerted effort" to include Anna "more actively." In other words, he tried to make her fit his ideal of verbal participation. When this did not work, he decided to remove her from the group, leaving as members those who fit his ideal. Believing in this ideal does not allow for students who are not as verbal or self-aware to participate and benefit from the group process.

Mark needs to go through a process of developing his personal awareness, his knowledge of other cultures, and his multicultural counseling skills as called for in the multicultural counseling competencies. Mark's personal awareness needs to come first: He needs not only to recognize that he has a culture and worldview through which he sees the world, but he also needs to understand that there are alternative worldviews. Awareness of other cultures can be improved through a variety of avenues including reading and other media, venturing out to various events that focus on other cultures, and getting to know members of other cultures. Mark could improve his multicultural counseling skills through taking a course, asking for help and/or receiving supervision from a counselor with more multicultural experience, and asking for (and accepting) feedback from a variety of his students.

REFERENCES

American Counseling Association. *Code of ethics and standards of practice.* (1995). Alexandria, VA: Author.

Association for Specialists in Group Work. (1998a). Best practice guidelines. *Journal for Specialists in Group Work, 23*(3), 237–244.

Association for Specialists in Group Work. (1998b). *Principles for diversity-competent group workers.* Retrieved from http://www.asgw.org

Association for Specialists in Group Work. (2000). *Professional standards for the training of group workers.* Retrieved from http://www.asgw.org

Helms, J. (1995). An update of Helm's White and people of color racial identity models. In J. G. Ponterotto, J. M. Casas, L. A.. Suzuki, & C. M. Alexander (Eds.), *Handbook of multicultural counseling* (pp. 181–191). Thousand Oaks, CA: Sage.

Sue, D. W., & Sue, D. (2003). *Counseling the culturally diverse: Theory and practice.* New York: Wiley.

LEADERSHIP TECHNIQUES

LEADER CONFRONTATION: "I'M NOT GOING THERE!"

This incident examines a situation in which leader confrontation of a member might be appropriate/necessary.

CRITICAL INCIDENT

Sheri Bauman

Background

Susan and Fred, experienced counselors and group leaders, cofacilitate a process group for eight male and female students in a high school. Many of the members struggle with relationships in their lives and have challenges relating to authority figures, peers, and parents. The group established norms in the first session, including honesty. The group discussed the importance of bringing concerns about the group to the group for discussion.

Henry is one of the members of the group. He is a sensitive, soft-spoken young man who joined the group to improve his interpersonal skills. He has participated in all sessions and has been very compassionate toward other group members. He has shared a bit about himself and appears to want to become more involved. Jim is also in the group and is a confident and self-assured young man. His voice is frequently heard in the group, offering advice and suggestions to other members, but revealing little about himself.

Incident

In the five sessions that the group has met, trust has been developing, and some members have begun to disclose their here-and-now reactions to each other. Most of these reactions have been positive, and some have shared that their initial impressions of others have changed as they get to know one another. One member of the group, Henry, came to the leaders after the last session to complain that he felt intimidated by Jim, whom he finds to be arrogant. Henry believed that Jim presents himself as better than the others in the group and that Jim implies he has no problems but is only in the group to help others. Henry wanted the leaders to "do something" about Jim's "attitude."

In their meeting with Henry, Susan and Fred emphasized the importance of honest feedback and stressed it would be helpful for Henry, and for Jim.

They also pointed out giving this feedback to Jim would provide Henry with the opportunity to discover if others in the group shared his concern. The leaders helped Henry role-play various scenarios in which he shares his concerns in the group and reminded Henry they would be active in supporting and protecting him in the group. Considerable time was spent in discussing Henry's concerns and preparing him to speak out in the group. Susan, Fred, and Henry decided the leaders would utilize a structured exercise that invited members to give feedback to one another in order to provide an opportunity for Henry to share his concerns. Henry left feeling prepared and confident, having made a commitment to bring up his reactions in the next meeting. The leaders were encouraged, believing that Henry, Jim, and the group as a whole would profit from the upcoming session, which they expected would bring the interactions into the here-and-now arena.

All members were present at the next session, and the exercise began. The leaders invited members to disclose their level of comfort with others in the group, and Henry said, "I like this group because I'm comfortable with everyone here." Susan suspected that Henry had had second thoughts about his ability to confront Jim, but felt she would be doing both boys and the group a disservice by ignoring the issue. So she said, "Henry, I know that is not true because you and Fred and I had a long talk about this yesterday. I know it's scary to confront someone, but the whole group will suffer if you aren't honest."

Discussion

Susan and Fred debriefed this interaction after the group left. Susan felt strongly that allowing Henry to gloss over his problem with another member would squander the opportunity to have a meaningful here-and-now interaction in the group. She felt that such interactions have the potential to move a group forward and to demonstrate the value of feedback. Fred did not agree. He felt that Henry was the one who needed to raise the issue, and if Henry was not ready to do so, the leaders should respect that. The two leaders discussed this at length and were unable to come to consensus about the best approach in this situation.

QUESTIONS

1. Should the leader confront a member when he or she knows the member is not being honest with the group?
2. Was Henry's disclosure to the leaders confidential? Did Susan violate his confidentiality by exposing him to the group?
3. How else might the leaders have handled Henry's concern and his later behavior in the group?
4. Was Susan exercising her responsibility as a leader to protect Henry? Did she set him up for attack and/or rejection by the group?

5. If Henry had responded to Susan's confrontation by saying, "What I told you yesterday is private, and I don't want to talk about it here," how might the leader(s) respond?

RESPONSE

John R. Culbreth

A key point in the concept of confrontation is the intent of the counselor. The typical understanding of confrontation is to highlight to a client some type of discrepancy in the message he or she has conveyed. In this situation, Henry conveyed a message to Susan and Fred about the behavior and lack of sharing from another group member, Jim. However, when provided with an opportunity to address this concern in the group setting, Henry stated he did not have any difficulty with any of the group members. Obviously, Henry is conveying two different messages to Susan and Fred. A confrontation in this situation, ideally, would be intended to highlight to Henry how what he has conveyed to Susan and Fred in a private meeting out of group is not consistent with what he has shared in the group.

Bringing attention to this discrepancy is not an unreasonable proposition for the group leaders. However, the intent of the confrontation, and how it is managed, is critically important. The way Susan brings attention to the discrepancy carries a tone of criticism for Henry. In this incident, it appears as though Susan does not approve of Henry's unwillingness to share his concerns, especially in light of the efforts made with him the previous day to prepare him for the discussion. If Susan's confrontation is an attempt to get Henry to come clean with his concerns about Jim, then this appears to be an effort by Susan to demonstrate her power as a group leader. If Susan believes that Henry is merely being dishonest with the group and she is trying to get him to be more honest in his feedback, then the method she chose might actually backfire, resulting in Henry feeling embarrassed or ashamed. Stating that the group will "suffer" from Henry's lack of honesty appears to promote a sense of shame in Henry for not sharing his feelings. Although it may be unfortunate Henry does not yet feel comfortable sharing his feelings about Jim, I think it is unfair to place the burden of the group's well-being on Henry's shoulders in this way. It is the group leaders' responsibility to manage the group process, not Henry's. Based on this interaction, I can understand why Henry might be much less inclined to share with the group and with Susan and Fred in the future.

Confidentiality of Henry's disclosure to Susan and Fred is an important question in this incident. A significant portion of this answer depends on how Susan and Fred set up out-of-group contacts and conversations for the group members. It is not uncommon for group members to have concerns or issues that they want to discuss with a group leader in a more private, individual setting. What is reported back to the whole group depends on how the leader structures this communication. If the communication has nothing to do with the group process or the group member within the group process, then a group leader can elect to not have the conversation disclosed to the group. If, however, the conversation is directly linked to the group process or to interaction with another group member, then group leaders will often expect the communication to be brought back to the group after the individual conversation is resolved. The critical element in this incident is that all group members have a right to be informed of this procedure, both at the outset of their group experience and as a reminder prior to any private conversation. This is a function of informed consent concerning group operational procedures. By allowing group processes and interactions to be discussed out of the group but not in the group, a group leader subverts members' efforts at learning appropriate and direct communication with other group members, which results in more harm than good for the group process.

If Susan and Fred did not explicitly state this procedure, then we could argue that Susan did violate Henry's confidentiality. However, it is not clear that this was a true violation in the strictest sense of the word. The result for Henry, though, is a feeling that his confidentiality was violated, which may be as detrimental for him as if it had really happened.

A different way to have handled Henry's concern was to have explained the group procedure for out-of-group communications between members and the leaders, as just outlined. An additional step that would have helped in the individual session with Susan and Fred would have been to discuss how the situation would be managed if Henry did not feel comfortable with disclosing his feelings in group. If Henry had known before group that Susan would bring up the issue if Henry did not, Henry might have been more forthright in his response to the group. This procedure results in a forcing of the issue, similar to what Susan tried; however, Henry is fully informed that this will happen prior to the events in the group.

Had Susan and Fred developed and explained the procedures for managing out-of-group communications, then Henry would have known what to expect and Susan's actions could be viewed as working to protect Henry's involvement in the group. However, because this was not the case, Susan's actions are not actually protecting Henry in this situation. In the debriefing of the interaction, Fred indicated he felt Henry should be allowed to determine for himself when he was ready to address this concern. So not only were Susan's actions not in the best interest of Henry, they created a difficult dynamic between the two group leaders.

In some sense, Susan did create a situation that may result in Henry being rejected from the group. Now the group knows that Henry has had some communication with the group leaders about some issue. They do not, however, know what the issue is or how it may impact them. This has created a dynamic of hidden information or secrets among select group members, namely the two leaders and Henry, resulting in what is referred to as *subgrouping*.

Responding to a statement from Henry about the privacy of his comments is a particularly difficult part of this scenario. As previously discussed, Susan and Fred have not created a procedure for dealing with this type of occurrence. Additionally, Susan and Fred appear to disagree on how the situation should be handled. Given these two challenging aspects of the situation, Susan and Fred might respond by describing what is and is not considered private communication between group members and the group leaders. This might be followed with a discussion about how the group is feeling about the issue of private communication with the group leaders. This may result in a clearer understanding among group members about how out-of-group conversations are handled. Another area to explore could be how group members address concerns they have with interactions in the group and with various group members. What-if situations could be presented to the group to provide ideas to consider and discussion material for how group members might feel in certain situations. This part of the conversation may make Henry feel more supported in his feelings toward Jim and in feeling that he has some element of control about his disclosure, possibly resulting in his sharing with the group how he perceives Jim as a group member.

RESPONSE

Judith A. Harrington

The answer to this question is complicated by two questions in this incident: Whom should the leader have confronted? and To whom did the burden of honesty belong? I believe the problem goes back to an even earlier need for confrontation within the group and with Jim. The leaders struggled with the line between letting the group behave as it was described, with some members participating wholly and others less than fully, and confrontation. Although Henry was a timid young man, he was carrying his weight in the group as contrasted with Jim, who was not disclosing. Perhaps they contributed to Henry's plea for help by failing to confront Jim about his advice giving and failure to disclose. Arguably, Jim was not being honest in his participation in the group. He may not have lied or told falsehoods, but he reportedly consistently did not participate authentically and actively by sharing of himself, choosing instead to serve as an advice giver. By contrast, Henry had stated goals for himself; he reportedly was participating fully; and rightly or wrongly, he was help seeking.

Especially with a group of this age, and with the history of personal relationship difficulties said to have existed among its members, the leaders have a responsibility to encourage healthy group behavior, to nudge the group to take care of itself as a whole, to model behaviors to members about how to confront each other appropriately, and, if all that fails, to confront a group member directly, empathically, and appropriately. I believe that Susan's confrontation of Henry was displaced, that he was scapegoated, and that confronting Jim should never have been his burden to carry alone. In this incident, I am concerned about Susan's own personal functioning, her own honesty, and her visiting of her own difficulties onto Henry while perhaps overidentifying with Jim.

I believe that it *is* within the scope of the counselor's job to reflect discrepancies and to hold the mirror of self-examination to clients, to confront. The question, then, is not "if" but "how."

The leaders blurred confidentiality principles by agreeing to meet with Henry and apparently not providing informed consent information to Henry or the group about the terms of confidentiality. Susan and Fred may or may not have clarified at the very beginning of group all the possible terms of confidentiality; but just as informed consent is an ongoing process, they should have clarified this at the beginning of group, at the beginning of Henry's consultation with them, and at the end of their consultation with him. They should not have entered into a secret with him, but they also did not inform him of what material would get launched into the group.

Confidentiality also has to do with what material disclosed in an individual session is privy across lines to a group session and vice versa (a dual relationship or dual function issue). Had they believed he should have shared his sentiments across lines from individual session to the group, it would have been preferable that they nudge, not force, him to speak on his own behalf, rather than to betray his here-and-now feelings as had been the precedent for earlier group sessions. When he resisted disclosing his feelings, I believe they should have respected this while also tagging it for a possible issue to return to later. The tension Henry had with Jim was likely to have increased, thus providing other openings for the conflict to be handled in the group session. What Henry did is fairly common among group members (perhaps more likely in a group of this age and in this setting) until expectations are normed and safety is achieved. The incident reveals that the leaders stated norms in the first session, but we know that storming may precede group performance and adherence to these norms.

The leaders should have prepared for the possibility of out-of-group contacts with its members, especially in a school setting, and developed some clinical guidelines and boundaries. Their approach might have focused on the dual relationship/function challenges in having individual sessions with persons who are also in groups; on terms of confidentiality; on possible triangulation, alliances, and scapegoating; and on leader/member division of responsibility.

When Henry approached them about his feelings of intimidation related to Jim, I think it was certainly appropriate to listen and to honor his help seeking. Reflection, clarification, and isolating the nature of the problem might have been an appropriate response. However, Susan and Fred turned the seemingly impromptu conversation into not only a counseling and coaching session but also a rush into problem solving and subgrouping.

Advisable in such a situation is first to clarify where boundaries of the group begin and end and the potential problems if they agreed to discuss group issues outside of group. Then Susan and Fred could have stated that they wanted to help Henry to further his confidence and overcome his stated sensitivities by promoting a steady response to Jim directly in the group so he himself could earn the victory of speaking on his own behalf. I think they should have also clarified with him in appropriate language how they might behave in group if he spoke up on his own behalf, how they would advocate for personal empowerment and the health of the group but not take sides. They should not have colluded with Henry by judging Jim, but kept the focus on Henry's own confidence and voice issues.

They might have explained that they had an obligation to the group as a whole, that they could not guarantee other persons' reactions or conduct, and that they were committed to the goals and needs of the group (process group ostensibly designed to assist students with relationship and authority problems). Had they recommended assertiveness training or related skill-building opportunities, I believe they could have referred him to other options that were not so tied in with the group's dynamics. Also, it is unclear if Henry had an individual counseling outlet apart from Susan or Fred, but that might have been an adjuvant option.

They might have given Henry some items to think about as homework and to consider bringing back to the group, such as

- Why am I fearful and sensitive and how can I overcome it?
- What help do I need from others when I feel intimidated?
- What do I feel when I am intimidated, and what choices do I have when I feel this way?
- What strengths do I have within myself that are a good match to these types of situations?
- When have I handled a situation in the past well and what can I draw on again in this situation?
- How did I learn to feel this way in the presence of strong personalities?
- Who am I reminded of when I am in the presence of a strong intimidating personality?
- What do I do or feel when people don't behave the way that I want them to?

They might have reframed the situation as an opportunity for Henry to try some new behaviors and to experiment with the help and safety of a group. They might have identified that there may be many people like Jim out there in the world and this might be a good time to practice his assertiveness skills. I believe both group leaders mishandled their responsibility to the group and to Jim by failing to hold Jim to the same standards as everyone else. They mishandled their responsibility to Henry in letting it go too far, and Henry should never have been left to function as a faux leader. It resembles dysfunctional families wherein a child is prone to overfunctioning in an effort to stabilize things.

Susan and Fred appeared to grasp, at least theoretically, the concept of individuals' responsibility to act on their own behalf in the group, but I believe they lost sight of where the line is, what *clinical judgment* means, and what *do no harm* means. Henry had evidenced relatively good judgment in the group in previous sessions, had been help seeking, and seemed to work from a position of honesty all along. Why did Susan take him to a place that he, in the here and now, did not want to go?

We know that rescuing and enabling are not good options, but careful clinical decision making and advanced empathy are essential in any counseling setting. Not only did she model hostile conduct toward him, thus suggesting by example that hostile confrontation is an appropriate option, but she also planted a seed that this is an option, by implication, that might occur to anyone in the group.

A glaring error, as already mentioned, was the omission of clearly stated informed consent, and also the leaders' choice to turn a help-seeking request into an individual session, perhaps even subgrouping. A priority should have been to be clear about the lines of confidentiality before Henry was encouraged to work on assertiveness skills outside of the group. Having missed that, Susan might have responded to Henry with reflection, engagement, and clarification rather than confrontation and betrayal. She might have said

- "I'm hearing you say that you consider our talk yesterday as a private conversation."
- "I'm hearing you say that you don't feel comfortable talking about our conversation yesterday."
- "When you say that our talk was private, I'm wondering what you're feeling about the prospect of sharing with the group?"
- "I'm wondering how I might be helpful to you at this time."
- "I'm wondering how you and I together can be open with the group about our conversation yesterday."
- "I'm aware that I feel an obligation to you and your need for privacy and also to the group and its need for open communication. I wonder how we might respect both of those needs."
- "I'm wondering if there's anything that you could ask of the group so that what you said in private might be shared with the group in a more comfortable way."
- "I'm aware that what you shared with me yesterday seems very important for the group, and I'd like to commend you for honoring your feelings. My hope is that, with more time, you might be able to share your feelings with the group."

In many ways, these replies are designed to talk-about-how-to-talk-about-it, which can be a way of doing risk management during conflict. No matter what Henry's responses to these statements may be, I believe the burden of extending unconditional positive regard belongs to the group leaders, and they are to model equal acceptance of him as they would with all group members.

In addition to the technical problems just discussed, there are additional therapeutic problems, such as countertransference, projective identification, and parallel process. Susan's response to Henry echoed Jim's style. Is this a case of parallel process, wherein she began to repeat a pattern or dynamic that had been transmitted from Jim to her? How did Susan find herself in the position of mimicking Jim's bossiness and defectiveness? Was it unintentional, was she sympathetic to Jim, was it unconscious and a part of her own psychodynamics, was she afraid to confront Jim, was she biased toward Jim's style? Is she herself really an unconfident and overly sensitive person, unable to confront others who she sees as stronger than she is?

Her reaction to Henry and choice of managing the situation crossed over the do-no-harm line and reflects poor clinical judgment and poor empathy. All these, and the seeming evidence of countertransference and parallel process, would be interesting, if not essential, to explore in clinical supervision.

CHAPTER 34

LEADER SELF-DISCLOSURE: "SHOULDN'T I BE A ROLE MODEL?"

This incident explores the appropriateness of leader self-disclosure and how it may harm the group process.

CRITICAL INCIDENT

Patricia Goodspeed

Background

Marie works as a counselor in an agency that provides services for unemployed workers. The clients who are referred to this agency are certified by the State Department of Labor as unlikely to return to their previous occupations. There are many personal issues that need to be addressed in addition to choosing another career, particularly those associated with anger, grief and loss, depression, and low self-esteem. Career and personal counseling is provided in small groups of five to seven people and augmented with individual sessions. The groups are semistructured, include a sequence of activities related to career counseling, and address personal issues. Although most clients find one to two individual sessions sufficient, occasionally several sessions are needed to resolve personal issues that impede progress relative to career issues.

Marie is very popular with her clients. She has always received excellent evaluations, which she attributes to her style. She typically self-discloses in the group relative to her own career transitions and crises, her experiences as an adult student, and her educational pathways, thereby modeling how she successfully manages transitions. Several clients have expressed to her how much they had been inspired by her successful transitions and by the risks she had to take in order to get where she is. Many clients related that they gained a great deal of insight into their own options and saw new possibilities for themselves as a result of this inspiration. Evaluations at the end of each 4-week group session, and at a 1-year follow-up, confirmed that the groups were highly successful for many of the members.

Incident

One group member, Steve, was a man in his early 50s who had experienced many problems in his life since he had been downsized 6 years previously. He had been a welder, and because this was a declining occupation, he decided to seek employment elsewhere. He had applied for many entry-level jobs, such as convenience store clerk and warehouse worker, and had become very discouraged at never being invited to interview for positions. After a while, Steve began to feel hopeless and helpless and he developed a sense of low self-worth. As he said, he couldn't even get a job at a convenience store, where they "hire just about anybody." He came into the group placing blame on everybody and everything outside of himself for causing his situation.

Marie suggested that Steve might benefit from some individual sessions, and because he felt he had nothing to lose after being unemployed for 6 years, he was open to the suggestion. During the individual sessions, Marie learned that Steve had experienced multiple, significant losses along with his job. He had lost his home, his wife had a divorced him, his children had grown and left the home, which left him feeling no longer head of a family. He was Italian, and being the breadwinner and the head of his household was an important part of his identity. Now that his roles had shifted, he felt empty, and life held no more meaning for him.

Steve began to make rapid progress in the individual counseling sessions and in the group. He came to some insights regarding his typical approach to solving problems, and he realized that he was casting himself as a victim. In addition, simple career interventions, such as help in rewriting his resume and instruction on job search methods, proved very beneficial. He began to identify new career possibilities based upon his transferable skills.

Marie was divorced, and she knew she needed support in her personal life separate from her professional life. One evening during the week she attended an open support group for divorced and widowed persons. On one particular evening, Steve was sitting in the group of about 20 people. She had never seen Steve at these groups before. She felt uncomfortable, but decided to stay. She reasoned that self-disclosure had proven extremely beneficial in the past with her clients, and this could give Steve an opportunity to see how she handled her own divorce issues. During the course of the evening, Marie shared with the group difficulties she was having, particularly around being shy in social situations, along with some other details of her divorce and fears about being single. Steve was not very talkative in the group, and Marie was so engaged in working on her issues that she seemed to forget about his presence.

Discussion

The next week, when Steve came for his usual appointment, he seemed more withdrawn than usual, and a bit uncomfortable and anxious. The rapport they had spent so long developing was not evident in this session. His progress seemed to suddenly stop. He stated he now felt funny because he knew the details of Marie's life. Marie tried to ease his discomfort and suggested he might be disappointed because he now saw Marie as a real human being with the same fears and weaknesses as anyone else. She rationalized that she saw herself as a role model for dealing with her issues in a positive way. After all, this practice had been extremely successful in producing positive results in her groups so far, and she felt she should go with what works. The following week, Steve called to cancel his appointment because he had started working at one of the jobs he had been exploring with Marie during previous counseling sessions. Because the ultimate goal of the agency was to help clients find work, Marie felt Steve was a success story because he had found employment related to his goals.

QUESTIONS

1. Was this a case of successful resolution based on the employment outcome, or did the counselor have a further obligation to the client regarding his personal issues?
2. Did the self-disclosure technique work equally well in both types of groups (career/transition and divorce/support)? Why or why not?
3. Are there any concerns with the way the leader handled either of the instances of self-disclosure?
4. Because self-disclosure occurred in a support group that was separate from the counselor's professional role, are there any ethical considerations?

RESPONSE

Vivian J. Carroll McCollum

Because Marie had not terminated with Steve either through group or personal counseling, it appears the work was unfinished. Much of Marie's success with her clients came with her self-disclosure and the augmentation of individual sessions. Through the individual sessions, Marie had a further obligation to Steve beyond what appeared to be a superficial resolution to his employment issues. Her obligation extends to helping him with personal issues that continue to plague his successfully finding and maintaining employment. Marie could continue to work with Steve on issues that keep him from holding a job for an extended period of time.

Self-disclosure worked well with the career/transition group because it did not jeopardize Marie's ability to lead the group, because self-disclosure was more fundamental and less personal in these instances, and because no ethical boundaries were violated. Self-disclosure is often successful with groups when the leader knows how much to disclose and when it is appropriate to disclose.

Self-disclosure in the divorce/support group was a failure for both Steve and Marie. Because the support group was separate from Marie's professional role, there were some ethical considerations. Marie voluntarily established a dual relationship with Steve. Marie placed herself in the conflicting role of group peer with Steve when she chose to remain at the support group meeting and work on her personal issues. She also remained his group leader and his personal counselor. As a result, both Steve and Marie felt uncomfortable, Marie appeared to have lost her professional image, and Steve felt it necessary to terminate by canceling his next appointment.

There are concerns about the way Marie handled self-disclosure in the divorce/support group. Marie tried to rationalize to herself why it was appropriate for her to remain in the support group. When Steve mentioned his discomfort, Marie then tried to comfort him by rationalizing to him why her actions were appropriate, indicating that she was demonstrating role model behavior. When Marie realized Steve was a member of the support group, there were decisions she should have more carefully considered. For instance, she should have asked herself if there was another group she could attend, and she should have considered skipping that meeting and getting Steve's opinion on how it might affect their working relationship. Marie should also have considered what amount of personal information, if any, to disclose for therapeutic purposes for herself and for Steve, and most of all she should have considered if the negative results of her self-disclosure might outweigh the positive ones.

RESPONSE

Sheri Bauman

What constitutes successful resolution of counseling is dependent upon the mutually agreed upon goals established collaboratively by the client and counselor. In this case, the initial goals apparently related to both career counseling (improving employability or job-seeking skills) and resolving personal issues. Once it became clear the incident in the divorce group had negatively impacted the individual counseling relationship, Marie had an ethical obligation to refer to ensure the client received appropriate treatment. Marie also had a professional obligation to provide an opportunity for Steve to discuss his reactions rather than to dismiss them with a perfunctory explanation. It appears that Marie was more interested in her own success than that of her client.

There are several questions a counselor should ask him- or herself prior to sharing personal material with clients: For whose benefit is this sharing? What is the therapeutic purpose of this disclosure? Will this disclosure deflect the focus from client to counselor? In this case, it appears the disclosures in the career group were offered as an example and incentive to the clients, and thus at first glance appear to be for the benefit of the clients. However, Marie should engage in careful introspection regarding possible other motives. For example, she may have a strong need to receive approval and affirmation of her worth from her clients, which is a possibility given that she attributes her popularity with clients to her style of self-disclosure. The American Counseling Association *Code of Ethics and Standards of Practice* (ACA, 1995), states that counselors "avoid actions that seek to meet their personal needs at the expense of clients" (section A.5.a).

In the career group, it appears that Marie's self-disclosures could be and were seen as examples to group members of successfully negotiating adult employment transitions. We hope and assume that Marie's experience was not the focus of the group and that excessively detailed information was not offered. It might have been more appropriate to have individuals not in the leadership position in the group, such as guest speakers, provide that kind of modeling. Utilizing a variety of guests could also have broadened the identification opportunities for clients.

In the divorce group, although Marie had sought this group for her personal issues (which is appropriate, particularly for counselors who are mindful of the importance of avoiding working on their issues with clients), once Steve was observed at the meeting, Marie would have been wise to leave. The situation created an inappropriate dual relationship. Assuming Steve observed her enter and leave, it would have been appropriate to process this with him individually. This brings up the question of whether therapists/counselors should seek such community self-help groups for their own treatment, or whether it is advisable to obtain treatment and support from closed groups or in individual therapy where such dual relationships can be avoided.

Because she had a therapeutic relationship with that client, the lines were blurred and this became a dual relationship. The ACA Code of Ethics states that counselors "make every effort to avoid dual relationships with clients that could impair professional judgment or increase the risk of harm to clients" (section A.6.a). The potential for Marie's professional judgment to be impaired as a result of interaction in the group is clearly present, and given the subsequent behavior of the client, the risk for harm was also present. Because other sources of personal support and treatment are available, Marie erred in proceeding to attend and disclose personal material at that group.

REFERENCE

American Counseling Association. (1995). *Code of ethics and standards of practice.* Alexandria, VA: Author.

CHAPTER 35

CUTTING OFF: "IT JUST FEELS IMPOLITE"

This incident addresses concerns that arise when the presence or absence of leader interventions fails to block inappropriate member participation.

CRITICAL INCIDENT

S. Lenoir Gillam

Background

Carson and Karen are new interns at a university counseling center. Their site supervisor understands that both have interest in group work, despite having little experience, so she works to ensure they will have an opportunity to develop and begin leading a group early in the semester. Carson and Karen have had two classes together during their graduate program, but they do not know each other well. Nevertheless, they seem to have similar personalities, and both are interested in working together. They decide to co-facilitate a personal growth group for traditional-aged college sophomores.

Incident

After several weeks of planning and screening prospective members, Carson and Karen are ready to start their 8-week group. The pregroup process went well, and the two interns are confident as members arrive for the first session. They ask members to check in briefly and share with other members their purpose for joining the group.

The first two members check in, keeping their comments focused and succinct. The third member, Roger, begins a long-winded account of his roommate difficulties and then shifts to family concerns. The leaders note that other members are attentive at first, but Roger's rambling soon leads others to lose interest. He finally winds down, and the rest of the members take their turns; but the first session ends before the discussion can proceed much beyond check-in. The interns stay to process the session and agree they will need to keep Roger on task.

The next few of sessions run fairly smoothly. However, Roger continues to monopolize conversations and take the group off track. The leaders struggle to keep him focused and hope that if they continue to use good attending skills when Roger speaks, then maybe they will be able to eventually confront him about taking over the group. They have a hard time gauging other members' reactions because of the frequent eye contact they are making with Roger.

With 5 minutes left in one session, another member named Sandra reveals to the group that she would like to talk about a serious concern. Other group members, seeming relieved to have the focus on someone other than Roger, are quite empathic as Sandra tells her story. The group runs 45 minutes late, but the leaders agree it is okay because Sandra needed the group time. Before the group ends, one of the leaders asks the group to summarize what had been discussed that day, looking at Roger as the question was being posed. Roger immediately volunteers to summarize but instead retells a story about an issue he had talked about earlier that day in group. After he finishes, the interns announce that time is up, and the group concludes.

The remaining sessions proceed along this same course. The interns become quite frustrated with having Roger in the group. The final straw occurs in the 7th week when Roger makes insensitive comments about interracial dating, failing to recognize that his values are offending other members. Carson and Karen breathe a sigh of relief after the final group ends and reassure themselves they will continue to improve with experience.

Discussion

The interns are asked by the center's director to present their group case at the next staff meeting. With the assistance of their site supervisor, who has been supervising them weekly, they discuss this experience with the staff. They realize that they have much to learn about group work, particularly with regard to their inability to cut off members who are long-winded, are off task, prevent a deeper focus on issues, or make harmful remarks to others. Although they once believed that cutting off, or blocking, was rude or harmful, they have learned that it is actually critical to a group's success.

QUESTIONS

1. How could the leaders have used cutting-off skills to make check-in run more smoothly?
2. What are examples of verbal interventions that the leaders could have made to shift the focus off of Roger or to make his contributions more focused?
3. What are examples of nonverbal interventions that the leaders could have made to shift the focus off of Roger or to prevent his immediate input?
4. How might the leaders have addressed the insensitivity to value differences?
5. How could the leaders have used cutting-off skills to prevent new business from being introduced at the very end of the session as Sandra shared about her history?

RESPONSE

Angela D. Coker

Dealing with a monopolizer in a group is often bothersome and problematic even for the most seasoned group facilitator (Carroll & Wiggins, 1997; Corey & Corey, 1997; Yalom, 1995). Although our human sensibilities tell us that it is not nice to cut others off when they are talking, our knowledge of group leadership reminds us of another reality. In group work it is more detrimental not to cut off a person who monopolizes its content and dominates the process of a group than to remain silent. New group members do not know what a good working group looks or feels like, so they look for direction from their facilitator(s). By allowing a monopolizer to continue with his or her destructive behavior, group facilitators quietly communicate and establish negative group norms. They indirectly role model for group members that it is appropriate for one member to dominate and that it is impolite to cut off members in the midst of dysfunctional group dynamics. In reality, it is these types of group dynamics that need to be addressed quickly to ensure that every group members' goals are being worked on. If this does not happen, group members get the impression that the monopolizer is the only one who matters.

Usually when individuals monopolize, they have issues with being in control, feel a high sense of importance/entitlement, or are so self-absorbed that they are truly oblivious to the feelings of others around them. Carson and Karen could have first dealt with the issue of Roger in a very indirect way and then gradually become more confrontational. In answering the questions, I advocate utilizing the following techniques:

- Use nonverbal cues such as periodically avoiding eye contact with Roger and smiling at others as a way of encouraging them to participate. Group facilitators should maintain eye contact throughout the group with all members to try to gauge reactions to various incidents that occur in the session.
- Structure the group by making statements and asking questions such as, "We only have a few minutes left until our group is over. Does anyone who hasn't shared want to say something now?" The group facilitator could also make statements such as, "Roger, you have a lot to share, but if you could wait a moment, I'd like to check in with others we have not heard from yet." The facilitators might also use a check-in exercise as a way to ensure that all members have an opportunity to speak. By keeping the check-in focused on a brief summary of what that member wants to discuss that day, the facilitators might try having members estimate how much time they will need in group and have them self-monitor.

- Use more process goals, such as working in the here and now, as a means of heightening the directness, intensity, and confrontation toward Roger. When checking in with members of the group, the leaders could go around the room and ask each member to use an adjective or two describing how they feel right after Roger monopolizes the group. The timing in the here and now is very important. It allows the group members to really tap into their current feelings about how the group is evolving. The group facilitators could stop and process in the here and now by asking group members how they are feeling about Roger's behavior. Also, Carson and Karen could ask members if they feel they have gotten enough time in the group that day.
- Use direct verbal communication. It may be necessary for the facilitators to openly, but gently, confront Roger. Karen and Carson may say something like, "Roger, I have noticed you tend to dominate the group and leave little time for others to contribute. Were you aware of this behavior?" The sole intent of this question is to give Roger feedback on how his behavior impacts the therapeutic growth and cohesion of the group. In the beginning stages of a group, it is natural for members to be quiet and reluctant to speak. However, if this behavior continues with Roger being the only vocal member, confrontations by the facilitator should be directed toward the compliant and tolerating silent group members. Karen or Carson might say, "I have noticed that many of you remain silent throughout Roger's monopolizing. What does that behavior do for you? Is it helping you meet your individual needs and goals? If not, what does your silence say about you?" These confrontations/approaches are twofold. They give both Roger and the other group members the opportunity to reflect on their in-group behavior. Chances are the members' in-group behaviors are being exhibited in their everyday outside lives. Ask group members how they are doing with meeting their goals in the group. Are they meeting them by allowing Roger to use most of the group's time?
- Set ground rules. Using a more structured approach, the facilitators can set ground rules—no monopolizing; have respect for other members' time and ownership of the group—at the beginning stage of the group and remind members to adhere to them. Other ground rules could include respect for differing opinions and no deliberately offensive remarks. This should also work nicely in dealing with Roger's insensitive comments about interracial relationships. In the event that Roger's offensiveness continues, the group members could exercise the right of asking Roger to leave the group as a consequence of his behavior. Further, use of here-and-now interventions might be particularly useful in addressing Roger's insensitivity. Another ground rule

might be to end on time unless a member has an emergency issue that can't wait. Encourage members to assert their needs during the check-in exercise, which should prevent members from bringing up new issues at the very end of group.

Coming in contact with difficult clients is a challenge that every group facilitator can count on. In fact, it is the problem-free group that should raise eyebrows among facilitators. Various degrees of conflict are part of the group process. Cofacilitators need to get to know each other's personalities and counseling strengths as much as possible. They need to talk about past group counseling experiences, confront their own personal issues (to guard against countertransference), and seek continued supervision. In fact, it was probably not wise to allow Karen and Carson to cofacilitate the group because they had little prior experience leading groups. Their supervisor should have insisted that Karen and Carson cofacilitate a group with a more seasoned group leader in order to develop their group leadership skills. Also, group facilitators need to be aware of how their facilitating style may contribute to the dynamics of the group. Are group members not confronting Roger because they think it is the facilitators' job and do not want to step on Karen or Carson's toes by doing so? Group leaders need to watch out for members who are very sensitive or who have a tendency to put the feelings or needs of others before their own. Remember that the purpose of any group is to assist its members with meeting their personal goals. It must never be about meeting the needs or fears of its group facilitators.

RESPONSE

Robyn L. Trippany

Carson and Karen have done a thorough job in the pregroup phase and are excited about the group beginning. However, it seems they did not anticipate a monopolizer as a member and are not prepared to deal with this particular group problem. The group leaders could have used a variety of cutting-off skills with Roger. One such skill would have been the statement, "Roger, it sounds like you have a lot to tell the group, and we will be able to talk more about that after we have had an opportunity to check in with the other members." The leaders might have used humor, as in, "Whoa, Roger! You have a lot of news today!" and hoped for him to respond to the cue and keep his comments to a minimum during check-in. The leaders might also have used the round-robin format to check-in, as in "I want everyone to rate their mood from 1 to 10," or "If you were an animal, what animal would you be today?" In addition, if using the round-robin format the leaders could start with the person to Roger's left and go around the group clockwise, leaving Roger to be the last to check in. Or the leaders could have asked members to bring in three things to talk about during the next session and then agreed to discuss at least one of those items for each member, more if time permits.

Shifting the focus from one group member back to the rest of the group is a delicate process. Certainly, a group leader never wants the members to feel rejected. However, in situations like this, it is crucial to maintain a group rather than an audience. The leaders could have reflected the feelings Roger described and then, looking at other group members, have asked, "Who else has felt like this?" or "Who else has had a similar situation?" The leaders could have also asked Roger to summarize what it is he wanted to share with the group so the other members have time to share. Further, the leaders could have used nonverbal techniques to minimize Roger's discussions, such as not making eye contact with him when posing questions to the group, not attending so thoroughly when he is being long-winded, making eye contact with other group members more frequently, and shifting their bodies to other members as an invitations for them to speak.

When any group member has made comments that appear to be offensive to the group, it is important to address them so as to not create a barrier that impacts the group bonding. The leaders could have commented to Roger, "It sounds like you do not agree with interracial marriages. However, I don't think this is how everyone in here feels. Although this belief might fit for you, it may be offensive to your comembers." If the other members need to respond, it is important the leaders not allow the discussion to become a debate, and intervene by stating, "This is a controversial topic and I am hearing a lot of different opinions. However, I think we should focus on the topic that we are here to discuss."

To minimize new material being introduced at the end of a session, humor could be used. In this incident, the group was already 45 minutes late, and the leader(s) could have said, "Roger, although I am sure everyone wants to stay here until midnight, we will get locked in the building if we stay any longer!" The leaders could also suggest that Roger remember what he wanted to discuss and then include it on his list of three items to discuss at the next group meeting. The leaders could also choose to simply state, "Roger, we are out of time for tonight."

REFERENCES

Carroll, M.R., & Wiggins, J.D. (1997). *Elements of group counseling: Back to basics* (2nd ed.). Denver, CO: Love.

Corey, M.S., & Corey, G. (1997). *Groups: Process and practice* (5th ed.). Pacific Grove, CA: Brooks/Cole.

Yalom, I.D. (1995). *The theory and practice of group psychotherapy* (4th ed.). New York: Basic Books.

CHAPTER 36

USING SILENCE: "SILENCE IS NOT ALWAYS GOLDEN"

This incident explores issues related to a novice group counselor who lacks appropriate use and implementation of effective silence within the group process. Supervisory interventions regarding these issue are also addressed.

CRITICAL INCIDENT

Jill D. Duba

Background

Jim has recently completed his course work and practica experience in a community counseling master's program. He has worked with several Caucasian and African American clients; however, he has not had much experience in working with clients from other cultures. Although Jim has had limited experience in leading groups, he feels especially confident in his counseling and leadership skills. Throughout his program, he has been encouraged and praised for his ability to demonstrate particular skills such as being able to empathize, interpret, question, support, and confront. Jim has recently begun his internship experience at a family-counseling agency in an urban setting.

Incident

Jim was recently assigned as leader for an adolescents-of-divorced-parents group. Eight adolescents, ages 13 to 16, comprise the group. Jim was excited to hear that these eight adolescents represent a range of cultural groups: Caucasian (three), African American (two), Native American (one), and Asian American (two).

During the first couple of sessions, each lasting 1 hour and 15 minutes, Jim implemented warm-up exercises in hopes of encouraging members to become comfortable and connected with each other. He felt these exercises proved to be successful, as all of the members were attentive to his instructions and seemed to be fairly participatory.

After a couple of sessions, Jim lessened the time he spent on warm-up activities and began to focus more on the group process and on the content of the discussion. By the sixth session, Jim felt especially proud of the sessions he was leading. There seemed to be continuous dialogue and discussion throughout the sessions. Jim also reported to his supervisor that he felt "accomplished" after each session.

During supervision, Jim showed his supervisor clips of videotape in which particular adolescents were interacting with each other, processing their feelings, and responding to Jim's seemingly empathic and encouraging interventions. He expressed to his supervisor that "the sessions are going just great! Everyone is participating and the discussion just never seems to die down. I never feel stuck in what to say and I feel so energized during that hour and 15 minutes!" His supervisor reported she was especially proud of him, and from what he was showing her, it seemed as if he was demonstrating strong group leadership and personal skills with the teenagers.

During the last group session, Jim asked the members of the group to share what they had learned through the group process. Jim was happy to hear that most of the members expressed they were able to see that their parents' divorce was not their fault. Upon leaving, Jim asked the members to write down anything in addition they had gotten from the group.

Discussion

Upon reading the responses from the group members, Jim's supervisor became concerned about two particular responses. Steve, an Asian American member, had written that it was "a good group because he didn't have to talk and Jim would end up saying what he was thinking" and he "hated to talk anyway." Another female member, Ellen, commented that she will miss having someone give her "such good advice all of the time." When the supervisor took it upon herself to view the last session in its entirety, she found that Jim seemed to talk either above or in an especially directed manner with these members in particular.

When Jim's supervisor addressed him with these concerns, Jim became confused and disheartened. He reported that he tried his best to allow all of his "members to feel as comfortable as possible." Jim further stated he "felt bad for Steve because he just seemed so uncomfortable when he was talking." He also reported that Ellen reminded him of his little sister, and he "figured that young girls could use as much feedback as possible."

QUESTIONS

1. How might the use of silence as a therapeutic intervention have worked with this group? In other words, what might it have encouraged?
2. What was sacrificed in the group process and member development by not implementing appropriate silence?
3. How might the use of appropriate silence have attended to cultural differences?
4. What role did Jim's supervisor play in Jim's lack of using appropriate silence?

RESPONSE

Patricia J. Neufeld

There are several aspects of this incident that require consideration. One is the role of supervision in the growth of the counselor in training. Others are the use of silence as a leadership technique, the understanding of cultural differences, and the need for greater supervisor involvement.

The purpose of supervision is to foster the professional growth and effectiveness of the counselor in training. Many times the role of the university supervisor is a combination of teacher and consultant. Like teaching, supervision requires higher order questioning in order to facilitate the growth and effectiveness of the supervisee. In this incident Jim seems to be reporting to his supervisor. This method of supervision is not always successful in promoting student learning. In the example with Jim, during supervision Jim is enthusiastic and reports that everything is "going just great." He also makes the statement that "everyone is participating and the discussion just never seems to die down." It is necessary when supervising interns to explore with them their perceptions of what is occurring within the group in order to understand and experience the stages of group counseling. Jim's supervisor might have asked him to interpret the active group discussion and what that means in the context of the growth of the group. The supervisor should have also explored, during the viewing of the video clips with Jim, how the interactions among the adolescents were therapeutic.

In regard to the use of silence as a therapeutic intervention, teaching interns or supervisees that silence is a necessary and integral aspect of counseling is imperative. Adolescents are often self-conscious about their interpersonal skills and typically find it easiest to respond to closed-end questions rather than questions that require thought and developed answers. For interns to understand that adolescents need time, or a period of silence, to develop their answer or reflect upon how they want to respond to the statement or question that was posed by the intern or another group member is important. Pauses of several seconds are necessary for the thoughts to be formulated in the minds of the group members.

Many times it is the discomfort of the counselor-in-training that limits or refutes the use of silence. Interns who talk too much or talk for their clients are guilty of rescuing, and thus prevent their clients from working through the difficultly they are experiencing. Using silence appropriately, in this situation of an adolescents-of-divorced-parents group, would have allowed the adolescents to develop and think through their responses.

Unfortunately, growth on the part of the group members was sacrificed or short-changed because of Jim's domination of the group process. Although Jim's supervisor only became aware of Jim's domination of the group near the end of supervision, the supervisor could have used the situation as a teachable moment. The supervisor could explore with Jim what he believes the role of a group facilitator is and when facilitating may cross the line and become preaching, or perhaps even self-promoting. The supervisor could also explore Jim's confusion and disheartenment with him. Perhaps this is the aspect of this situation that is most important and holds the possibility for growth in Jim as a counselor in training. Jim might be very uncomfortable to learn that his talking over, specifically, several group members might have actually impeded their growth within the group. This learning experience for Jim may be the impetus that encourages him to explore within himself his need to "help" and "rescue" his clients. If Jim can understand that, he is on his way to using silence more appropriately in counseling and also to increasing his effectiveness as a counselor.

The understanding of cultural differences within the group experience is another aspect that was missing from the supervision. Although generalizations cannot be made about the group member that was Asian American, or to the female member, it is necessary and important that supervision include a discussion of the role that culture may have played into the manner in which those two particular group members interacted within the group. More importantly though, Jim must gain an understanding of how his race may be viewed by the group members. Alarmingly, Jim may be unaware that the directed manner in which he spoke to the two group members could be construed as condescending and biased.

Jim's supervisor needs to be more involved in the supervisory process. Self-report and video clips are not the most effective means of providing supervision that assists counselors in training in assessing their skill level. The supervisory process should have included the opportunity for Jim to explain how facilitating the group for adolescents would be an intervention for adolescents of divorced parents. Jim should have also been required to conceptualize what was occurring within the group and explain the group process. Growth and learning often occur as a result of a struggle or dilemma. In this incident, an opportunity exists for both the supervisor and supervisee to examine themselves and their effectiveness.

RESPONSE

Joyce A. DeVoss

The use of silence could have been instrumental as a therapeutic intervention in this group to encourage the members to self-reflect and develop insight and a sense of self-direction as opposed to dependence on the formal group leader. Silence could also serve as a challenge for group members to consider taking risks in the group by disclosing about themselves. Furthermore, silence could have been used to allow for the natural process of the group to unfold. Silence is not unusual in the early stages of a group as members are unsure of how to behave and interact. Allowing for it offers the group members the opportunity to work through trust issues and begin developing a sense of ownership in the group.

By not providing the opportunity for appropriate silence, the group leader sacrificed important aspects of group process. The group did not have the opportunity to learn by struggling with silence without the leader stepping in. By not allowing appropriate silence, the leader did not instill a sense of faith in the group process and in the group members' abilities to solve their own problems. Instead, the leader took responsibility for the group process by providing advice to group members.

Some group members who were hesitant or slow to respond may not have had the opportunity provided by a period of silence to take risks that may have led to significant personal growth. Some cultural minorities in the group who were accustomed to silence and indirect communication may have felt alienated by the constant verbalization with no pauses. Some cultural minorities may value silence and appreciate its inclusion in the group as a sign of respect. Using appropriate silence could contribute to the comfort of these clients in the group and build a sense of trust in them. Silence could demonstrate to minority clients both patience and willingness to listen for an extended time. Using silence in this manner may have facilitated greater participation by Steve, the Asian American member. In addition, it may have been useful in assisting a female group member, Ellen, in developing her own ideas instead of depending on the leader for advice.

The American Counseling Association *Code of Ethics and Standards of Practice* (ACA, 1995) states that "Counselors, through ongoing evaluation and appraisal, are aware of the academic and personal limitations of students and supervisees that might impede performance" (section F.3.a). Jim's supervisor did not provide adequate supervision for him in the group experience and, therefore, played a major role in Jim's lack of using appropriate silence. Jim had limited experience both in leading groups and in working with diverse cultural groups. Whether he had experience working with adolescents is also in question. By conducting supervision merely based on videotape clips that Jim chose, the supervisor not only failed to observe Jim's lack of appropriate use of silence but also missed other deficits in Jim's counseling skills. For example, Jim's statements about the group indicated that he acted on his countertransference toward a female member in the group and behaved toward her based on what he thought girls her age needed. Also, only after viewing the entire last session of the group on videotape did Jim's supervisor's observe that Jim tended to either talk above or in a directed manner to an Asian American group member and to the female group member previously mentioned.

Jim's supervisor could have arranged to have Jim start out by co-leading the group to help him become more experienced with group facilitation skills as well as with counseling skills for working with a culturally diverse group of adolescents. In the group, she could model appropriate use of silence as well as other skills, and in supervision sessions, she could address his countertransference issues and his tendency to talk above or in a directed manner to certain group members. In addition, she could have used videotaped clips of the group sessions to highlight Jim's strengths and address areas for improvement.

REFERENCE

American Counseling Association. (1995). *Code of ethics and standards of practice.* Alexandria, VA: Author.

CHAPTER 37

ESTABLISHING TRUST: "TRUST ME, I'M YOUR COUNSELOR"

This incident highlights the responsibility that group counselors share in the development and maintenance of a trusting relationship between themselves and their clients.

CRITICAL INCIDENT

Kelly A. McDonnell and Stephen E. Craig

Background

Ann and Scott are counselors in a community mental health agency located in an urban setting. After completing a 6-month premaster's internship at the agency, Ann was hired as a full-time counselor and has been working in that capacity for almost a year. She has worked with a diverse group of clients and has a particular interest in group work. As a master's student, Ann had a class in group dynamics and theory, participated as a member of a personal growth group, and co-led an 8-week depression group in the counseling center of her university. Since then, she has gained more experience leading and co-leading counseling groups at the current agency. Scott has extensive experience working in community mental health agencies and has been in his current position for the past 5 years. His area of expertise is working with children and adolescents, primarily in individual treatment.

Recently, the agency where Ann and Scott are employed has experienced an increase in the number of domestic violence cases referred from the court system. As a result of the increase in cases and some financial support from the community, the agency formed a domestic violence treatment team to explore ways to better serve people affected by this issue. Both Ann and Scott are working on the team. Ann expressed an interest in being involved with this newly formed team because of a growing interest in the impact of domestic violence on women and children. Scott's background in working with perpetrators and victims of domestic violence makes him well suited to serve on the team.

Ann had been working with the team for about a month when her supervisor approached her about facilitating a new counseling group for children (ages 10 to 12) who experienced domestic violence. The supervisor chose Ann because of her experience with group facilitation and her expressed interest in working more with people facing this difficult issue. Initially Ann was apprehensive about taking on this responsibility because she had limited experience in the area of domestic violence. After voicing these concerns in supervision, Ann's supervisor suggested she co-lead the group and recommended her colleague and fellow team member, Scott, who has had considerable experience in this area. Though they had not previously worked together, Ann approached Scott about cofacilitating the group, and he was enthusiastic about the opportunity.

Ann and Scott met on several occasions to structure and plan the group. During the pregroup planning meetings, they talked about their clinical backgrounds, individual counseling styles, and expectations for the group. They began to know one another better and to develop a working relationship. They discussed how their individual strengths could complement one another and subsequently provide a good experience for the group members. Together, Ann and Scott made some decisions about group design, content, and process. Group participants would consist of boys and girls, ages 10 to 12, who have experienced domestic violence. The group would meet once a week for 90 minutes. Ann and Scott decided to have an open group, which would allow members to enter at any time. This structure seemed to be the most appropriate way to respond to the immediate needs of potential members, as opposed to asking the children to wait several weeks or even months to join a cyclical group. Although the group would be open, members would generally participate for about 10 to 12 weeks, though sometimes longer. The group design reflected a combination of psychoeducational and counseling group formats. The goals of the group were to increase member knowledge about domestic violence, discuss how it can impact individuals and families, help group members develop personal safety plans, and provide a supportive environment in which the children might feel comfortable talking about their experiences, fears, and concerns.

Ann and Scott announced the formation of the group to their fellow clinicians and felt fairly confident they would be able to fill the group (approximately six to eight members) through internal referrals from intake staff and other counselors. In about a week they had received enough referrals to begin the group. They contacted the parents/caregivers of the referred children and notified them about the date and time of the first group meeting. They asked the participants' parents/caregivers to arrive 15 minutes early for the first session so they could receive an informational handout and sign a consent form for their children's participation.

During the planning meetings, Ann and Scott talked about how they would organize and structure the group sessions to help create a comfortable and safe atmosphere within the group. The leaders attempted to provide sufficient structure, but also make the group interesting and fun for the young members. They began the initial group session with introductions, an orientation to the group, and an icebreaker activity. Ann and Scott talked with group members about the importance of maintaining confidentiality within the group. They also outlined circumstances under which they, as leaders, might need to go outside the limits of confidentiality. Ann and Scott attempted to address this important issue using age-appropriate language and examples to which the preadolescents could relate. The leaders were aware of the important role that confidentiality plays in creating and maintaining a comfortable and trusting environment in the group. Also, in an effort to help build trust within the group, the facilitators sought to establish other norms like honesty, listening, taking turns, and mutual respect (such as respecting personal space and not making fun of other group members). Scott, knowing that preadolescents may have a difficult time verbalizing their thoughts and feelings, suggested the use of therapeutic games and role-plays to help the group members work through emotions related to their situation. His training and experience in working with this age group was invaluable as the leaders planned activities that would help the children express themselves and work on the issues that brought them to the group. The leaders, anticipating that the group members might need to talk about the difficulties at home and how they are feeling, provided ample time during the initial session for the members to talk about these issues.

Subsequent sessions followed a format similar to the initial session. Because open groups can result in different constellations of members across sessions, Ann and Scott included a reminder about confidentiality and other norms at the beginning of each group meeting. The leaders used structured activities and exercises to help members address domestic violence issues and to share with one another. In order to nurture group members and to end sessions on a positive note, they closed each session with a fun activity and a snack.

Incident

Following the sixth session, Ann and Scott were walking some of the children into the lobby where a significant number of parents had gathered to pick them up. Some group members took a seat in the waiting room, as their parents had not yet arrived. Meanwhile, a mother of one of the children approached Ann and Scott asking for information about her son's (Chad) progress during group counseling. They discussed the situation, and the following exchange occurred in the waiting room:

> Mother: I was hoping to get some information about how my son is doing in the group.
> Ann: Well, Mrs. Williams, perhaps we could schedule a meeting for a parent consultation. When would be a good time for you this week?
> Mother (unimpressed with Ann's offer): Look, I have a busy schedule, and it's difficult for me to come back here between appointments. I just want to know how he is doing.
> Ann: You're right, scheduling a different time would be too challenging for both of us. Why don't we just walk over to this corner of the waiting area, and I would be happy to share with you some of what he has been working on in the group.
> Mother: Great....

> Scott (with some hesitation as he notices the child watching them): From my perspective, your son has been working very well with the other children. I have noticed him working more cooperatively with his peers, and this is considerably different from his earlier tendency to boss his fellow group members.
>
> Ann (continued): And today, he talked about how he sometimes feels angry and wants to hit or throw something, but has been able to control himself.
>
> Mother: I hope he hasn't gotten in trouble again because of some angry outburst.
>
> Scott: No.

The exchange continued for several more minutes and consisted of more questions from Mrs. Williams and feedback from the counselors. After several minutes, Chad walked over and insisted he wanted to leave. Ann and Scott had apparently satisfactorily addressed Mrs. Williams' questions, and she and her son turned to leave the clinic. Ann and Scott said goodbye to them, but only the mother acknowledged their goodbye gesture. Ann and Scott were confused by Chad's failure to say goodbye, especially since at the conclusion of all previous sessions, he had devised a handshake ritual with Scott as a way of saying goodbye.

The following week, the group met for its seventh session, and Ann and Scott had a group activity planned. Ann instructed the children to use the art materials provided to construct something that shows what anger looks like. For children who were willing, Ann and Scott requested they show their work and talk about it with the group. In previous sessions, Chad had been an active group member; however, today, he was much more quiet and reticent about participating in the activity. He was also less responsive to queries by Ann and Scott. This behavior continued throughout this session. Ann and Scott spent some extra time after the group session talking about the change in Chad and the resulting impact on the group.

QUESTIONS

1. Once trust with a child (like Chad) is jeopardized, how could Ann and Scott intervene to try and resolve the problem and reestablish trust?

2. If you were in this situation where a parent/caregiver approached you in front of other children and caregivers, how might you have responded, and why?

3. What did Ann and Scott do to establish and maintain trust with the individual children in the group? With the group as a whole? With the parents/caregivers? What might they have done in addition?

4. How might Ann and Scott have used informed consent at the very beginning of the process (e.g., pregroup meetings) to assist in establishing a trusting relationship with the caregivers? With the group members?

5. What did Ann and Scott do to establish trust between them, and what else might they have done?

RESPONSE

Robin Wilbourn Lee

Ann and Scott began this group experience with forethought and planning. They worked to establish a healthy and trusting environment for themselves and their group members, and to provide an appropriate group experience for members, by recognizing and discussing openly their individual limitations as well as by preplanning the group structure, format, and purpose. To establish trust with the group members, Ann and Scott attempted to make the group a safe environment for members to disclose difficult concerns by addressing some of the issues that adolescent boys and girls are susceptible to, such as name calling and ridicule. This was accomplished by establishing rules such as sharing, mutual respect, listening, and honesty. To establish trust with the parents and caregivers, Ann and Scott provided them with an informational handout about the group and had them sign an informed consent document.

There are several ways that Ann and Scott could have improved the trust between themselves, the group members, and their parents and/or caregivers. First, Ann and Scott could have ensured that trust remained strong between themselves by developing a plan designed to protect each other when their personal and professional limitations impinged on the success of the group. If one leader identified that the other was not functioning appropriately in the group, that leader should feel free to confront the other, and each should be open to honest discussions about the situation. Second, Ann and Scott could have improved trust with the group members by explaining more thoroughly not only the circumstances under which they may need to go outside the limits of confidentiality, but also how they might reveal such information. Particularly, group members should be told that if their parents and/or caregivers want to know about their progress in the group, the group member would be notified and presented with the opportunity to give his or her permission. In addition, the group member would be given the opportunity to be present and even participate in the sharing of information. Third, Ann and Scott could have improved trust with parents and/or caregivers by holding prescreening interviews with both parents/caregivers and group members to discuss the parameters of the group, including confidentiality as it relates to minors. Although children do not have legal or even ethical rights to confidentiality, professionals suggest that counselors encourage parents and/or caregivers to honor the privacy of the child. According to the American Counseling Association *Code of Ethics and Standards of Practice* (ACA, 1995), counselors are encouraged to act in the best interest of their clients, taking measures to preserve and maintain the confidentiality of clients. Measures to safeguard the confidentiality of minors can be implemented by developing and presenting a specific informed consent document addressing confidentiality, limits to confidentiality, the importance of confidentiality to the group process, and procedures for sharing information with parents/caregivers. It is crucial that all parties concerned (group leaders, parents/caregivers, and clients) are in agreement as to how confidentiality will be handled for the duration of the group sessions.

It is apparent that Ann and Scott, while having good intentions, have damaged their relationship with Chad by sharing information with his mother. Not only did Ann and Scott violate Chad's right to privacy, but they did so publicly, risking that other children would hear their discussions. More than likely, Chad feels as if Ann and Scott did not show him the respect that they have encouraged group members to show while in group. Ann and Scott did not follow the very rules they developed. One way they might repair the relationship with Chad would be to hold a private meeting with him to discuss his feelings. By doing so, they can begin to show Chad they do respect him and recognize the difficulty the incident may have caused him. In addition, this incident has provided Ann and Scott an excellent opportunity to improve the procedures for dealing with confidentiality. They can now address confidentiality with the group members and the parents and/or caregivers.

Confidentiality should be discussed in the group. Ann and Scott can also call a meeting with parents. Because informed consent is an ongoing process, Ann and Scott can explain these additional circumstances of confidentiality and ask for the cooperation of all concerned.

RESPONSE

Cheryl W. Forkner

Reestablishing trust is a difficult but not impossible task. First, we need to review what went wrong and why Chad felt the need to withdraw from his relationship with Ann and Scott and the group. As group leaders, Ann and Scott can be commended on their preplanning activities. Their preparation is a good example of co-leaders building and establishing a working relationship. As a co-leader team, they had the counseling experience and interests to offer the group to preadolescents who have experienced domestic violence. They determined how they could work together by discussing their counseling styles, made joint decisions on structure of the group, and engaged their young clients in the group process. They were sensitive to the issues of safety and trust among children who experienced domestic violence. Ann and Scott understood how the changing constellation of an open group could threaten the feelings of safety and attempted to create a safe environment for group members by reviewing confidentiality at the beginning of every session. As co-leaders and protectors of the group environment, Ann and Scott created an opening ritual for their group that was symbolic of the trust and security of the counseling relationship.

The problem occurred when Chad witnessed Ann and Scott breaking the rule of the group concerning maintaining confidentiality within the group. Providing feedback to a minor client's parent or caregiver is inevitable. Discussing the child's progress with the parent or caregiver falls within the limits of confidentiality and all parties (parent, minor client, co-leaders) should understand the limits of disclosure and what information will be conveyed to the parent. Whether Ann and Scott discussed this situation with their group members and their respective parents or caregivers or included it in the written materials distributed to the adults is unknown. However, although Ann and Scott requested parents to arrive 15 minutes before the first group session to sign the consent form for their child to participate in the group, there was little time for Ann and Scott to discuss this aspect of confidentiality with both parent and child.

Once trust is jeopardized between client and group leaders, there are several steps group leaders can take. The group leaders can admit that a breach of trust occurred and discuss the situation openly in the next group session. Ann and Scott can open the session in their traditional manner and inform the group they want to change the session slightly to talk about a serious matter. Ann and Scott can then explain the situation as it occurred. They can explain how they were caught off guard by a request from a parent wanting to know how her child was doing in group and how they responded to the parent in the moment. They can point out how they made a mistake and why it was a mistake. Ann and Scott can process with group members their thoughts and feelings, in hindsight, about the situation, the consequences of their behaviors, and their concerns or fears of breaching the trust and hurting the group member and the entire group. They can facilitate a discussion with the group of (a) what group members think or feel about their parents or caregivers asking Ann and Scott about their progress in the group, (b) what type of feedback is appropriate and comfortable for all parties (group members, co-leaders, and parents), (c) the circumstances in which Ann and Scott believe it is necessary to reveal more than the basic information to parents/caregivers, and (d) whether group members should or want to be present when feedback is given to the parent/caregiver. Furthermore, Ann and Scott, together with the group, can devise a protocol for giving general feedback to parents/caregivers. For example, one protocol is that they can agree that when a parent requests feedback, a brief meeting will be arranged with the parent and the child following the next group session when the parent is at the agency to pick up the child, and another protocol is that all parents will receive a progress statement after the 10th or 12th session.

These recommendations only address the pragmatic aspect of this problem. However, the emotional aspect must also be addressed in the group. Ann and Scott should apologize to Chad within the group session. The apology should be in front of the group for several reasons: First, Ann and Scott's discussion with Chad's mother occurred in the public view where Chad's fellow group members witnessed the group leaders speaking with his mother.

Other children may have developed feelings of mistrust for Ann and Scott after witnessing the discussion. Second, acknowledging the obvious in group is therapeutic for the children as opposed to ignoring it or maintaining an aura of secrecy. Third, in their roles as group leaders, Ann and Scott should model healthy behaviors. As children who experienced domestic violence, the group members have been exposed to unhealthy adult behaviors and experienced betrayal from an adult they trust and love. Ann and Scott are adults with power and authority in the lives of these preadolescents, and it will be an invaluable learning opportunity for the children to see that adults do make mistakes (unintentionally), are willing to discuss the issues without blame or excuses, are aware of the impact on the child, and are willing to correct the situation (when possible) or deal with the consequences. By apologizing to Chad, Ann and Scott are modeling healthy, interpersonal behavior. After the apology, Ann and Scott can attempt to invite Chad back into the group by asking him if he wants to express his thoughts or feelings about the situation.

Because Ann and Scott have success in working with planned activities, they can plan group activities that focus on issues of trust and betrayal and try to reengage Chad through the group activities. Ann and Scott face a delicate balance of inviting him back into the group process and giving him the personal space to experience, own, and trust his own feelings (one of the group's goals for the children). The difficulty of this situation is that reestablishing trust requires time. Ann and Scott do not have much time with Chad if he will terminate from the group after the 10th or 12th session. They have two more sessions to process the situation. Completely restoring Chad's trust to its original level within this brief period of time may not be possible. However, mending the relationship is possible.

Being approached by a parent who wants immediate information in the manner Ann and Scott were approached is a difficult situation. If approached, my initial response would be similar to Ann's: I would offer Mrs. Williams a scheduled appointment. My preference would be to consult with my co-leader and inform the child of our plans to speak to his parent. If the parent rejects the suggestion to meet between group sessions, I would offer her a brief parent consultation immediately following a next group session when the parent is at the agency to pick up the child. If the parent insists on discussing her child at the moment she approached me, I would try to explain how the waiting room is an inappropriate place to discuss her child's treatment because the waiting room is a public area and jeopardizes confidentiality. I would convey my ethical responsibility and role in protecting the child's and family's confidentiality within the limits of the law and stress that discussing treatment information, regardless of how innocuous the information may be, in a public area, is a breach of confidentiality. I would insist that we talk in the privacy of our offices or the group room. My next step would be to ask the parent to give me a few minutes, excuse myself, and briefly consult with my co-leader so we can determine the type of feedback we are comfortable giving to the parent. I would then go back to the waiting room and ask both the parent and child to meet with us in a counseling room. Again, I would stress our position on confidentiality and give the parent feedback on the child's progress.

I disagree with the information Ann and Scott gave to Mrs. Williams. I think the first part of Scott's feedback, describing the behaviors he has observed in Chad over the course of the group sessions, was appropriate with the exception of his last comment about Chad exhibiting bossy behaviors. I doubt if Ann and Scott had an opportunity to discuss this observation with Chad. Overhearing Ann and Scott describing him in this manner to his mother was probably distressing for Chad. Ann's statement was a direct breach of confidentiality because she explicitly revealed what the client discussed in that day's session. A more appropriate report to Mrs. Williams would have been, "The group is working on identifying and expressing feelings. Chad is a good group member who participates in the group activities and is learning more about identifying and expressing his feelings." If the parent prefers not to have the child present for the feedback, I would highly recommend the child be present for the purpose of not having secrets between the parent, child, and co-leaders. If the parent disagrees with this recommendation, I would wonder if the parent's agenda is to actually reveal to us sensitive information about the child or the home situation as opposed to receiving feedback on the child's progress. I would ask this question directly to the parent. If this were the case, I would still encourage the parent to meet with us at her convenience with the child in our office in order for us to ensure confidentiality. Other suggestions I would make if the parent rejects these options are to schedule a meeting before the group session or to arrange a phone consultation (this is my least favorite preference because the child will not be involved; however, it would occur after we had an opportunity to talk to the group member). Ann and Scott were cognizant of how the changing constellation of an open group could jeopardize the feel of safety for group members.

Their decision to start each group session by reviewing confidentiality and group norms reminded the children of the seriousness of valuing confidentiality and being respectful to fellow group members. Ann and Scott created opening and closing rituals, which provided the children with a sense of predictability, consistency, and stability associated with the group. The children may not have experienced these conditions in their familial environment. The rituals symbolized a safe arena for members to express their experiences and were critical in establishing and maintaining trust within the entire group. There is little information about how the co-leaders established and maintained trust with individual group members. Obviously, Scott and Chad had a special connection because they created a good-bye handshake used after every session. Whether Ann and Scott had a similar connection with each group member is unknown. However, I believe Ann and Scott did connect with the group members and were able to establish trust with the members because they appear successful in reaching out and helping members meet their goals.

Pregroup meetings are a good way of establishing trust with individual group members. Pregroup meetings are used to determine a client's appropriateness, identify individual goals, and orientate prospective members to the group process. Additionally, the pregroup meeting is a good opportunity to connect and begin a therapeutic relationship with individual members. If Ann and Scott had met the children individually before the group's first session, they would have begun establishing their trust and used the group to continue building trust with each child. Ann and Scott did very little to establish trust with the parents or caregivers. The referrals for their group came from their colleagues, not from Ann or Scott's caseloads. It is assumed the parents had a relationship with other clinicians or with the agency itself and may have felt comfortable with their children participating solely because of their relationship with the agency or their belief the group would be helpful for their children. Ann and Scott's only contact with the parents or caregivers occurred 15 minutes before the first group session, which was for the purpose of receiving their signed consent for the children to participate in the group. A pregroup meeting with both the parent or caregiver and child would have given the co-leaders an opportunity to meet the parents face to face and tell the parents about the nature and goals of the group. The results of having a face-to-face meeting with a parent or caregiver are qualitatively different from handing the adults written material. I realize clinicians working in community mental health agencies are responsible for a large caseload and provide many direct hours of clinical services. However, the preplanning stage is vital for the group's success. Ann and Scott did a good job planning the group and could have established and maintained trust with the parents and the children if they had allocated time to establish working relationships with the families prior to the start of the first group session, determined how information regarding the child's progress would be provided to parents, and revealed that information as part of the informed consent.

Informed consent is essential in establishing trust with clients. Informed consent provides clients with full knowledge of the parameters and limits of the counseling relationship. Even though it includes detailing all the logistical information and risks of the relationship, it also has a relational dimension that is critical in establishing a working alliance. If Ann and Scott had conducted pregroup meetings with each parent or caregiver, they could have discussed Ann and Scott's credentials and professional experiences, how information with minor clients is managed, the type and frequency of feedback, and how the parent or caregiver can convey to group co-leaders any concerns that may arise with his or her child during the intervention. Parents could use that time to get acquainted with the clinicians who will be working with their children, ask questions about the process, and make an informed decision about their child's participation. Ann and Scott assumed the internal referrals, the signed consent forms, and the written materials about the group were sufficient information for the parents and caregivers. Unfortunately, more efforts were required for the parents and caregivers.

As previously stated, Ann and Scott did a very good job in building a working relationship as co-leaders and colleagues. The time they spent getting to know each other's strengths and determining how they can work together as a team is essential for group co-leaders. Yalom (1995) believed co-leaders offer more advantages than groups led by a single leader. One advantage is that co-leaders can explore how their skills can compliment each other for the benefit of the group process. Another advantage is having two or more observers of the group process and using the joint observation to further the group's development. Yalom highly discouraged colleagues who do not know each other or dislike each other from working together. It appeared Ann and Scott liked and respected each other's professionalism and skills. They were good candidates for a co-leader team. They both worked at the same agency and had an interest in domestic violence.

They were different in their clinical experience. Ann had group experience, and Scott had experience with children and adolescents and with domestic violence. Both of them invested in the preplanning time, explored how they could work together as cofacilitators, and valued postsession processing. Ann and Scott shared in the duties and responsibilities of the group. But they appear to have made one error. They did not discuss how to manage the parents or caregivers. Throughout the incident, Ann and Scott appeared to share the responsibilities of the group. However, in the situation when they were approached by Chad's mother, Ann and Scott did not consult each other, and consequently, they did not function as a team. If they had, the outcome of the situation might have been different. For example, Ann could have referred to Scott as she was talking to Chad's mother. Speaking for both of them, Ann stated that scheduling an appointment between group sessions would be difficult. She did not refer to Scott or inquire if he had other suggestions before offering to speak with Mrs. Williams in the corner of the waiting room.

Similarly, Scott did not mention to Ann his apprehension about having the conversation with Mrs. Williams even after he noticed Chad observing the exchange. Additionally, Ann and Scott did not have any idea of what information would be appropriate to reveal to Chad's mother. They provided her with information that appeared fragmented, with Ann providing specific information from the day's session and Scott providing a broader assessment of how Chad's behavior had changed since he started the group. If Ann and Scott had a chance to recapture their sense of being a team before speaking with Mrs. Williams, the information they provided would have been more appropriate and integrated and probably less alarming to Mrs. Williams. Ann and Scott could have taken a time out or a break from the situation after Mrs. Williams approached them. By saying something like, "Mrs. Williams, can you please give us a few minutes and we will be glad to speak to you," Ann and Scott could have devised a plan of how to jointly manage the situation. This is an example of how co-leaders can extend support and maintain trust with each other outside of group. By each counselor knowing her or his co-leader will not make unilateral decisions that affect the group or their working relationship, co-leaders establish and maintain trust within their relationship, and this sense of trust and collaboration is modeled within the group session.

Ann and Scott can use supervision or peer consultation to build and maintain their trust with each other. Through supervision, the co-leaders can learn more about how each person observes or experiences the group and how their perceptions affect their working relationship. Many times, post-session processing focuses on what occurred in session and discussion of individual group members or group dynamics. Supervision provides the space and time for co-leaders to focus on developing their co-leadership skills and building a stronger, collaborative relationship. Ann and Scott would benefit from discussing the situation that occurred with Chad, from the moment they were approached by his mother in the waiting room to their observation of Chad's behavior in the next session, with a supervisor or consultant who can help them learn from this critical incident in their group experience.

REFERENCES

American Counseling Association. (1995). *Code of ethics and standards of practice*. Alexandria, VA: Author.

Yalom, I. D. (1995). *The theory and practice of group psychotherapy* (4th ed.). New York: Basic Books.

CHAPTER 38

TRANSITIONING: "RETICENCE RUN AMOK"

This incident presents some of the issues associated with the transitioning during various stages in group counseling.

CRITICAL INCIDENT

Mark B. Scholl

Background

Elizabeth and Jessica are counselors working in a public high school. Elizabeth has a PhD with a specialization in school counseling and 4 years of experience as a school counselor. Jessica has a MEd in school counseling with a postmaster's certificate in student development practices in higher education. In addition to her graduate internships, Jessica has 6 months of experience working as a school counselor in the same high school with Elizabeth. Elizabeth is Jessica's superior, and they are still in the process of getting to know one another and developing a comfortable working relationship.

Incident

The two counselors have collaboratively formed a group to prepare high school seniors for the transition to college. The group is comprised of 12 seniors and is intended to give them the opportunity to explore and resolve issues and feelings related to this difficult transition. In addition, the group will give the students the opportunity to problem solve and develop interpersonal skills related to successfully adjusting to the demands of a college environment.

In the first session, Jessica and Elizabeth conduct a session designed to provide the students with a broad overview of the group process over the next 8 weeks. The session includes introductions of group members, icebreakers, and an invitation for the group members to share their college plans as well as their feelings about moving into a less familiar academic and social environment. In general, the members appear to be formal and reticent in this first session.

As the students are leaving, a member named Allan stops at the door and asks Jessica and Elizabeth if he can talk to them privately. They agree, and he shares his anxiety over the strained relationship he is experiencing with his girlfriend. He has been anxious over whether this relationship will continue after he leaves town to attend college. His anxiety has been compounded by a recent argument he had with his girlfriend. After Allan relates his concerns and feels somewhat better, Elizabeth tells Allan this relationship concern would be a good issue to share within the context of the group. She points out this is the type of issue the group is meant to address and encourages him to share his concerns with group members in an upcoming session. Allan is noncommittal, saying only that he will think about it.

During a planning session between the first and second meeting, Jessica and Elizabeth discuss Allan's self-disclosure and possible approaches to encouraging him to talk openly about his concerns in the next group meeting. Jessica feels that Allan should self-disclose only if he is comfortable; Elizabeth is more adamant, insisting they should do everything they can to get him to talk about his issue.

In the second session, the two counselors attempt to facilitate a discussion of the group members' issues. Primarily they do this by asking the members to respond to open-ended prompts such as, "The one thing about college I am most looking forward to is...." and "The one thing about college I am least looking forward to is...." These prompts are fairly successful in generating discussion among the 12 members. The students are still rather reticent, but there does appear to be some cohesion as the students have themes in common and are supportive of each other's statements. Jessica and Elizabeth comment on similarities among the issues raised by the students with regard to their worries such as the fear that they will not be able to handle the increased workload or that they might not have the self-discipline needed to succeed in the first semester. They assure the members these concerns are common among high school seniors, and they should not consider these concerns to be signs of a lack of ability or maturity. At the end of the session, Elizabeth asks Allan to stay and talk for a minute. She reiterates her invitation, this time more strongly urging him to share the issue related to his romantic relationship. After Allan leaves, Jessica suggests that maybe they should allow Allan to have some more space and that he might be feeling too much pressure to self-disclose comfortably. At this point, Elizabeth and Jessica disagree, but they fail to arrive at a mutual understanding of how to proceed.

At the third group session, Elizabeth briefly summarizes the previous session and then asks the members if anyone has any unfinished business from the previous session that they would like to discuss. When this question is met with awkward silence, Jessica asks, "Are there any other issues you have?" Again there is an awkward moment of silence before Elizabeth states, "In that case, I have a problem that I would like for the group to help me with. Allan has shared a personal relationship issue with Jessica and me, and we feel this issue is appropriate for sharing with the group. However, Allan has been reluctant to share his issue. I would like for each of you to help me with this problem." This statement is met with awkward silence from

Allan and the other members. Elizabeth continues, "I would like to hear how some of you are affected by hearing this about Allan." Jessica attempts to help the group by stating, "There are certain personal issues I feel uncomfortable discussing in front of a group. I feel self-conscious when I talk about these things in front of people I don't know very well." However, no progress is made in terms of facilitating Allan's self-disclosure to the other group members. Instead, the group moves on to a discussion of open-ended themes presented to the group such as feelings about making the social adjustment to college life. The members respond to the facilitator's prompts in a manner that is superficial and impersonal.

Discussion

During the transition stage, Elizabeth and Jessica experienced contrasting attitudes. Elizabeth felt a great deal of responsibility for motivating the participants while Jessica felt a need to allow the participants to move at a comfortable pace. After the third session, Elizabeth felt frustrated by Allan's refusal to self-disclose while Jessica sympathized with his feelings of embarrassment and reluctance to share. Although Jessica had disagreed with the way Elizabeth had handled the session, she did not confront Elizabeth on this issue. Elizabeth was similarly reluctant to bring up the issue. Instead they discussed what had happened in abstract terms such as the importance of facilitating the natural organic development of the group and trusting the process. In later sessions, the group members did have meaningful activities including role-plays of hypothetical difficulties with college roommates and problem-solving activities related to how to effectively deal with unexpected academic setbacks. However, the group lacked spontaneity, and the members appeared to be too dependent upon the leaders to provide structure for their work.

QUESTIONS

1. What could the two counselors have done differently with regard to dealing with Allan at the time of his "doorknob disclosure"?
2. What are some possible explanations for the contrasting responses of the two counselors to Allan's reluctance to share as well as for their contrasting approaches to transitioning?
3. How might the group leaders' interpersonal dynamics have influenced the dynamics of the group? What recommendations do you have for improving their working relationship?
4. What recommendations do you have for more effectively approaching Allan's resistance in the context of the group?
5. What additional recommendations do you have for the two counselors with regard to more effectively transitioning and dealing with the group's resistance?

RESPONSE

Emily Phillips

Several issues were at play here that kept this group from being effective. One of the key issues was that Elizabeth and Jessica did not know one another well, nor had they developed a working alliance either before or between sessions. This is further compounded by the fact that Elizabeth has more power, which was inherent in the relationship because she was the superior. In addition, it appeared they each had very different goals and theoretical orientations, and these issues were never addressed before they began the group.

A support group for seniors leaving the familiarity of high school to attend college is a valuable service for school counselors to provide. The counselors were clear in stating, during the first session, that the purpose of the group was to explore this transition, to problem solve, and to develop interpersonal skills related to the demands of a college environment. Nowhere did they state that the goal was to share personal relationship issues. Students learned of the goals, unfortunately, at the first session, instead of before it. As part of informed consent, members have the right to know what the goals are, and trust in the early stages of a group comes partly from leaders keeping their word. Although they maintained their focus on their original goal in the second session with their open-ended questions focusing on college, Elizabeth shifted goals in the third session toward a more intimate focus. This could have been a goal the members were not interested in pursuing.

In order for a group to be successful in the transition stage, the formation and orientation stages need to be addressed and worked through. This did not happen effectively in this group. The counselors did not seem to address confidentiality issues with members, nor did they do much to provide an atmosphere of safety. Indeed, the third session could very well be too soon for them to expect such a high level of self-disclosure, especially if students were still struggling with basic issues of trust and cohesion. It is easy to make an incorrect assumption that just because students are in some classes together that they know and trust one another.

Elizabeth and Jessica did not appear to respect or to deal with one another's polar-opposite approaches to group process and goals. They needed to work out what they would do about Allan's doorknob disclosure outside of the sessions, not during them.

Elizabeth's bringing up that Allan had an issue not only had the effect of shutting him down but also seemed to have a spillover effect on the other students. Allan did not give permission for his material to be shared. To the other teens, this could be taken as a sign that opening up and sharing highly private and emotionally charged information was not safe in this group. This would explain the rather superficial nature of the discussion that occurred in each session.

In addition, it was evident to the students the leaders were not in agreement with one another, and this added another dimension of mistrust. Resistance on Allan's part could have come from many levels, and they did nothing to find out what the basis was. If he was unwilling to discuss the girlfriend issue within the group, they could have asked him if he wanted to meet with either counselor privately. It was acceptable to encourage him to consider sharing with the group and to allow the group to help him. The choice to reveal information, though, should rest with the client, both for the sake of personal autonomy and out of respect. Corey and Corey (2002) stated, "For group leaders not to respect the members' resistances is akin to not respecting the members themselves" (p. 109). The American Counseling Association *Code of Ethics and Standards of Practice* (ACA, 1995) states that members should be free from coercion and undue pressure. Elizabeth not only pressured Allan to share personal information, but she also enlisted the group members to, in effect, gang up on him. This was highly inappropriate.

If the leaders believed Allan's issue was a valuable topic for group discussion, in that they thought that it was a common theme among many of the group members, they could have brought it up in a more general sense. They could have said something such as, "There are many losses associated with leaving home. What are some that concern you?" They could have been more specific by saying, "When we move away we leave both places and people. Our relationships with others can and often do change—not always for the negative—but they become different. Would you like to talk about your current relationships and what might change?" In this way, the members had a choice, and Allan might have felt freer to share once he heard others felt similarly about changes among their relationships.

It was clear that Elizabeth and Jessica had competing goals for the group and for Allan. This conflict became evident to the group and prevented cohesion. Resistance is common in the transition stage of a group, but as Corey and Corey (2002) stated, this can often be because group leaders were not successful at the orientation stage. Resistance can also exist and continue when there is friction between the co-leaders. This was clearly the case with Elizabeth pushing for self-disclosure and Jessica's comment regarding comfort level with others before disclosing. It appeared that Jessica, although the less experienced counselor, seemed to be more familiar with the ethics involved with this situation and more aware of group development. The stage was never set for establishing and building trust or safety, and Elizabeth's decision to corner Allan reinforced this to the group members.

Sometimes we mistakenly assume that if members aren't emoting and talking about heavy issues, then nothing valuable is going on. Perhaps Elizabeth expected more out of this developmentally oriented group, or maybe she was unclear about what kind of group she was running. These counselors needed to spend the time necessary before and between group sessions ironing out their differences and planning for sessions. It could be that

Elizabeth's high need to be directive and confrontational did not mesh well with Jessica's style. This does not mean that either approach is better, but perhaps this is a less effective match for a co-led group, especially if they did not intend to put the time in to developing a positive therapeutic alliance. Unfortunately, the negative experience of co-leading this group may taint their general working relationship.

RESPONSE

Ginger L. Dickson

Elizabeth and Jessica might have suggested, at Allan's first mention of a personal concern related to leaving for college, that he save his concern for discussion with the group. They could have explained how his concern could be addressed effectively and appropriately within the group, conveying their trust and belief in the value of the group. This approach might have helped Allan to understand how he could benefit from the group and that he was responsible for asking the group for help. Instead, Allan disclosed part of his issue to Elizabeth and Jessica, and experiencing a sense of relief, was less compelled to share this concern with the group.

Elizabeth and Jessica apparently differed in their leadership styles and their views of the role and responsibilities of group leaders. Jessica appeared to prefer a less directive style of leadership that allows the members to navigate the group process more on their own. Conversely, Elizabeth appeared to prefer a more directive style of leadership that assumes much of the responsibility for the actions of the members. These differences may explain the counselors' contrasting reactions to Allan's reluctance to share his issue with the group. Elizabeth assumed the responsibility to do what it took to get Allan to disclose his issue to the group, while Jessica defended Allan's right to disclose only if he felt comfortable.

Unfortunately, the counselors did not address and work through their differing views of leadership. This seemed to prevent them from acknowledging their mutual belief that Allan's disclosure to the group would be beneficial and developing a plan to help the group establish an environment that was safe and inviting for him to do so. Consequently, their disparate views were exhibited in the group and remained unfinished business both within and outside the group.

By stepping back to examine their interpersonal process, Elizabeth and Jessica might have been able to improve their working relationship. For instance, had Elizabeth and Jessica recognized their attempts to avoid conflict between themselves, they might have been better able to address and work through issues, such as the supervisory nature of their relationship and trust, that might have been contributing to their avoidance of conflict. Through this process, Elizabeth and Jessica might have established clear expectations, ground rules, and boundaries for their roles as co-leaders. This might have freed them to respond collaboratively and more effectively to the needs of the group.

Similarly, Elizabeth and Jessica might have approached the group's resistance to share personal issues by illuminating the group members' process of avoidance. This would have precluded singling out Allan as the one member who had an issue but refused to share and would have maintained the onus on the group members to address conflicts that might have been holding them back. The leaders could then have invited the group members to examine the issues (e.g., trust, safety) that were contributing to their reluctance to share personal issues with the group. As group members began to share their concerns of trust and safety within the group, the interplay of several therapeutic factors, particularly universality, cohesiveness, and interpersonal learning, could have progressed. Sharing and working through these issues might have helped the members to engender the trust necessary within the group to begin taking risks such as Allan sharing his concern. Conflict and resistance arise within every group.

By recognizing and illuminating these processes, group leaders can increase the therapeutic potential of the group and more effectively help group members examine issues that contribute to their resistance. Additionally, co-leaders who discuss their differences and potential issues in advance are less likely to allow these issues to interfere with the process of the group.

REFERENCES:

American Counseling Association. (1995). *Code of ethics and standards of practice.* Alexandria, VA: Author.

Corey, M.S., & Corey, G. (2002). *Groups: Process and practice* (6th ed.). Pacific Grove, CA: Brooks/Cole.

CHAPTER 39

DEEPENING THE FOCUS: "PEELING THE LAYERS OFF THE ONION"

This incident addresses how a counselor decides how far to engage clients in disclosing their feelings and thoughts.

CRITICAL INCIDENT

Jane Goodman

Background
A group of women in their 50s have been meeting for 3 weeks at a community college women's center. The focus of the group is career decision making, but the discussion has also focused on the limits they have felt because of their gender. All of the women are full-time homemakers until returning to school. Some need to work because they are recently divorced; others want or need to contribute to the family income as children enter college or because they wish to be a fuller participant in their household support. Others want to find a way to use their time more productively now that their children do not demand as much attention. The leader is a counselor in the community college counseling center who spends 2 days a week at the woman's center, running groups as well as seeing individuals. The women have discussed their interests, skills, values, and lifestyle preferences. They have analyzed their past work experience and looked at transferable skills. The week prior to the incident was spent looking at their support systems. The women drew a picture of their supports and then discussed who and what provided support for them as they faced this transition. The discussion also included who they felt created barriers for them or acted in nonsupportive ways. They were encouraged to think about this topic further in the following week.

Incident
When the women returned to the group a week later, one of the divorced women asked to have some time to talk about her thinking regarding her support system. She said she had been thinking all week about how some of the supports identified by the other women were people who created negative energy for her. She told a story of her parents and later her husband who told her that a woman's place is in the home. She says this statement always made her feel less valuable than her brothers or her husband. She begins to cry as she relates how inadequate she feels to face the challenges

of the workplace. The other women rush to reassure her she is valuable. The leader asks them to wait a minute and invites her to talk more about her feelings of inadequacy. She then asks the other women if any of them have ever felt less than the men in their lives, or working women.

In the ensuing discussion, each woman begins to reveal her vulnerability, and the discussion deepens beyond the barriers in the workplace and moves to the internal barriers many of the women feel. They are able to discuss not only their fear of failure but also their fear of success.

Discussion

After the session, the leader thinks about the appropriateness of her actions. Her invitation to discuss inadequacy certainly opened up a lot of wounds. Was this the right setting to do that? Was she violating the implied contract with the women to stick to a narrow interpretation of career decision making? The counselor is aware that without her intervention, the women would have reassured the woman who was distressed, and they would have returned to the more surface level of conversation. The time together would than have been spent on the career exploration they signed up for. But she also believed that without examining these issues, the women might find it hard to make the kinds of decisions they needed to and move successfully through the college experience and make the transition to work. She was afraid that they would get close to their objective and find a way to fail, by dropping out or otherwise, consciously or unconsciously sabotaging their own efforts. She was also afraid that if they did not discuss these issues they might let others sabotage their efforts.

QUESTIONS

1. Was it appropriate to invite a deeper level of disclosure at this point?
2. Might it have been better to allow the group to reassure the woman?
3. Would it have been better to acknowledge her pain but refer her to individual counseling?
4. Did she violate her implied contract to stick to the more obviously career-related topics?

RESPONSE

Jennifer C. Lewis Jordan

In order to reaffirm that the leader of this group had indeed deepened the focus of the group appropriately, we must look at several factors. These factors include the implied contract, the needs of the group members, and the appropriateness of the leader's processing skills to take the group to a deeper level. First, we consider the contract to which members of the group consented. In this case the leader mentions the contract was implied, apparently based on the topic or name of the group. This appears to be causing her a great deal of stress because she did not use a formal or informal contract. By using a contract, either written or verbal, she would have been able to prepare her group members for certain topics or issues that might come up as a result of their career exploration. The group members then would have the chance to provide feedback and to state their commitment to the amount of involvement they wished to contribute to the group.

Second, we must look at the needs of the members in the group. In this particular session it seems as if the members of the group were experiencing the need to explore their career decisions at a deeper level. The members were asked the week before the incident to think more about the activities they had participated in for the following week. Because the women were prepared to relate back to this topic and share any new insights they may have had, I believe the discussion was warranted. When one member spoke of her issue, it seemed to strike a chord in the other members, allowing them to process their feelings as well. It seems that the group leader sensed that the other women were also dealing with the same issues and might benefit in sharing them with the group. Although the issue was painful for the women in the group, it also presented itself as a catharsis for further growth in their personal and professional career decisions.

Third, the appropriateness of the leader's processing skills to take the group to a deeper level needs to be addressed. In this particular situation I feel the leader would have been neglectful to the group if she had not let them explore their concerns at a deeper level. Might it have been better to allow the group to reassure the woman? No. I believe the leader acted skillfully by not allowing the other members to rescue the member experiencing emotional pain. Thus she allowed them all to explore the issues at a much deeper and more meaningful level.

In conclusion, I feel the leader of this group may wish to be more formal in group introductions. This may include informing clients of the types of issues that may arise, the potential risks and benefits to being in a group, and the expectations of group members and the leader. This will also allow the leader to obtain the level of commitment each member brings into the group. A leader must utilize their ethics, skill, knowledge, and instincts in order to process a group to a deeper level and be successful.

RESPONSE

Robyn L. Trippany

It seems the discussion in the third group meeting, although not concretely focused on career decision making, certainly dealt with such issues as success/failure, adequacy/inadequacy, and value as a worker, which are legitimate issues many people face when considering entering into or changing careers. For anyone making changes in how they have focused their time on a daily basis, insecurity is natural. These women are leaving a secure livelihood and entering a world in which men of their generation have had the most successes and in which they will most likely be competing against younger men and women. Thus a discussion regarding one's vulnerabilities and fears is beneficial. In addition, as this was the third group meeting, group bonding is a reasonable step for this phase. The women have had an opportunity to get to know each other to some extent, and as evidenced by each woman sharing on such a deep level, there was a sense of security for the group members.

Allowing the other group members to simply reassure this group member might have been countertherapeutic as it would have minimized her personal struggle and left no sense of validation. The discussion that ensued served to normalize her feelings as well as bring those issues to the surface so that not only the group member who initiated the discussion but also all group members had a chance to own and process those feelings such that they are less likely to interfere in an actual job search or setting. Certainly if this group member needs to process these issues further and on a deeper level, a referral for individual counseling would be appropriate.

It is difficult to discuss whether this was a violation of an implied contract as little history is given in regard to the discussion of what was stated in the first group meeting regarding the content of the group. However, if the group leader was able to tie the discussion back into career-related topics, it seems an appropriate topic. Further, the group leader may have asked how the group felt about continuing the discussion as a check-in for the comfort level of all members before allowing the discussion to get to such a deep level.

CHAPTER 40

GROUP ASSESSMENT: "AS INEXPENSIVE AS POSSIBLE"

Counselors are bound by ethical standards for assessment in both individual and group work. This incident points to issues created when group leaders fail to follow some essential ethical guidelines.

CRITICAL INCIDENT

Pamela A. Staples

Background

Janet and Brian are counseling interns in an at-risk middle school. They are under the supervision of both a university supervisor and an on-site school counselor. They provide various types of counseling services, such as group guidance, parent/teacher consultation, individual counseling, and group counseling. The on-site supervisor assigns their duties for five out of the six periods during the day. The two interns are not assigned specific tasks during the sixth period. They typically use this time for planning and other administrative functions.

Incident

The principal of the school bumped into Brian in the lunchroom and told him there were a number of students in the sixth-grade study hall who were interested in learning more about careers. The principal asked Brian what he thought about leading a career group with these students. Brian said he thought it was a good idea, but he wanted to discuss it with Janet and the on-site supervisor. Janet was favorably inclined, but the on-site supervisor said she would only have time to get the informed consent forms for them, and that was all. Janet and Brian agreed to be responsible for the content of the weekly sessions.

The groups began a week later. Janet and Brian asked members to introduce themselves during the first session and also asked each of them to share their personal goals for the group. One of the members said she had heard there was a career test that could tell her what type of career she should go into. Janet and Brian said they would try to find some instruments for their next session.

After the session, Janet and Brian agreed to make their search for career instruments their first priority. Each of them went home and looked through their files. Janet found an old copy of an instrument that measured career interests. There was no name on it, but she remembered her appraisal instructor said the results of the instrument could be correlated to the Holland codes. She knew the Holland codes were used a lot for career assessment and decided to look up Holland on the Web. Her memory refreshed, Janet found an occupations finder that links Holland codes to occupations. Janet spent an hour pouring over the career interest inventory and figured out a way to match the results to the codes. She could make copies of the inventory for group members, help them score it, correlate the score to a code, and then they could link the code to occupations. And she could do so on her budget, which for her meant as inexpensively as possible.

Brian had two types of instruments at home. One measured self-esteem, the other math anxiety. He thought the math anxiety instrument would be good for those group members who might be thinking of going into a job in which they would use math. But he decided there were probably several members who wouldn't really care about it. Because he was sure about the correlation between self-esteem and academic achievement, he could just present self-esteem as also being important to job success. Brian was very familiar with the self-esteem inventory because he had administered it to over 50 participants for his thesis research. And as an added bonus, he had enough copies of the instrument on hand for each member of the group.

Janet and Brian met before school the next day to discuss the instruments. Brian agreed to use Janet's, but Janet was hesitant to administer a self-esteem instrument. She argued that it was a career group, not a self-esteem group. Brian decided he would bring the idea up again later because they were not going to have time to use both of them in one session.

In the next group session, Janet and Brian told the members they were going to take an interest inventory. It would identify interests they could match to occupations. After the members completed the interest inventory, Janet and Brian explained how to self-score it. They then spent a few minutes moving around the room to answer individual questions, but the session was almost over.

Discussion

Later that day, the on-site supervisor asked Janet how the session went. Janet told her it went well and then rushed out to her internship class at the university. As was customary during class, each intern related a couple of highlights from his or her week. When Janet and Brian related the details about the career inventory, their university supervisor looked disgruntled and asked them to meet him after class.

QUESTIONS

1. Do you think the university supervisor's negative reaction to the inventory was justified? As you discuss your view, also consider the questions that follow.

2. Do you think the interns went outside their limits of competence with regard to the design and/or use of the inventory? If so, why or why not?
3. Were there any infringements upon client welfare involved by administering the inventory to the group? If so, what were they?
4. What suggestions would you give Janet and Brian with regard to assessment in future groups?

RESPONSE

Craig S. Cashwell

This incident highlights the problems of unprofessional behavior in the assessment process. The university supervisor was quite justified in looking "disgruntled," but waiting to discuss the problematic behaviors with Janet and Brian after class is debatable. On one hand, it seems appropriate to discuss this in the group supervision meeting as it presents a teachable moment. On the other hand, the group supervisor must make this decision ultimately based on what will be most beneficial to Janet and Brian. It is clear, however, that Janet and Brian are working outside the scope of their competence because of the number and variety of errors they made in the assessment process.

The incident illustrates a number of common mistakes made in the assessment process that merit discussion. Most notably, there are issues related to consultation, copyright infringement, psychometric properties of assessment instruments, focus of assessment techniques, and inappropriate methods of interpretation.

Consultation. Many of the problems highlighted in this incident could have been avoided if Janet and/or Brian had consulted with the university supervisor. The university supervisor could have helped them develop a plan of action for getting the group started that would be consistent with best practices in both group counseling and assessment.

Copyright infringement. Though the details are not specified in the incident, it is likely that Janet and Brian were guilty of some type of copyright infringement in copying these tests and/or using tests for reasons other than originally intended. If the career interest instrument was a copyrighted instrument, Janet has broken copyright law in photocopying the instrument. Similarly, it is not uncommon for permission to be granted for using an instrument for research purposes. If, however, Brian only received permission to use the self-esteem instrument for research, his use of the instrument within the group was a contractual violation. Fortunately, this instrument had not yet been used and the university supervisor can address this.

Psychometric properties of instruments. There are a number of additional potential problems associated with using the career interest instrument at the outset of this group. The instrument is described as *old,* and thus may be outdated. Janet has no information on validity and reliability studies, so it is not possible to determine if the instrument is psychometrically sound. Further, without a test manual or a review of external research on the instrument, Janet has no way of knowing if the instrument is appropriate for middle-school students. It is possible that the instrument was established only for adult populations and never normed for adolescents. Further, it is possible that the reading level of the instrument is higher than the reading level of some of the students in the group.

Focus of assessment techniques. When considering the use of any assessment technique, it is important to first consider the type of information that is wanted and then determine the most effective method of collecting this information. That is, the assessment technique (e.g., type of instrument, interview format) should be selected based on the type of information that is being collected. In this instance, there are three focus problems with the approach that has been used. First, the decision to use paper-and-pencil measures appears to have been made based on a statement by one member of the group. It may have been more useful to tell the group members they would consider paper-and-pencil measures for future sessions and continue with didactic psychoeducation and process-oriented meetings until an appropriate assessment instrument could be identified. Second, Janet used an instrument that appears to provide information related to specific occupations. Coupled with the failure to provide an adequate interpretation (discussed in the next paragraph), the focus on specific occupations is developmentally inappropriate with middle-school students. For students at this age, particularly those at risk, the focus of the assessment and counseling process should be to help them consider a broad range of potential occupations (i.e., encourage divergent rather than convergent thinking). The approach taken by Janet and Brian may identify foreclosure for some students by focusing on specific occupations. Further, though Brian did not administer the self-esteem instrument, he also was making a basic mistake. Rather than determining how to assess information that would be useful, Brian was in essence allowing instrument availability to determine the focus of the questions that would be asked and discussed in the group.

Inappropriate methods of interpretation. In addition to the focus problems, there are issues related to how Janet and Brian handled the interpretation process. Leo Goldman coined the phrase *plop phenomenon* to describe the process of plopping test results in front of a client without an interpretative process. Without time spent interpreting the results, it is impossible to ensure that the client understands the results and can make appropriate use of the information. Though Janet and Brian took "a few minutes" to answer individual questions, it is likely that some students did not understand the results, what they meant, and how to make use of the information.

In addition, information gathered from paper-and-pencil measures is generally best used as one source of information in a multimethod assessment process. In this way, it is possible to integrate the information gained from the paper-and-pencil measure with other available information. In this instance, such information might include data from student cumulative folders, self-reports from students, and reports from others (e.g., teachers and parents). Further, waiting until later in the group process to administer the instruments would allow more time for rapport and trust to develop among the group members.

In conclusion. Though well intentioned, Janet and Brian have committed some serious errors in the early stages of this group, notably in the manner in which they have chosen to collect assessment data. Their work clearly is not consistent with best practices in assessment, and potential harm to clients is not unlikely.

RESPONSE

Patricia J. Neufeld

There are several aspects of this incident that require discussion. One is the ethical behavior and limits of competence of the interns. Another is the facilitation of a successful and age-appropriate group experience. Yet another aspect that needs to be considered is the role of supervision in the growth of the counselors-in-training.

Providing a meaningful group experience for students requires planning and careful reflection. Janet and Brian failed to plan adequately for the students who were interested in learning more about careers. There is no mention of interviewing potential group members or developing a group format, and most importantly, there is no mention of Janet and Brian planning and/or discussing the group experience with their university supervisor. As a result, the group begins without any structure. It seems that Janet and Brian are taking a fly-by-the-seat-of-your-pants approach with little or no thought as to what they want to accomplish with the group of students. It also seems Janet and Brian have a limited understanding of the maturity of sixth-grade students. Counselors in training working with children must be knowledgeable of children's developmental stages. It cannot be assumed that group experiences will be appropriate for use with any population or all children.

Sixth-grade students have a limited perception of the world in which they live. Career awareness and education would be more age appropriate for this level of students than administering an interest inventory. Students at this age will benefit from opportunities to explore who they are and their personal characteristics. Awareness of what they like to do, and what their talents, interests, and skills are, could begin to provide the basis for exploring jobs and careers. This information along with a discussion of the changes that have taken place in the world within the last century might provide a basis for the students to understand the importance for career and educational planning as they enter middle school and high school.

Janet's creation of her own career interest inventory raises several concerns. Copyright laws may have been violated. Photocopying instruments without permission in some instances is not only unethical but also illegal.

In addition, her creative endeavor to match the Holland codes to the inventory creates an instrument that is an invalid measure, has not been validated, and yields unreliable results. This kind of behavior in a counseling intern raises several ethical questions as to the potential for harm. Client welfare must always be central and foremost in delivery of counseling services. There is potential for harm in presenting a cut-and-paste interest inventory that infers to the sixth-grade students that this instrument can identify occupations that match their individual interests. At the very least, Janet exercised poor judgment in creating her inventory. Brian's consideration of administering a self-esteem and math anxiety instrument reiterates the fact that planning for the group experience is an integral piece of group counseling. His judgment, too, is questionable. Being familiar with an instrument, having administered it frequently during his thesis research, and having enough copies on hand are hardly sufficient reasons for using the instrument as part of the group experience.

The extent of the relationship between Janet and Brian and their on-site supervisor is unclear. The on-site supervisor was involved in the group experience only to the extent of securing the informed consent forms. There is no mention that the university supervisor was consulted prior to the first group meeting. Janet and Brian should have been required to meet with either or both supervisors, and ideally both, in order to successfully plan for the group experience. One aspect of the supervision might have focused on the fact that sixth-grade students are at the age when they are easily influenced. Special consideration and planning for peer pressure or the influence of group leaders during the group experience might have been included.

In summary, both supervisors have an ethical responsibility to ensure that appropriate planning and levels of competence exist in order for the best interest of clients to be served. The purpose of supervision is to foster the professional growth and effectiveness of the counselor in training.

CHAPTER 41

LEADER COMPETENCY: "SCARED AND UNPREPARED"

This incident explores the ethical issues surrounding the collaboration between and the preparedness of a school counselor and a mental health counselor.

CRITICAL INCIDENT

Jackie M. Allen

Background

Claudia, a new high school counselor, is asked by her principal to start academic success counseling groups at her school. The principal has also asked Jesse, a community mental health counselor he knows, to work with Claudia. Pressed by the Board of Education's emphasis on improving academic performance, the principal has asked the counselors to start the group the next week. He has invited the two counselors to his office to discuss the possibilities of such a project. The counselors do not know each other, and this will be their first meeting.

Claudia is concerned, as an untenured counselor, to say no to her principal and agrees to start the group the following week. She discovers Jesse will be out of town on business for the entire week, and he says he is unable to meet with Claudia before the first session. By phone they agree that 8 to 10 ninth-grade students who are failing in at least two classes will be invited to participate in the group. Claudia accepts the responsibility of sending out invitations, contacting teachers, and gaining parental permission. Jesse agrees to show up for the first session, a week from Wednesday, and help Claudia facilitate the first group counseling session. The principal agrees to be supportive of the new program and give credibility to the activity by cosigning the invitation letter. Claudia decides to go to the Student Success Team (SST) the next day to ask for the names of students who need help and might be interested. Claudia prepares the letter, using a format she found in one of her counseling books, and sends out the invitations. The SST recommends 20 students, and 12 students return their slips, agreeing to attend the group counseling sessions. With only 2 days left before the first session, Claudia sends out notes to the teachers announcing that the group counseling sessions will take place weekly during fourth period. Claudia is very nervous and gets out her text from group counseling class and tries to prepare herself for the first session. The day arrives for the initial counseling group, and eight students arrive for the group; the other four students were not released from class to attend. The participating students complain their teachers might not let them come every week. Jesse arrives early and hopes to talk with Claudia about the agenda for the first meeting, but Claudia has had a drop-in crisis counseling situation with a pregnant minor and her boyfriend and is unavailable to talk with Jesse before the session.

Incident

The counseling group meets in the main office of the high school, in a conference room, next to the vice principal's office. Group members can be seen entering the room, and a window in the door of the room allows others to look in. The group begins with Claudia explaining the purpose of the group: to help students improve their grades. She discusses the general rules of group participation, member responsibility, leader responsibility, and confidentiality issues. Jesse talks about wanting to help students with their personal problems and invites them to contact him personally if they need further counseling beyond the group sessions. Neither counselor discusses the concern about releasing students from class or how this might affect the counseling sessions and what might be done.

The students are asked to introduce themselves, and an icebreaker activity prepared by Claudia works well. Students begin sharing about their academic problems, and one female student, Julia, shares she has been accused of copying a paper she submitted to her history teacher and was subsequently given an "F" on the paper. She talks more about the incident and finally confesses she really did copy the material directly from a Web site. When she expresses concern about the counselors keeping her information secret, Jesse promises that information shared in the group will be confidential. The students seem reassured by his words and begin to comfortably share other personal information.

Later in the week, Julia's history teacher wants to know how Julia is doing in the counseling group and approaches Claudia. In talking with the teacher, Claudia shares that Julia admitted plagiarism during the counseling group and asks the teacher to keep the information to herself. On Wednesday, when it is time for the group counseling session, only four students show up and Julia is not among them. Jesse asks to talk with Claudia before the session begins and mentions some of the students have talked to him about the lack of confidentiality. Jesse asks Claudia to leave while he talks with the students. Claudia agrees and lets Jesse run the group that day.

Discussion

Claudia realizes she has broken confidentiality and becomes very unsure about her role as a leader of a group counseling session. After Claudia has had some time to think about the incident, she questions her dual role as faculty member and group leader. She decides to tell her principal that she cannot continue leading the group. Her principal is very disappointed and suggests she become trained in leading group counseling sessions because it is an important counseling service he wants the students to have. Claudia agrees that she will take a professional development class and some supervision at the local university to improve her counseling skills as a group leader. After a couple of class sessions, she begins to realize her responsibilities as a group leader. She lets her principal know that she was not prepared and should not have accepted the group counseling leadership without further training.

QUESTIONS

1. What training must counselors have before starting group counseling with students?
2. What responsibility do group counseling leaders have to meet and discuss roles and techniques before the first session?
3. What rights of confidentiality do students have in a group?
4. What responsibility does a counselor have to share student information with a faculty member?
5. How can co-leaders prepare themselves to work together, without having competing purposes?
6. How should co-leaders handle a group problem?
7. How might Claudia have responded to her principal's request to lead a group? To the history teacher's concern about Julia?
8. What was Jesse's responsibility as a co-leader in supporting Claudia and in working with the students?

RESPONSE

Emily Phillips

There are multiple issues involved in this incident. A primary concern is that Claudia, a new counselor, felt unprepared to run groups. It appears her only group training was during her school counselor preparation. Although academic success is not generally thought of as a "heavy" topic, the reasons for students' failure can be very complex and serious. To those outside of the counseling field, an academic success group may not seem like a deep and personal topic. Claudia should have let her principal know that she felt unprepared and that it would be unethical for her to run a group with such feelings. She could have told him then that she was willing to seek additional training to become prepared.

There are many reasons for the lack of success of this group. We do not know the experience of Jesse, the community mental health counselor, but his decision to just show up at the first meeting without any prior commitment or work suggests he was unfamiliar with the particulars of group counseling. Claudia was put in a lose-lose situation in which she felt one down to another counselor, and this could have had a negative effect on group process. She was left with all the clerical, administrative, and planning responsibilities with little prior experience from which to draw. In addition, she had no choice in the matter and no insight into how her style matched with Jesse's, or even if they had compatible foci. Although differing orientations can be meshed, no work was done before the group to iron out the agenda or even to discuss their vision and beliefs. This left the leaders with friction between them and at cross-purposes, with no planning between sessions to work any of this out. A co-led group does not simply mean two leaders.

Another key concern is that the principal wanted the group to start in a week. This was not a reasonable expectation. The Association for Specialists in Group Work *Best Practice Guidelines* (ASGW, 1998) is clear about the myriad activities that should occur during pregroup planning and the additional work required with co-leaders before and between sessions. With only 1 week before the first meeting, there was no time to become sufficiently ready for this group. Although the child study team referred students, and it appeared that students agreed to attend, no work was done to allow for informed consent (section A.7.b) or to assess whether the members' goals were compatible with the group leaders' goals (section A.7.a).

Claudia, due to inexperience, simply sent out letters to teachers telling them which students would be missing class. Unfortunately, this is not the most effective way to gain support for a group that will interfere with class time, especially for students who are at academic risk. This could set up an adversarial relationship with the faculty. Claudia could have handled this differently. First, she should have explained to the principal why she needed more time to screen, to prepare, to inform, and to develop a comprehensive program with goals for academic success. Second, she needed either to meet with the teachers involved or to prepare a flyer that explained the purpose of the group so teachers could understand the benefits of students being out of class. In addition, no mention is made of how many sessions were planned. If there are numerous sessions, it is not realistic to expect high school teachers to release students weekly for months. If students are already in academic distress, this will just add to the situation. A system whereby the group met at different periods of the day on a rotating basis would be fairer to the teachers involved. The group could have also been arranged at lunchtime, during a common study hall, or after school if there was a late bus available. Giving teachers 2 days notice was not sufficient. The lack of face-to-face discussion probably also added to teachers not releasing students as they were unfamiliar with this new school counselor and the goals of the program, and they did not have an opportunity to understand the purpose of groups. Claudia needed to discuss with teachers what they saw as interfering with students' academic success. If the principal was insistent about her having the group, she could also have asked him to inform teachers that he wanted this group to be run right away and that teachers were expected to cooperate with releasing students from class. Even the students who did show for the first session were stressed, not knowing if they would be allowed to come each week. This in and of itself can become a distraction because group cohesion and trust are built through regular attendance.

The location of the group in the main administrative area, next to the vice-principal's room (a negative connotation) with a view from the central office, might have hindered group process. In schools, there are often few alternatives for group meetings. Perhaps, if another location could not be found, a curtain or some visual shield covering the window in the door might have helped students feel less self-conscious.

Adolescents are, in general, nervous about meeting with a counselor. Meeting with two, one being from a mental health facility, could have been perceived as more threatening. Additionally, pregroup screening did not take place in order to assess if students understood what exactly they were volunteering for. This could have created a situation in which the members' and the leaders' goals were not the same. Also, Claudia spent most of the first session setting the ground rules and goals. It did not sound as if much was done to involve the teens in this process. Jesse's invitation for students to contact him personally for counseling was divisive to this new group and could have given the adolescents the impression they were in the group because they had mental health problems. The group began with the leaders providing mixed messages about the purpose of the group, and with Jesse appearing to have more power than the school counselor.

Claudia's breaking of confidentiality was only one of the issues in this incident. The group was in trouble before that took place. It is inappropriate and unethical for school counselors to break confidentiality except in cases of clear and imminent danger (American Counseling Association [ACA], 1995, section B.1.c; American School Counselor Association [ASCA], 1998, section A.2.b). Once confidentiality is broken, it has a ripple effect, not only for the student involved but for the other group members as well. An additional outcome could be that word would spread through the student grapevine that a counselor cannot be trusted. Without trust, which is the cornerstone of the counseling relationship, students will not seek or use counseling services. Perhaps this is why only four students showed up for the session following Claudia's disclosure to the teacher. If members do not trust the leader(s), the group becomes an unsafe place; and even if members do continue, talk may remain at a superficial level (Corey, 2000). Claudia's goal should have been to get the student to disclose the plagiarism to the teacher. She should have asked the history teacher what his or her concerns were and talked in general terms about Julia's progress. She could also have suggested sitting in on a meeting with the two of them to facilitate discussion. In this way, she could have worked with Julia to help her decide how to approach this topic.

A background element of this situation is that Jesse appears to be engaged in a power struggle with Claudia. To "ask Claudia to leave while he talks with the students" was not only highly inappropriate and divisive, but also made Claudia appear powerless and incompetent. Jesse, however, was made to look like the good guy, the real counselor, and her superior. That Claudia agreed to leave showed her lack of experience, self-confidence, and knowledge of group process. That Jesse arranged for this display of disrespect for Claudia to occur demonstrated he also was ignorant of group process and unfamiliar with issues of co-leadership. Without mutual respect, they could not create an effective working relationship. Group members can sense disharmony. The group became fragmented, and these adults were doing little to model effective communication and interpersonal relationships.

As a school counselor, Claudia cannot avoid dual relationships. In and of themselves, they are not negative; however, she needs to be careful the information shared in one setting does not contaminate the other relationship(s) she may have with students. Her first role is as counselor/student advocate. Her first allegiance is to the counseling process and the students she was hired to serve, not to the teachers.

It is also unreasonable to expect that a mental health counselor employed in the community will be available on a regular basis throughout the school year, or from year to year. Given time/work constraints, the need to travel to and from a school, and reimbursement issues, it is highly unlikely these opportunities will be frequent. These constraints add to the difficulty of co-leading and planning together for groups, both before and between sessions. Jesse was an invited guest in the school. Guests do not have comprehensive day-to-day responsibilities for the students. Claudia needed to have positive relationships with these students so she could work effectively with them throughout the school year and through the students' entire high school experience. Given this, Jesse needed to support Claudia's growth and relationships with students. Instead, he undermined her.

Claudia's struggles with skill development, lack of clinical supervision, and role identity are common with new school counselors. If she had focused first on establishing and marketing a comprehensive, developmental program focusing on personal/social, vocational, and academic success in accordance with the *National Standards for School Counseling Programs* (Dahir, Sheldon, & Valiga, 1998), faculty and the principal would have better understood her goals. She would have had a clearer vision of her role, and goals for various foci would have been established. In this way, her school counseling services would have better been integrated into the overall educational system. She would have been able to explain to Jesse how his services fit with her program, rather than passively following his lead and floundering. If she had reviewed her group texts and codes of ethics before agreeing to facilitate this group, she could have presented to her principal concrete reasons why she was not ready and why it would not be in students' best interests for her to provide this service. In all likelihood, once her principal understood that her reluctance was not simply based on anxiety, he probably would not have seen her in the negative light she feared he might.

Administrators may be unaware of the specifics of our codes of ethics and best practices guidelines and unfamiliar with the complexities of group process. Claudia could have used this as a teachable moment, potentially increasing the principal's respect for her as a professional school counselor.

RESPONSE

Carol A. Dahir

Acquiring knowledge and skills. Effective group counseling requires a strong foundation in theoretical approaches, a solid understanding of appropriate applications, and a repertoire of skills and techniques that are intentionally applied in various situations. Group counseling is a challenge to the most veteran of school counselors. Groups take on characteristics and personalities of their own. Group members form relationships with the leaders as well as with each other, explore concerns collaboratively, and support each other's decisions and strategies.

As a new counselor Claudia is probably not sure of her skill fluency because she has not yet faced all of the challenges that are presented in working with high school students. Eager to please her new principal, she may not have properly thought through all of the nuances and dynamics that surround group counseling. Because her principal sought to initiate the academically at-risk ninth-grade group within a week, we can only surmise that neither the principal nor Claudia or Jesse were aware of the logistics involved, the preparation and planning required, and the potential conflict of confidentiality issues that differ from school to agency setting.

Co-leader relationships. From the onset, Claudia and Jesse set themselves up for challenges. There was no time allocated for planning, preparation, or having a solid discussion about establishing goals for the group. Although Jesse made an attempt to connect before the group began, even that would not have allowed the two of them to get to know each other's theoretical orientation and repertoire of techniques. It would have been wiser to delay the initiation of the group until a planning session could take place. Co-leaders have an obligation not to just plan and debrief, but also to provide feedback and supervisory support for each other.

Conflicting purposes. Claudia explained the academic success purpose to the group of students. Perhaps the academic focus of the group was not what Jesse had in mind because his offer to address personal problems also extended beyond the group setting (to his office). Immediately a dichotomy between the co-leaders' intent was established. Is the group for academic success? Or is it to resolve personal issues? Experienced counselors know the interrelationship of the two. Perhaps a commitment to collaborative planning and solid preparation on the part of Claudia and Jesse would have brought this connection to the surface. Claudia could have openly discussed this at the next group counseling session with the students, and collectively, she and Jesse could have clearly delineated the parameters of confidentiality. In the orientation stages of group development, members are clearly focused on the behavior of the leaders.

Confidentiality. This was broken the moment group members were seen entering the room in a very public setting. There was no attention paid to ensure the students' privacy entering the room or while in the room. Community agency and school counselors collaboratively seek solutions as partners in prevention and intervention. Confidentiality is always an influencing factor in individual and group counseling, and in school it is internally guided by state and board policy. Community agencies, especially those federally funded by alcohol and substance abuse grants, are guided by federal law.

Although Jesse promised that information shared in the group would be held confidential, Claudia did not respond, which may have been interpreted by the students as concurrence. If that were not the case, Claudia should have immediately expressed her reservations by interjecting the need-to-know factor that requires us to consult and collaborate with teachers on individual student situations.

Should Claudia have broken the student's confidentiality? ASCA's *Ethical Standards for School Counselors* (1998) remind us of our responsibilities to students and our obligation to reveal information with the informed consent of the counselee. Additionally, this must be consistent with the obligations of the counselor as a professional. Julia had already been reproached by the teacher for plagiarism and received an "F." We do not know if a specific school policy required Claudia to reveal the student's confession. Claudia should have discussed the dilemma with Julia if under obligation as a faculty member.

Respect for students' concerns. Although student assignment to the group was based on the recommendation of the SST, two important concerns should have been addressed. Students need to voluntarily participate if the group is to succeed. Counselors need to take the time to carefully explain to teachers the purpose of the group, what they hope will occur, and gain the teachers' support by asking for permission. Neither counselor discussed the concerns expressed about the students' ability to be released from class, or how this might affect the counseling sessions, or what might be done.

Ethical behavior. Claudia's decision to tell her principal that she cannot continue leading the group may have been premature. If a collaborative working relationship was established with Jesse, this would have provided her with both the experience and supervision needed to co-lead effectively. Conceivably, her presence could have assured that the group would stay focused on the goal of improving academic success. Claudia acted ethically when she informed her principal that she was not prepared to lead a group and needed further training.

Supervision. School administrators need to be aware of the challenges of working with youth in groups that go well beyond a desire for expediency or efficiency. School counselors have an obligation as leaders and advocates not only to clearly articulate to their principals the support needed to organize and plan a group, but also to discuss the nuances of student behavior and potential conflicting motivations. Building administrators may not be aware that the ethics of confidentiality may be governed by conflicting sets of rules and regulations.

REFERENCES

American Counseling Association. (1995). *Code of ethics and standards of practice.* Alexandria, VA: Author.

American School Counselor Association. (1998). *Ethical standards for school counselors.* Alexandria, VA: Author.

Association for Specialists in Group Work. (1998). Best practice guidelines. *Journal for Specialists in Group Work, 23*(3), 237–244.

Corey, G. (2000) *Theory and practice of group counseling* (5th ed.). Pacific Grove, CA: Brooks/Cole.

Dahir, C. A., Sheldon, C. B., & Valiga, M. J. (1998). *Vision into action: Implementing the national standards for school counseling programs.* Alexandria, VA: American School Counselor Association.